HISTORY, HISTORIOGRAPHY
AND INTERPRETATION

The Hebrew University of Jerusalem
The Institute for Advanced Studies

HISTORY, HISTORIOGRAPHY AND INTERPRETATION

STUDIES IN BIBLICAL AND CUNEIFORM LITERATURES

Edited by

H. Tadmor

and

M. Weinfeld

THE MAGNES PRESS, THE HEBREW UNIVERSITY, JERUSALEM
E. J. BRILL, LEIDEN

First Edition 1983
Reprinted in 1984, 1986

Distributed by
E.J. Brill, Leiden, Holland

By The Magnes Press
The Hebrew University
Jerusalem 1986

ISBN 965–223–459–1

Printed in Israel

Typesetting: S.T.I. Jerusalem

CONTENTS

Editors' Note

The papers presented in this volume originate from seminars and colloquia conducted at the Institute for Advanced Studies, the Hebrew University of Jerusalem, Mt. Scopus, during the academic year 1978–1979. Almost all of the authors were Fellows of the Institute during that period and participated in the symposium held in May 1979 on problems of history and historiography in the Bible and the Ancient Near East.

The present volume is organized in topical fashion: the essays on the Ancient Near East precede those devoted to biblical topics, though several studies integrate both the cuneiform and biblical fields. These papers are the product of the fruitful discussions and scholarly cooperation which characterized that year. The manuscripts were presented for publication by the authors in 1979–1980 and updated, after editing, in 1981–82.

On behalf of the authors, the editors of this volume wish to express their gratitude to the Institute, its Director, Professor A. Dvoretzky, Mr. M. Bitan, the former Associate Director, Dr. S. Gairon, the present Deputy Director, and its staff for the hospitality and congenial atmosphere which made this enterprise possible.

D. Satran assisted in preparing copy and drew up the list of abbreviations; proof in its entirety was read by Ms. Adelle Zarmati, and in part by Professors M. Cogan and I. Eph'al. The help rendered by all these persons was indispensable and the editors acknowledge it gratefully; responsibility for the work and such faults as may remain is, of course, their own.

H. Tadmor
M. Weinfeld

SUMERIAN HISTORIOGRAPHY

WILLIAM W. HALLO

Yale University

I am going to use the expression "Sumerian historiography" in a double sense here – one to describe the Sumerian texts dealing with history, and the other to identify the attempts of modern scholars to reconstruct Sumerian history.* My object is to test the validity of the proposition that literary sources may be used, with due caution, in historiographical reconstructions. In the case of ancient Israel, this proposition is virtually axiomatic. For many periods, institutions and topics of Biblical history, the Bible is our only resource, and it is a literary source. The debate over its admissibility in evidence has raged long and hard all the same, and I have reviewed it at length elsewhere.[1] I will not dwell on it here except to note that my recent animadversions on Assyrian historiography were in part an attempt to bring that analogy to bear on the debate.[2]

On the Egyptian side, I may perhaps cite the opinion of Gun Björkman who, in an article entitled "Egyptology and historical method," argued against the uncritical use of New Kingdom literary texts to

* Presented to the Third Assyriological Colloquium, Hebrew University of Jerusalem, May 9, 1979, on "Aspects of Cuneiform Historiography" under the sponsorship of the Institute for Advanced Studies. For an earlier treatment of the subject, see Samuel Noah Kramer, "Sumerian Historiography," *IEJ* 3 (1953), pp. 217–232.

1. See my "Biblical history in its Near Eastern setting: the contextual approach," in Carl D. Evans, William W. Hallo and John B. White (eds.), *Scripture in Context: Essays on the Comparative Method (Pittsburgh Theological Monograph Series* 34), 1980, pp. 1–26.

2. W.W. Hallo, "Assyrian Historiography revisited," *Eretz Israel* 14 (H.L. Ginsberg Volume), 1978, pp. 1*–7*. Of other recent contributions, note especially J. Krecher and H.P. Müller, "Vergangenheitsinteresse in Mesopotamien und Israel," *Saeculum* 26 (1975), pp. 13–14, and B. Hruška, "Das Verhältnis zur Vergangenheit im alten Mesopotamien," *Archív Orientální* 47 (1979), pp. 4–14.

9

William W. Hallo

reconstruct the history of the First Intermediate Period.[3] Two of these are commonly used for this purpose, the Admonitions of Ipuwer and the Instructions of Merikare. But "since the date and historical value of the literary composition called Admonitions is not established, it should consequently not be used," – not at all it appears.[4] And as for the Instructions, confronting them with an elaborate list of sources contemporary with the period in question leads to the conclusion that while they rarely contradict each other, neither do they confirm each other since, on the whole, they do not cover the same ground.[5]

To me, this view seems a little bit naive. It implies that, in the first place, our sources are abundant enough even for so obscure a time as the First Intermediate Period to enable us always to weigh contemporaneous documentation against later literary formulations. (In fact, of course, we cannot even be sure that the Admonitions refer to the First Intermediate Period and not the Second.) In the second place, it suggests a degree of objectiveness and infallibility for contemporaneous sources which flies in the face of abundant examples of their own tendentiousness and other subjective features.

I still prefer the principle I enunciated in the preface to *The Ancient Near East: a History*, namely that the modern historian's function is to write "not only a history but a commentary on ancient history and historiography."[6] If, with Huizinga, "history is the intellectual form in which a civilization renders account to itself of its past,"[7] then we must listen to the native traditions in which these accounts are rendered. In this enterprise, a critical attitude is of course desirable, indeed essential; but it must be applied to all the textual sources, contemporary as well as later, documentary as well as literary. And it cannot be applied to the later, literary sources unless these are included in the enterprise in the first place.

This does not imply indiscriminately equating all sources, and I doubt anyone would accuse me of wanting to do that. In fact, I have

3.   Gun Björkman, "Egyptology and historical method," *Orientalia Suecana* 13 (1964), pp. 9–33.
4.   *Ibid.*, p. 16 (citing J. van Seters, *JEA* 50 [1964], pp. 13–23).
5.   *Ibid.*, pp. 20–31. For a different view, see R. J. Williams, "Literature as a medium of political propaganda in Ancient Egypt," in W.S. McCullough (ed.), *The Seed of Wisdom: Essays in Honor of T.J. Meek*, Toronto, 1964, pp. 14–30, esp. pp. 16–19.
6.   W.W. Hallo and W.K. Simpson, *The Ancient Near East: a History*, 1971, p. vi.
7.   J. Huizinga, "A definition of the concept of history," in R. Klibansky and H.J. Paton, (eds.), *Philosophy and History: Essays Presented to Ernst Cassirer*, Oxford, 1936, p. 9. See further to this point Hallo (above, n.1).

devoted a good part of my Assyriological efforts to identifying and demarcating the broad categories of cuneiform writings. For the loose and purely functional distinctions such as Gadd's "sacred, ceremonial, or everyday,"[8] I substituted categories based on form as well as function,[9] defining these respectively as canonical,[10] monumental,[11] and archival.[12] Within these broad categories, I have been at pains to delineate the individual genres into which they could be broken down,[13] to trace the evolution of these genres over time,[14] and thus to reconstruct the separate genre-histories from which a literary history of Mesopotamia could ultimately be assembled.[15] To a growing extent, my classification system has been gaining acceptance in the field.[16]

Classification is not, however, the be-all and end-all of our efforts. Even if our modern taxonomy tallies with the native categories, it remains no more than a working hypothesis, a means to an end, or to diverse ends. One of these is to reconstruct a literary and cultural history of Mesopotamia, juxtaposed with the political, social, and economic history of the area, to the reciprocal illumination of both. Another end is closer to our purpose here. For, having once defined and distinguished our categories and genres, we can more safely aspire to re-unite them, in other words to draw on all of them jointly and severally in order to reconstruct the historical reality lying behind them.

I made a first conscious attempt in this direction with "The House of Ur-Meme," the aristocratic family which held some of the highest political and priestly offices at neo-Sumerian Nippur for five generations.[17] My reconstruction of the genealogy of the family and the

8. C.J. Gadd, *Teachers and Students in the Oldest Schools*, London, 1956, p. 6.
9. Hallo, (above, n. 6), pp. 154–156; previously e.g. in *JNES* 17 (1958), p. 210 n. 6.
10. *Idem*, "New viewpoints on cuneiform literature," *IEJ* 12 (1962), esp. pp. 21–26.
11. *Idem*, "The royal inscriptions of Ur: a typology," *HUCA* 33 (1962), pp. 1–43.
12. *Idem, Sumerian Archival Texts (TLB* 3), Leiden, 1963–1973.
13. *Idem* (above, n. 11) for monuments; cf. "The neo-Sumerian letter-orders," *Bib Or* 26 (1969), pp. 171–175 for an archival genre.
14. *Idem*, "Individual prayer in Sumerian; the continuity of a tradition," *JAOS* 88 (Speiser Memorial Volume; *AOS* 53), 1968, pp. 71–89.
15. *Idem*, "Toward a History of Sumerian Literature," *Sumerological Studies in Honor of Thorkild Jacobsen (AS* 20), Chicago, 1976, pp. 181–203.
16. I.J. Gelb, deploring the lack of "any comprehensive study of the typology of written records in ancient times," singled out my studies (above, nn. 10–11) "for preliminary thoughts on the topic as applied mainly to ancient Mesopotamia" in his "Written records and decipherment" in Thomas A. Sebeok (ed.). *Diachronic, Areal and Typological Linguistics (Current Trends in Liguistics* 11), 1973, p. 254. Cf. previously E.C. Kingsbury, *HUCA* 34 (1963), p. 1, n. 1.
17. "The house of Ur-Meme," *JNES* 31 (1972), pp. 87–95; cf. *idem*, "Seals lost and found," *Bibliotheca Mesopotamica* 6 (1977), p. 57 and nn. 18–20.

William W. Hallo

careers of its members drew in equal measure on account-texts, seal inscriptions, and literary letters, and served incidentally but happily to confirm the essential historicity of the later canonical texts by means of the contemporaneous archives and monuments.

The same purpose was pursued on a more ambitious scale by my student Piotr Michalowski in his dissertation on "The Royal Correspondence of Ur." He demonstrated that the literary letters to and from the neo-Sumerian kings of Ur constitute an essentially authentic record of the events they describe, though preserved in copies postdating these events by two to three hundred years. All of the letters deal with the same general theme, namely the coming of the Amorites, which leads one to suspect that they were selected from the surviving royal records of the Ur III empire for use in the scribal school by pupils (or professors) with some interest in this particular subject. And their personal names, geographical names, events, and other data are repeatedly corroborated by the evidence of the Ur III archives and monuments.[18]

A companion piece to this corpus is formed by "The Royal Correspondence of Isin," which is so far represented by two pairs of letters to and from the kings Iddin-Dagan and Lipit-Ishtar[19] and possibly one from Enlil-bani.[20] Though the focus of interest changes (from the coming of the Amorites to the struggle over water rights), this corpus shares with the Ur correspondence a sober style and matter-of-fact tone appropriate to authentic letters on affairs of state.

But even while the royal correspondence developed along these prosaic lines a more poetic format was evolving for private letters. Petitions addressed to superiors,[21] to kings,[22] and to gods[23] combined an epistolary format with a hymnic style which apostrophized the addressee and enumerated the petitioner's wants in ever more elaborate terms. Thus the literary letter developed along two separate but

18. See, for now, P. Michalowski, "The bride of Simanum," *JAOS* 95 (1975), pp. 716–719.
19. M.B. Rowton, "Watercourses and water rights in the official correspondence from Larsa and Isin," *JCS* 21 (1967), pp. 267–274.
20. So according to M.E. Cohen, "The Lu-Ninurta letters," *WO* 9 (1977), pp. 10–13.
21. E.g. the letter of Lugal-murub to Enlil-massu his son (!) = No. 16 in "Letter-Collection B" (below, n. 57); it can be dated to the time of Ibbi-Sin (more or less) if the author's father is Zuzu; cf. Hallo (above, n. 17).
22. E.g. Letter-Collection B_6, from Ur-shaga to Shulgi(?) (below, n. 57); cf. Hallo (above, n. 14), p. 75f.
23. E.g. Letter-Collection B_{17}, from Inannakam to Nintinuga, which can perhaps be dated to the time of Amar-Sin; cf. Hallo, (above, n. 17), p. 91f.

parallel lines in neo-Sumerian (Ur III–Isin) times: one the royal letter and the other the letter-prayer.

The two lines converged under the Larsa dynasty, when we have no less than four royal letter-prayers addressed by King Sin-iddinam (ca. 1849–1843 B.C.) to Utu, the patron-deity of Larsa, and (in one case) to Nin-Isina, goddess of Isin. Since I have dealt with these letters in some detail on previous occasions here in Jerusalem in 1973[24] and 1977,[25] I will pass over them now and turn instead to a fifth letter-prayer which follows directly on one of the Sin-iddinam letters to Utu in a prism from Oxford recently published by Gurney and Kramer,[26] and which thus forms part of the Royal Correspondence of Larsa. It is, in fact, in many ways the pièce de résistance of this correspondence.

The new composition is a letter, not from the king but to the king, and that king is Rim-Sin, last and longest-lived member of the "Larsa dynasty." It is addressed to him by a woman, Ninshatapada. Like the famous Enheduanna, she is a princess, priestess and poetess in one. Like her predecessor more than four centuries earlier, she was born to the founder of a new dynasty, in her case, the founder of the Old Babylonian dynasty of Uruk, Sin-kashid. She was removed from her office and exiled from Durum, the city in which she served, when it fell to Larsa. Now she pleads with the conqueror to spare her city and restore her to her priestly office. The text is complete, in six duplicates and 58 lines. Its elaborate structure features a three-part salutation and a three-part body so disposed that each portion of the body is twice as long as the corresponding section of the salutation.

There is little difficulty in correlating the newly recovered letter with the history of southern Babylonia in the late nineteenth century B.C. as this is known from monumental inscriptions and date formulas.[27] But in addition it gives us precious new insights into the period.

24. Hallo, "The royal correspondence of Larsa: I. A Sumerian Prototype for the prayer of Hezekiah?" *S.N. Kramer Anniversary Volume* (*AOAT* 25), 1976, pp. 209–224.
25. *Idem*, "The royal correspondence of Larsa: II. The appeal to Utu," C.B.F. Walker in G. van Driel *et alii* (eds.), *Zikir Šumim*, Assyriological Studies Presented to F.R. Kraus on the Occasion of his Seventieth Birthday, Leiden, 1982, pp. 398–417. Cf. *idem*, "Letters, prayers, and letter-prayers," *Proceedings of the Seventh World Congress of Jewish Studies, 2: Studies in the Bible and the Ancient Near East*, Jerusalem, 1981, pp. 17,27.
26. *OECT* 5:25. A full edition of this text and its duplicates will appear shortly as "The Royal Correspondence of Larsa: III," together with a study of its historical implications. My remarks here will be confined to its literary, and specifically its historiographic dimensions.
27. For this history, see especially A. Falkenstein, *Bagh Mitt* 2 (1963), pp. 22–41.

Sin-kashid's solicitude for the southern city of Durum, expressed in our letter by the appointment (either by himself[28] or less likely by one of his successors) of his own daughter to be high-priestess there, now adds new significance to the title "viceroy of Durum" which he affected on recently published inscriptions in honor of the chthonic deities worshipped there.[29] Apparently he himself served there as an appointee (or perhaps even a member) of the dynasty of Isin, much as Ishme-Dagan, fourth king of the dynasty, had served as viceroy of Durum in the lifetime of his father Iddin-Dagan,[30] thus carrying on a tradition that can now be traced back as far as Ishbi-Irra, first king of Isin,[31] and Ibbi-Sin, last king of Ur III.[32] But what is most revealing in the new letter is its use of repeated allusions to historical events known from the Larsa date formulas and even in the very words of those formulas. There are also many phrases in the letter taken from, or shared in common with, the inscriptions of Rim-Sin.

To begin with, Ninshatapada addresses Rim-Sin as "shepherd" (sipa) or possibly even as "good shepherd" or "faithful shepherd" (sipa-zi)[33] an epithet used attributively, i.e. *before* the royal name, by only two rulers throughout what I call the "Classical Period" of Mesopotamian history (ca. 2100–1600 B.C.): Gudea of Lagash in his cylinders[34] and Rim-Sin of Larsa in his date formulas and one of his hymns.[35] In between, it was used predicatively, i.e. *after* the royal name, by Shulgi of Ur in his royal hymns, by An-am of Uruk in his inscriptions, and by Nur-Adad and Sin-iqisham of Larsa in letter-prayers and hymns respectively.[36] The Akkadian equivalent *rēu kīnu*

28. Note that he appointed another daughter, Nish-inishu, as high priestess of Lugal-banda at Uruk; cf. Sin-kashid 6 (republished Falkenstein, above, n. 27, Pl. 8); P. Weadock, *Iraq* 37 (1975), p. 125.
29. C.B.F. Walker, AfO 23 (1970), pp. 88f.; G. Pettinato, *Oriens Antiquus* 9 (1970), pp. 105–107; David I. Owens, *JCS* 26 (1974), pp. 63f.; H. Steible, *Archiv Orientální* 43 (1975), pp. 346–352.
30. YOS 9:22f. (=Ishme-Dagan 6) (written BÀD.KI).
31. The high-priestess (nin-dingir) of Lugal(g)irra installed according to "Isin Date C" presumably functioned at Durum, probably under Ishbi-Irra.
32. In view of his hymn to Meslamtaea and Lugalgirra, edited by Å. Sjöberg, *Orientalia Suecana* 19–20 (1970–71), pp. 140–178, No. 11a.
33. Hallo, "Royal titles from the Mesopotamian periphery," *O.R. Gurney Anniversary Volume* (*Anatolian Studies* 30, 1981) n. 75.
34. Perhaps in an effort to translate Akkadian *rē'ûm epšum*; cf. Hallo, *Early Mesopotamian Royal Titles* (*AOS* 43), 1951, p. 148 and n. 2. Is the comparable $utul_9$-zid applied to one of the earliest "Rulers of Lagash" a parody on this epithet? Cf. E. Sollberger, *JCS* 21 (1967), pp. 281, 284, 289 (line 113).
35. Hallo (above, n. 33), n. 74.
36. *Ibid.*, nn. 68, 71–73.

occurs in a fragmentary literary letter reminiscent in many ways of our Sumerian letter.[37] Now Rim-Sin used the attributive title only in the date formulas of his 23rd to 26th years (1800–1797 B.C.); before that (year 22 = 1801) he called himself simply "shepherd" (sipa) and afterwards "obedient shepherd" (sipa-gištug) (year 27 = 1796) and "reliable shepherd" (sipa-gi-na) (years 28ff. = 1795 ff.). Thus our text reflects the official designation of the years following the capture of Uruk (year 21 = 1802).

In the second (really: third) salutation, Rim-Sin is apostrophized, among other things, as "natural-born son of the lord Nergal." This epithet occurs verbatim in a fragmentary literary letter also, presumably, addressed to Rim-Sin,[38] and less literally, in several inscriptions of the king.[39] It assumes special significance in the present context in view of the equation of this chthonic deity with Meslamtaea, the god whom the writer served as high-priestess.

The body of the letter begins with a 15-line hymn praising Rim-Sin's magnanimous treatment of the defeated Uruk which is so far unique in cuneiform literature, but which draws everywhere on the official diction of the conqueror's scribes. Larsa is referred to as "the city lofty like a mountain" (uru-hur- sag-gim-íl-la), a simile used exclusively in the inscriptions of Warad-Sin and Rim-Sin during this period.[40] The king "takes the field at the command of the gods An and Enlil" (du$_{11}$ ^{d}An En-líl-lá-ta mu-un-da-an-zi-ga), the phraseology of his date formulas from his 22nd year (1801) on; previously, notably in date formulas 17–21 (1806–1802), only Enlil was invoked. The implication is that the conquest of Uruk commemorated in year 21 (1802) entitled the king to invoke An, the tutelary deity of Uruk, in his subsequent date formulas, the more so if his treatment of the conquered city was magnanimous.[41]

And so indeed it was, as is clearly stated in the next three lines, where we read (i.a.) "of Uruk: its king . . . you captured (but) spared its

37. J. van Dijk, *UVB* 18 (1962), 61f. and pl. 28c; Falkenstein (above, n. 27), and n. 91; R.D. Biggs, *ANET*, p. 604. All tend to associate the text with Sin-kashid.
38. Line 19 of BE 31:7 (= Letter-prayer G in Hallo, above, n. 14, p. 89), republished as *OECT* 5:31 (dumu-tu-da en-^{d}Nè-iri$_{11}$-gal-la-ka).
39. Hallo (above, n. 34), pp. 134–136. For Nergal as Rim-Sin's personal god (dingir-ra-ni) cf. Rim-Sin 12 (UET 1:141) and Hallo, *JCS* 20 (1966), p. 136 n. 53; for Nergal as divine begettor (dingir-sag-du) of Rim-Sin cf. Rim-Sin 10 (*UET* 1:144), 30f., Rim-Sin 12:21f, and *UET* 8:85:23.
40. Cf. I. Kärki, *Studia Orientalia* 35 (1967), pp. 232f.
41. Some date formulas add Enki to An and Enlil, implying a similar "conquest" of Eridu. Cf. also Rim-Sin 7, which has all three deities giving Uruk to Rim-Sin.

populace" (unu^{ki}-ga lugal-bi...mu-un-dab$_5$-bé u-gù name-lú-u$_x$-lu-bi šu-gar mu-un-gar-ra). The captured king may be Irdanene, whose defeat Rim-Sin recorded in his 14th year formula (= 1809 B.C.) and whose capture he claimed in his inscriptions.[42] But the sparing of the population is surely a reference to the events commemorated in identical terms in the 21st year formula (= 1802 B.C.); our letter even makes it possible to improve on the currrent reading and understanding of the date formula,[43] which seems to be quoted once more three lines later on.[44]

In the second 15-line strophe of the letter, the writer turns to her own plight, speaking of the exile from her city and her priestly office which she has endured for five years[45] or, in a variant, for four years.[46] If she met this fate upon the defeat of Uruk in 1803, then her letter was composed, or at least worded as if composed, in 1798, or 1797 according to the variant. If "inclusive reckoning" is involved, the corresponding dates are 1799 or 1800 respectively. All these dates fall within the time span – 1800–1797 – already argued above on the basis of the royal epithets.

But more likely her exile began one year earlier, for in the concluding 9-line stanza of her letter she speaks of Durum as "my city"[47] and as cult-seat of the twin-gods of the underworld, Meslamtaea and Lugalgirra.[48] This Durum is undoubtedly the same city whose capture in 1804 Rim-Sin recorded in his 20th date formula (= 1803).[49] Its location has been much disputed, but was clearly close to Uruk,[50] for its

42. Rim-Sin 10 and 15 (from Ur); cf. D.O. Edzard, *Die "zweite Zwischenzeit" Babyloniens*, Wiesbaden, 1957, p. 155, and the additions of E. Sollberger, *UET* 8 (1965), pp. 31f. (*sub* Nos. 28 and 32).
43. ugu nam-lu-ulu$_x$-bi šu-gar mu-un-gar-ra. Edzard (above, n. 42), 156, read egir instead of ugu but ugu is clear in the date lists as well as some of the attested texts (e.g. *YOS* 5:79). M. Stol, *Studies in Old Babylonian History*, 1976, p. 23, does not comment on Edzard's reading.
44. Cf. line 27: ur-sag-bi (var. -e-ne,ø) ...šu-zu (var. -šè, ø) sá bí (var. am-mi)-in-du$_{11}$-ga with the date formula's erín-á-dah-bi sá bí-in-du$_{11}$-ga. Cf. also *UET* 8:82 as read by Michalowski, (below, n. 50), p. 87.
45. Cf. line 36: mu-5-kam-ma-(ta) uru-mà nu-me-a etc. So *OECT* 5:25:92; *TCL* 16, no. 46:1.
46. So with M. Çığ and H. Kızılyay, Sumerian Literary Tablets *and Fragments in the Archaeological Museum of Istanbul I*, Ankara, 1979, p. 181 (Ni. 9729).
47. Cf. line 51: BÀD.KI uru$^{(ki)}$-mu.
48. Cf. line 53: é-mes-lam-<ma> dingir-min-a-bi.
49. A. Falkenstein, "Zur Lage des südbabylonischen Durum," *AfO* 21 (1966), pp. 50f. On this date formula, see most recently Stol, (above, n. 43), pp. 22f., but read there Dūrum, not Dēr.
50. P. Michalowski, "Dūrum and Uruk during the Ur III period," *Mesopotamia* 12 (1977), pp. 83–96.

capture ushered in the fall of Uruk itself in the following year. The confusion is due in part to the almost generic character of the city-name, whose full form may have been Dur-Sinkashid.[51] An analogy is provided by Dunnum, a synonymous toponym;[52] of the many sites so named, one lay close to Isin and its fall precipitated the capture of that capital by Rim-Sin in the following year.[53]

Our letter, then, illuminates the linked fate of Durum and Uruk. Ninshatapada has drawn an accurate picture of her life and times that enables us to refine and correct the historical record based on monumental and archival sources. If it be asked how her letter-prayer came to be incorporated into the scribal curriculum, I would answer that it did so via the Royal Correspondence of Larsa, to which it found entry because its complimentary portrait of King Rim-Sin suited the ideology of that semi-official corpus. Its very language was that of the royal scribes who formulated the hymns, inscriptions and date-formulas of the dynasty. We may also assume that the princess and her plea found favor with Rim-Sin, and that he spared Durum as he had previously spared Uruk. Nor need we look far for the source of her inspiration. For between her princely birth and her priestly appointment, she was trained as a scribe (l.16) – indeed she is one of the few women outside of Sippar[54] known to have borne that proud honorific in the Old Babylonian period.[55] She thus stands in a long tradition of princely women of Sumer who enriched Sumerian literature with their creative talents: the daughter of Sargon, the widow of Ur-Nammu, the mother of Shu-Sin among them.[56]

What are the implications of these findings for our topic? If we retrace our steps for a moment, we will recall that the general reliability of canonical texts known only in copies of the 18th century (more or

51. *Ibid*, p. 88, n. 27. Previously Falkenstein (above, n. 27), pp. 28f.; Steible, (above, n. 29), pp. 347f.
52. For the possible equivalence of *dunnum* and *dūrum*, see now Jean-Marie Durand, "Notes sur l'histoire de Larsa," *RA* 71 (1977), p. 21, n. 1; Dominique Charpin, *RA* 72 (1978), p. 18 n. 25. Cf. also *MSL* 13 (1971), 69:89; 84:14.
53. Hallo, "Antediluvian cities," *JCS* 23 (1970), p. 66 and nn. 110–114.
54. Rivkah Harris, *JESHO* 6 (1963), pp. 138f.; B. Landsberger and M. Civil, *MSL* 9 (1967), pp. 148f.; cf. Civil, *MSL* 14 (1979), p. 135.
55. B. Meissner, *Babylonien und Assyrien*, II, 1925, p. 329 with references to *ABL* 1367 rev. 4 and 1368 rev. 6; R. Harris, *Orientalia* 38 (1969), pp. 140 and 145; *idem, Ancient Sippar*, 1975, pp. 196f. For dub-sar as an honorific, see Hallo *apud* B. Buchanan, *Early Near Eastern Seals* 1981, pp. 490f. There is an extensive "correspondence féminine" from Mari but its authors do not claim the scribal title; cf. G. Dossin and A. Finet, *ARMT* 10 (1978).
56. Hallo, "Women of Sumer," *Bibliotheca Mesopotamica* 4 (1976), pp. 29 and 31f. with nn. 49 and 66–69.

William W. Hallo

less) was defended by comparing them to and integrating their data with the evidence of monumental and archival texts of the 21st century. Specifically, one could point to numerous prosopographic correspondences (names, patronymics, professions etc.) between the "House of Ur-Meme" and the literary letters generally grouped with the "Royal Correspondence of Isin" in support of this assessment of the so-called "Letter-Collection B."[57] Much the same could be said for "Letter-Collection A" and the "Royal Correspondence of Ur"; here, indeed, the points of convergence go beyond prosopography to historical context and details. But the "Royal Correspondence of Larsa" now offers something more: verbatim identity between the very diction of this canonical corpus on the one hand, and the building inscriptions and date formulas of the dynasty on the other. What does this imply?

Ideally, I would like to be able to draw the conclusion that our case authenticates the literary correspondence as a primary historiographic source, i.e., as a group of documents copied with little or no change from originals on deposit in the royal archives. For it would be stretching credulity to suppose that a scribe would so accurately imitate the diction of the court if he was composing far away from it, in time or space.

But in fact the letter-prayer of Ninshatapada does not warrant this conclusion. Of its six extant exemplars, two come from Nippur, the others are of unknown provenience and, though none is dated, all are likely to belong to the same 18th century whose opening years are described in the text. This contrasts with the two and three centuries that separate the extant copies of the Isin and Ur correspondence from the events described therein. Thus we cannot simply "validate" that correspondence on the strength of the Larsa evidence. But we are entitled to draw another conclusion, equally important from the historiographic point of view.[58]

I submit that Ninshatapada, or whoever was the "author" of our letter-prayer, wrote it in response to a real, historical situation, and wrote it, moreover, in full knowledge of the requirements of royal phraseology. This phraseology of the court scribes I would like to

57. F.A. Ali, *Sumerian Letters* (University Microfilms), 1964. Cf. Claus Wilcke, "Die Quellen der literarisch überlieferten Briefe," *ZA* 60 (1970), pp. 67–69 with 4 tables.
58. The importance of Ninshatapada's letter for Sumerian historiography was recognized, on the basis of my remarks in "Women of Sumer" (above, n. 56) by Hruška (above, n. 2), p. 11.

designate the "chancery style,"[59] and I further suggest that it applied, if not equally then at least with due allowance for generic distinctions, to all three categories of cuneiform texts.

In this connection I find it necessary to reiterate a hypothesis advanced more than a decade ago: "There are striking and sometimes even literal parallels between the date formulas and the royal inscriptions, between the date formulas and the royal hymns, and between the royal hymns and the royal inscriptions. I am, therefore, inclined to reconstruct an annual or biennial ceremony, perhaps related to the New Year's celebration, in which one and the same event was memorialized in three distinct formulations: at its most concise in the official proclamation of the date formula; more fully in an appropriate building or votive inscription; and at its most elaborate in the royal hymns."[60]

The significance of this observation was not entirely lost on our Assyriological colleagues,[61] and indeed, a couple of years later I was invited by F.R. Kraus to enlarge on it for the Rencontre Assyriologique at Leiden devoted to "The Temple and its Cult." To do it justice would, however, have required more than the sampling of documentation which I was then able to offer for my hypothesis; it called for a systematic survey of all three genres during the "Classical Phase" of Mesopotamian civilization in order to establish all the attested correlations among them. Meanwhile, such a survey has now been completed as a doctoral dissertation at Yale.[62] It is not my purpose here to duplicate this investigation or anticipate its results. Suffice it to say that the original hypothesis quoted above seems to be confirmed at numerous points along the 500-year span for which its validity is claimed.[63]

What I am proposing here is that this very hypothesis can be extended to include not only the royal hymns but also the royal letter-prayers, and, presumably, other historiographical genres such as the so-called "triumphal inscriptions," in short, all the vehicles of the

59. Cf. F. Charles Fensham, *VT* 13 (1963), p. 133 on "the impact of the royal chancellery language in the latter part of the second millennium B.C. on the greater part of the ancient Near East," citing Klaus Baltzer, *Das Bundesformular* (1960), p. 28.
60. "The cultic setting of Sumerian poetry," *RAI* 17 (1970), pp. 118f.
61. Cf. Michalowski (above, n. 18), p. 716, n. 2; J. Renger, *RLA* 6 (1980), p. 68.
62. D.R. Frayne, *The Historical Correlations of the Sumerian Royal Hymns (2400-1900 B.C.)* (PhD dissertation, Yale University, 1981).
63. With this important proviso: that we do not insist "that *all* royal hymns were written to commemorate events recorded in year formulae, or that *all* year formulae were commemorated in hymns" (Frayne, *ibid.*, p. 500).

"chancery style." Together, they constitute impressive evidence that, already in Sumerian-speaking times, or should I say in Sumerian-writing times, the great political, military and cultic events of the court were chronicled as they happened. As this evidence grows, it may yet have to be thrown into the balance in the search for the origins of later, more sophisticated cuneiform historiography. But already it allows us to reclaim at least some of the finest examples of Sumerian literature from the realm of legend or historical tradition and claim it instead for historiography.[64]

64. Comparable conclusions were reached for some Akkadian literary texts by J.J.M. Roberts, "Nebuchadnezzar's Elamite Crisis in Theological Perspective," in Maria de Jong Ellis (ed.), *Essays on the Ancient Near East in Memory of Jacob Joel Finkelstein* (Connecticut Academy of Arts and Sciences, Memoirs 19), Hamden, Conn., 1977, pp. 183–187.

HITTITE HISTORIOGRAPHY: A SURVEY

The Oriental Institute, University of Chicago

When asking myself: what significant contributions did the Hittites make to the cultural history of the world, I can only think of two fields: art and literature. Yet even there their contributions are limited. Their art, while having a marked style of its own, owes most of its subject matters and modes of expression to the general tradition of the Near East, and in quality it cannot be compared to that of Egypt, although it does, in its best products, match that of other parts of Western Asia. Literature, too, is in great part an adaptation of foreign works. This is true of hymns and prayers as well as of the more elaborate epic compositions. As original works of mythological literature there remain those of truly Anatolian, i.e., most probably Hattic origin: the various stories about a lost or hiding god and that of the conflict between the Stormgod and the Dragon. In the field of mythology, the Hittites were transmitters rather than creators, as has been shown by a comparison of the Kumarbi myths with the *Theogony* of Hesiod and other works.

In contrast, it seems to me that the Hittites made original contributions in the field of historiography. It is true that the Hittites produced neither a Herodotus nor a Thucydides. Some of our colleagues in Classical studies consider this enough to dismiss all Hittite and – for that matter – other near-eastern historical texts as unworthy of their consideration. If this standard is employed, there is no point in arguing. But we should not apply extraneous standards to a period and a civilization to which they are not applicable. Leaving them aside, we shall see that the Hittite historical texts have merits of their own.

What kinds of historical texts do we find? There are first-person accounts of kings, a type well known from Babylonia. There it grew out

21

Hans G. Güterbock

of the dedicatory inscription styled in the *inūma – inūmišu* pattern: "I am king so-and-so. *When* I had conquered land X and done such and such deeds, *then* I built this temple for the god Y", where the historical account is in the "when" clause; the end consists of blessings for him who would preserve the building and curses against him who would destroy it.[1] It is noteworthy that this type was not taken over by the Hittites. Almost all their royal accounts begin with the Akkadian formula *umma* NN *šarru rabû* "thus speaks NN, the Great King," a formula that is common to royal edicts and letters. Some historical texts are indeed introductions to royal edicts or decrees, as we shall see. One cannot say that Hittite historiography grew out of royal edicts, since other texts are also introduced by the *umma* formula, for instance magical rituals which begin "Thus speaks Anniwiyani" or "Tunnawi" and many other incantation priests. What can be said is that the *umma* formula puts the historical accounts on the same level as any other pronouncement of the king.[2]

The only exceptions to this form are found at the very beginning and end of Hittite history. A text of Šuppiluliuma II, the last known king, begins with the words "I am Šuppiluliuma, the Great King, son of Tudḥaliya, the Great King, grandson of Ḫattušili, the Great King." This is identical with the beginning of the hieroglyphic Luwian inscription of the same ruler, as pointed out by Professor Laroche,[3] and is the standard form of introduction of all such inscriptions, which, thus, follow the Akkadian and especially the West-Semitic model.

The other exception is the much discussed text of Anitta of Kuššar. Its introduction is still a crux, since it only consists of his name, patronymic, and title followed apparently by *qibi*, the imperative "speak", which is common in letters but makes little sense without saying "to whom" the reader should speak. Here it almost sounds as if the command were addressed to Anitta! Be that as it may, what is perhaps more interesting is the fact that at one point the text says that this account was inscribed on the gate – a reflex of the Babylonian type

1. S. Mowinckel, "Die vorderasiatischen Königs-und Fürsteninschriften," *Eucharisterion* (H. Gunkel Festschrift I, *FRLANT* 19), Göttingen 1923, pp. 278–322; W. Baumgartner, *OLZ* 27 (1924), pp. 313–317.
2. In *ZA* 44 (1938), pp. 94f., I only spoke of historical texts which have the form of edicts, but did not derive all Hittite historiography from edicts. Nor did I do so in a paper read before the Turkish History Congress of 1937 (published in Turkish only): *Ikinci Türk Tarih Kongresi (Türk Tarih Kurumu Yaınlarından IX.* Seri, N°.2), Instanbul, 1943, pp. 177–181.
3. E. Laroche "Nisantas", *Anatolica 3* (1969–70, pp. 93–98.

of building inscription. But strangely, this mention of an inscription comes very early in the text, and the narrative continues after this, as though the author had added the accounts of the most important events to an existing short text.

The Anitta text is now available in the German translation of Erich Neu;[4] Vieyra gave excerpts in French.[5] A few of the better preserved sections follow as samples:

> Anitta, son of Pidhana, king of Kuššara, speak!
> He (i.e., Pidhana) was dear to the Stormgod of Heaven,
> and as he was dear to the Stormgod of Heaven
> the king of Neša [. . .] to the king of Kuššara.

> The king of Kuššara came with might down from (his) city
> and took Neša at night by assault.
> He captured the king of Neša
> but did no harm to the people of Neša;
> he [rather] treated them as mothers and fathers.

> After my father Pidhana I defeated an uprising in one year:
> By (the help of) the Sungod, whatever country rose up, I
> defeated them all.

> (there follows a fragmentary section dealing with various
> towns, among them Hatti)

> These words [I put] on my gate with a tablet.
> In all future, let no one destroy this tablet!
> Whoever destroys it shall be (counted as) enemy of Neša!

> For the second time Piyušti, king of Hatti, ca[me],
> and his helper whom he brought along,
> I [defeated(?)] them at Šalampa.

> All countries from Zalpuwa, from the sea on [I
> defeated(?)].
> Formerly Uhna, the king of Zalpuwa, had carried the god
> Šiušmi from Neša to Zalpuwa.
> Finally I, Great King Anitta, brought Šiušmi from

---

4. E. Neu, *Der Anitta-Text* (*StBoT* 18), 1974.
5. M. Vieyra, in R. Labat, *et al.*, *Les religions du Proche-Orient asiatique*, 1970, p. 467.

Zalpuwa back to Neša.
But Huzziya, the (present) king of Zalpuwa, I brought
alive to Ncša.
But Hattuša ...; I left it alone.
When it finally was plagued by hunger,
my god Halmašuits handed it over[6] (so that)
I took it at night by assault
and sowed weeds in its place.

Whoever becomes king after me
and settles Hattuša again,
let the Stormgod of Heaven hit him!

There follow a campaign against Šalatiwar, a report on building activities, a royal hunting expedition, and *another* campaign against Šalatiwar. The last paragraph reads:

When I went to war [against . . .], the ruler of Purušhanda
[brought] gifts to me: he brought me a seat of iron and a
staff(?) of iron as gifts. When he goes into the inner cham-
ber, he sits down in front of me on my right. (End of text)

In the past I thought that since Anitta's name occurs in Old Assyrian
documents from Kültepe and even in one from Alishar said to bear his
seal, his chancery would have only used the Old Assyrian language and
script. I argued that if Anitta had wanted to have the Hittite language
written down, his scribes would have employed the Assyrian script for
it, too. I could only explain the fact that Hittite was written in the
Babylonian type of cuneiform by assuming a time lapse between Anitta and the first writing of Hittite. Therefore the Anitta inscription,
which makes the impression of an authentic document, would have
been originally written in Assyrian and later translated into Hittite.[7] I
have changed my mind. First, Neu has demonstrated that the text
shows no trace of being a translation.[8] Secondly, we now know from the

6. In this interpretation I now follow F. Starke, "Halmasuit im Anitta-Text . . .", *ZA*
 69 (1979), pp. 47–120.
7. H.G. Güterbock, *ZA* 44 (1938), pp. 139–143; idem, *JAOS* 84 (1964), p. 109.
8. Neu (above, n. 4), pp. 132–135. His main arguments are the fact that the language
 of the Anitta Text is good Old Hittite, which he contrasts with the un-Hittite word
 order observed in translations from the Hattic, and a few details, such as the non-
 occurrence of the particles -*za* and -*kan*. Neu also thinks that the divine name
 Sius(mis) here still means "Sun" in contrast to the normal (according to him: later)

sealed bullae and inscribed dockets found at Acemhüyük shown by Mrs. Nimet Özgüç in lectures in New York and Chicago[9] that about the time of Anitta central Anatolia was in contact with Mari, and that some of those dockets are inscribed in Babylonian characters, not Assyrian. If, as is likely, Acemhüyük is the site of Purušhanda, the special honors accorded its king by Anitta gain in importance. And it is by no means impossible that Anitta employed Assyrian-trained scribes when dealing with the Assyrian merchants, but Babylonian, or rather Syrian-trained ones for writing Hittite. We do not know Anitta's own ethnic background, but there is no reason why he could not have been a Hittite and spoken that language, which is attested in Kültepe even long before his time. I, for one, do not call him a "Protohattian"!

The main exemplar of the text is written in the kind of handwriting which we now know to belong to the Old Hittite kingdom and may well be a copy made at that time, that is, some 100 to 150 years after Anitta.

From the Old Kingdom we have a number of historical texts of different nature. Of Hattušili I two texts were handed down and copied until the time of the New Kingdom. In character they differ: one is a highly personal document in which the ageing and ailing king installs his adopted son Muršili as successor.[10] Its aim is not to write history but to show the reasons for the old monarch's decisions. In doing so he draws upon the past, tells what happened before in order to justify what he did, in the form of short episodes inserted into the body of the edict. This method is characteristic of a number of Hittite works of later times as we shall see. The other text is the oldest example of what may be called Annals in that it reports the king's military exploits

meaning "god" of *sius*. This theory, unconvincing as it was, has now been aptly refuted by Starke (above, n. 6). The "good Old Hittite" could also be explained if the text were a free version of an Akkadian text rather than a translation. In so far the objections to Neu's dating voiced in the general discussion by Dr. Aaron Kempinsky are valid. On the other hand, since recent finds at Kültepe (still unpublished) tend to extend the duration of the *karum* IB period, to which Anitta belongs, to some time after Hammurapi, the time lapse between Anitta (late 18th century?) and Labarna I (middle of 17th century) is much shorter than previously assumed, so Anitta would not be that much earlier than the Old Kingdom. For possible contemporary Akkadian models, see below n. 12.

9. A Turkish version appeared in *Belleten* 41 (1977), pp. 357–381; an English version in E. Porada (ed.), *Ancient Art in Seals*, Princeton 1980, pp. 61–69.

10. F. Sommer–A. Falkenstein, *Die hethitisch-akkadische Bilingue des Hattusili I (Labarna II) (Abhandlungen der Bayerischen Akademie der Wissenschaften*, Philologisch-Historische Abteilung, Neue Folge 16), 1938.

year by year, covering the first five of his reign.[11] The term "annals" is here used in the same sense as for the later Hittite and Assyrian annals which also cover military activities only and say nothing of other events.

Two points attract our attention here. One is the fact that both documents of Hattušili I exist in an Akkadian version alongside the Hittite. The language is not Assyrian but Babylonian, and obviously "made in Hattuša"! Why or for whom were the Akkadian versions written? Was this one of the requirements of the scribal school? Maybe texts had to be put into the classical language simply because it was the basis of all learning? We do not know.

Professor Tadmor has suggested[12] that Babylonian or Syrian inscriptions similar to the building inscription of Yahdun-Lim might have served as model for the "Annals" of Hattušili I (and, by extension, we may add also for the text of Anitta?). If so, Hattušili's scribes changed the format: his text is not a building inscription. The style is much drier; the narrative consists of a simple enumeration of the cities conquered and the booty taken. The fragmentary inscription of Zimri-Lim, mentioned by Professor Tadmor as another possible model, is closer to this dry style. Only in the last paragraph, where Hattušili stresses his most glorious deed, is the style more elaborate:[13]

> No-one had crossed the Euphrates, but I, the Great King Tabarna, crossed it on foot, and my army crossed it [after me(?)] on foot. Sargon [(also) crossed it]; he defeated the troops of Hahhum [but] did nothing to [Hahhum] and [did not] burn it down, nor did he show the smoke to the Storm-god of Heaven. I, the Great King Tabarna, destroyed Haššuwa and Hahhum and burned them down with fire and [showed] the smoke to the [Storm]god of Heaven. And the king of Haššuwa and the king of Hahhum I harnessed to a wagon.

This shows that the Sargon stories were known to the king or his writers. In the light of the discoveries at Tell Mardikh the famous expedition of Sargon of Akkad against Nur-Dagan of Purušhanda has

---

11. H. Otten *MDOG* 91 (1958), pp. 78–83; F. Imparati and C. Saporetti, *Studi Classici e Orientali* 14 (1965), pp. 40–85.
12. H. Tadmor, in *Essays on the Ancient Near East in Memory of J.J. Finkelstein* (Connecticut Academy of Arts and Sciences, Memoirs 19), 1977, p. 213.
13. H.G. Güterbock, *JCS* 18 (1964), pp. 1–6.

a better chance now of reflecting a real event, but this would have taken place seven centuries before Ḥattušili. Since there existed a literature about the kings of Akkad already in the Old Babylonian period, it is likely that Ḥattušili knew of this famous king through some literary texts of the so-called Historical Tradition. The Hittites themselves also produced works of this genre. Leaving aside the popular story of *šar tamḫari*, The King of Battle, about Sargon's campaign to Anatolia,[14] I want to dwell on those texts of the Tradition literature which must be dated to the Old Kingdom on the basis of their archaic language.

Fragments of this literature were known for a long time, as they were included in Forrer's *Boghazköi–Texte in Umschrift*, First part, of 1922. But new finds of recent years restored those texts and added new ones. The most striking new find is the beginning of the story about the city of Zalpa. The second half of the text was known, but the beginning was a new find, ably published by Professor Otten.[15] The story deserves being read:

> The queen of Kaneš gave birth to thirty boys in one year. She said: "What a crowd did I give birth to!" She filled boxes with manure, put the boys inside and entrusted them to the river. The river carried them to the sea, into the country of Zalpuwa. The gods lifted the boys out of the sea and raised them.
>
> When years had passed, the queen again gave birth, (this time) to thirty girls. Those she raised herself. The sons set out to go back to Neša, taking a donkey along. When they came to Tamarmara, they said (to the people): "You heated the house so that the donkey will mount!" The townspeople replied: "Wherever we come, a donkey will mount [once]." The boys said: "Wherever *we* come, a woman gives birth to [one] child [or two children], but she had *us* [all] at once!" The townspeople answered: "Once our queen of Kaneš gave birth to thirty girls, but her sons got lost!" The boys said in their heart: "Our mother, whom we were seeking, we have found! Come, let us go to Neša!"

14. H.G. Güterbock, "Die historische Tradition und ihre literarische Gestaltung . . . ", *ZA* 42 [N.F.8], (1934), pp. 1–91; 44 [N.F.10] (1938), pp. 45–149. For *šar tamḫari* see *ZA* 44, ppp. 45–49; P. Meriggi, *Gedenkschrift W. Brandenstein*, 1968, pp. 259–269; H.G. Güterbock, *MDOG* 101 (1969), pp. 14–26.
15. H. Otten *Eine althethitische Erzählung um die Stadt Zalpa (StBoT* 17), 1973.

> When they went to Neša, the gods gave them different
> features, so that their mother did not recognize [her sons].
> So she gave her daughters to her own sons. The sons did not
> recognize their sisters . . .

The only one who senses the danger of incest is the youngest, and he warns his brothers; but a gap in the text leaves it to us to guess what happened. Since the continuation deals with hostilities lasting through three generations of Hittite kings one may guess that the sin committed by the sons was considered the cause of the ensuing evil. But this remains speculation.

You may dismiss all this as legend, hence not historiography. But so many nations counted sagas, the tradition of Before the Flood, or the tales of the Heroic Age as real part of their history, that we may allow the Hittites the same. What matters is that they wrote such a story down, probably after it had lived in oral tradition, and that it is a good story.[16]

Not all stories of this literary genre are as unreal as this one. The story of the siege of Uršu, in Akkadian,[17] and the Old Hittite account of the war against Ḫaššuwa and its ally, the general Zukraši from Aleppo,[18] are apparently dealing with real events in a literary style that employs the device of relating the speeches of the protagonists. The events fall into the reign of Ḫattušili I, and the Old Hittite story, according to its language, must have been written relatively soon after the events, under the next king at the latest. Unfortunately the text is too fragmentary and too difficult to be presented here.

But let us turn to the best known historical text of the Old Kingdom, The Proclamation of Telipinu.[19] I consider it a most remarkable piece of writing. To be sure, it is not "pure" historiography for history's sake, but rather an account that serves the purpose of showing reason for political action. The purpose is the regulation of the dynastic succession and the establishment of jurisdiction over the royal family. The introduction is to show that these measures were necessary because in the past, whenever there was unity at home there was success abroad, but when there was strife and murder in the royal family then disaster befell the whole country. The text has been criticized for being

16. In the discussion, Judg. 12:8–9 was mentioned, which simply states that the Judge Ibzan had 30 sons and 30 daughters and acquired 30 daughters-in-law.
17. *ZA* 44 (1938), pp. 114–125.
18. H. Otten, *MDOG* 86 (1953), pp. 60 f.
19. E.H. Sturtevant and G. Bechtel, *A Hittite Chrestomathy*, 1935, pp. 182–193.

repetitious, even for having introduced a non-existing first king. I cannot share this view. The repetitions are an impressive stylistic device[20] telling us that under the second and third king things went as well – or nearly so – as under the first; equally impressive is the use of corresponding phrases for the description of the bad times. For reasons that lie outside our discussion here I maintain that Labarna I was a real king and not an invention of Telipinu's scribes. The ability of the author to organize a narrative covering many generations under one theme deserves our admiration.[21]

The use of historical narrative for "showing cause" for action is a device used more often, particularly in the vassal treaties. Although the history as told in these is one-sided, one has to acknowledge the clarity of these accounts and how they 'make their point'. One of the best examples is the treaty between Tudḫaliya IV and Šaušgamuwa of Amurru.[22] Its introduction starts with the statement that Amurru was not conquered by force of arms, but that Aziru rather sought Šuppiluliuma's overlordship by his own free will and remained faithful also to Muršili. Skipping Duppi-Tešub, the text then turns to the time of Muwatalli; it says that "the people Amurru" simply declared that they had been vassals by free will and now chose to terminate the relation and sided with the king of Egypt. So then "Muwatalli and the king of Egypt fought about them, and Muwatalli defeated him" (the laconic Hittite reference to the battle of Qadesh!), subjugated Amurru and installed Šapili as its king. Ḫattušili then replaced Šapili by Bentišina, who remained faithful, and now Tudḫaliya concludes this treaty with Bentišina's son Šaušgamuwa to whom he gives his sister in marriage.

There follows the usual admonitions to acknowledge only the direct descendants of the king, and in order to show clearly what the vassal is *not* to do, Tudḫaliya tells a story. This is not part of the introduction but rather one of those illustrating anecdotes which we briefly mentioned as being used in the edict of Ḫattušili I. It reads:

> Do not act like Mašturi! This Mašturi, who was king of
> the Šeḫa River Land – Muwatalli took him, made him his

20. A device discussed by J. Licht, *Storytelling in the Bible*, Jerusalem, 1979. His simplest examples (pp. 57ff.) come closest to the Hittite text.
21. An analysis of the Telipinu text was given by H. A. Hoffner, Jr., in H. Goedicke and J. J. M. Roberts (eds.) *Unity and Diversity*, Baltimore, 1975, pp. 51–56; he describes it as an apology.
22. C. Kühne and H. Otten, *Der Šaušgamuwa-Vertrag (StBoT 16)*, 1971.

Hans G. Güterbock

brother-in-law by giving him his sister in marriage, and installed him as king in Šeḫa. But when Muwatalli became god, his son Urḫitešub became king. [But my father] took the kingship away from Urḫitešub. Mašturi, however, joined the plot, and he whom Muwatalli had made his brother-in-law, did not protect the latter's son Urḫitešub but rather sided with my father, (saying) "Should I protect a bastard?" (referring to the fact that Urḫitešub was the son of a lesser wife of the king). Would you ever act like Mašturi?

The frankness with which Tudḫaliya here refers to his father's action is quite surprising; it shows how far objectivity was on occasion carried.

There are other examples of the use of historical narrative to explain political action. From Ḫattušili III we have a number of edicts written with the stated purpose of granting exemption from feudal duties to certain estates. In some of these the narrative is no longer an introduction but has become the essential part. The best known of these is the so-called Apology or Autobiography of the king,[23] in which he ascribes his rise to power to the favor of Ištar, who protected him from the beginning and finally helped his against the transgressions of his nephew Urḫitešub. In his gratitude he donates the estate of one of his opponents to the goddess, appoints his son Tudḫaliya as its administrator, and exempts it from all duties. This is the "edict" part of the text, which otherwise is a masterpiece of political propaganda, but impressive by its logical development of events.[24]

So far I have mainly talked about historical texts written for a purpose. If you wish, you may exclude them from historiography, if you define it as only the writing of history for its own sake, for telling "what really happened". The Hittites came close even to such "real" historiography in the class of texts which we call Annals because of the arrangement by successive years. The Hittites called them *pišnadar*,

23. Sturtevant–Bechtel (above, n. 19), pp. 64–83. A new edition is: H. Otten, *Die Apologie Hattusilis III.* (*StBoT* 24), 1981.
24. On the propagandistic and apologetic character of the text see A. Archi, "The Propaganda of Hattušili III", *Studi Micenei ed Egeo-Anatolici* 14 (1971), pp. 185–216; Hoffner, (above, n. 21), pp. 51–55; cf. the paper by Prof. Tadmor in this volume on "Autobiographical Apology in the Royal Assyrian Literature".

literally "manliness", meaning Manly Deeds.[25] If we say "Deeds" for short, we should remember that the Hittite term is not the same as *res gestae*, but rather has the connotation of *virtutes*. We mentioned one such work of the Old Kingdom, but the best examples come from the New Kingdom, and especially from Muršili II, who reigned shortly before 1300 BC.

It is strange that those annals texts that have been preserved are so unevenly distributed among the known kings. We have fragments of the Annals of Tudḥaliya, the first ruler of the New Kingdom, and of a similar text about his co-regency with his son Arnuwanda I.[26] The great Šuppiluliuma did not write annals; his Manly Deeds[27] were written by his son, Muršili II, who must have felt it necessary to fill the gap. Muršili's own Annals are by far the best preserved of all.[28] After that we only find a few fragments which may or may not be parts of annals of Ḥattušili III.[29]

It is hard to explain this phenomenon. Is it really by chance that all the other annals were destroyed? Is there another archive hidden underground at Boghazköy with all the 'missing texts'? One might also think that some kings did not care to write about their deeds, and that Muršili, whose personality speaks to us from his numerous texts, was more than others given to conscientious and detailed reporting about what happened and why.

I just spoke of kings as 'writing' their annals. I know that most kings were not able to write, and I do not mean that the king wrote in person on a tablet. But there is no denying that some texts make the impression of vividly expressing the views or feelings of an individual, and Muršili's texts, especially his prayers, have this quality. One may argue whether such texts were actually dictated by the king or whether he would only give guidelines to his 'scribes' who would then use their own words. In this connection the question of sources comes up. A text like the Ten-year Annals of Muršili must have been conceived as a whole and written at one time, which obviously could not have been

---

25. Usually written partly logographically as LÚ-*natar*; see J. Friedrich, *Hethitisches Wörterbuch*, s.v. For the Hittite reading see E. Neu and H. Otten, *Indogermanische Forschungen* 77 (1972), pp. 181–190. (In the discussion, M. Weinfeld compared גבורה, as used, e.g., in 1 Kings 16:27).
26. Listed in E. Laroche, *Catalogue des Textes Hittites*, 1971, nr. 142–143.
27. H. G. Güterbock, *JCS* 10 (1956).
28. A. Götze, *Die Annalen des Mursilis (MVAG* 38), 1933 [Nachdruck: Darmstadt, 1967] (Hereafter: *AM*).
29. Laroche (above, n. 26), nr. 82.

earlier than the tenth year of his reign. It is unlikely that it was then all written from memory; there must have been some records on which the writers could draw. It has been observed that some parts of the Deeds of Šuppiluliuma, which only list the conquest of one city after another, look like simple quotes from such records. The search for, and use of, archival material is mentioned. The best examples are in the Deeds of Šuppiluliuma and in one of the Plague Prayers of Muršili.[30] Both texts quote verbatim from the same old tablet that told how the Stormgod had led the people of Kuruštama to Egypt, and how on that occasion the Hittites and Egyptians had concluded a treaty. The context of these quotes is different: in the Deeds it serves as background to the new ties expected from the marriage of a prince with the widow of Tutankhamun; in the Prayer it serves to show that the Hittite attack on Amqa, which preceded the Egyptian queen's request for a prince, was a breach of that old treaty, causing the plague as divine punishment.

The three works of Manly Deeds composed under (or by) Muršili deserve special attention. (The following remarks are largely based on the careful analysis by Professor Cancik of Tübingen in his recent book.)[31] There are, first, the Manly Deeds of Šuppiluliuma, written in the third person with the word "my father" as subject (and "my grandfather" where actions of Šuppiluliuma's father are reported). Thereby Muršili makes it quite clear that this is *his* account of his father's deeds. Second, the so-called Ten-year Annals, which deal with the first ten years of Muršili's reign, and third, his Comprehensive Annals which did (or at least were meant to) cover his entire reign. But the time span covered is not the only difference. The Ten-year Annals have a prologue and an epilogue in which it is stated that this is an account of how the king defeated the enemies who challenged him upon his accession, that he accomplished this within ten years, and that he left out of this account all the military operations conducted by "the princes and lords".[32]

Comprehensive Annals also cover the first ten years and then continue for several more. Where for an episode both versions are preserved, the difference is striking. Not only are the activities of the princes and generals included in the Comprehensive Annals,

30. Plague Prayer: A. Götze, in *Kleinasiatische Forschungen* 1 (1930), pp. 208–213; idem, in *ANET*, p. 395; Deeds: Güterbock (above, n. 27), p. 98.
31. H. Cancik, *Grundzüge der hethitischen und alttestamentlichen Geschichtsschreibung (Abhandlungen des Deutschen Palästinavereins)*, Wiesbaden, 1976.
32. Götze, *AM*, pp. 23, 137, Cancik (above, n. 31), pp. 102ff.

but in most cases much more detail is given. Also, the Comprehensive Annals describe simultaneous events and how they were related to one another. Stylistically, much use is made of quoted speech, messages, complex syntactical periods including conditional and temporal clauses, and the mode of the non-real for actions that were contemplated but not carried out. Time does not allow for verbatim quotes, so let me give a summary of the account of part of the ninth year.[33]

There was trouble in Palā, that is, Paphlagonia, north-west of Hattuša, and Muršili sent the general Nuwanza there, who was successful. The king himself went to Kizzuwatna (Cilicia) to worship Hebat of Kummanni. While he was there, his brother Šarrikušuh, king of Carchemish, joined him but fell ill and died. Now first the body was (or rather, the ashes were) taken to Hattuša for the funerary rites, but Muršili apparently stayed in Kizzuwatna and mourned his brother there. Now he got news of a revolt in Nuhašše (in North Syria). He decided to send a general named Kurunda with troops to Nuhašše, with the order to destroy the crops. We are told that the gods punished the kings of Nuhašše for having broken their oaths, and that Aitakama, the king of Qadesh, was killed by his son Niqmaddu.[34] Niqmaddu then submitted to Muršili, but the latter did not accept him as vassal, rather expressed the wish that the divine punishment should take its course. Someone, presumably Kurunda, then goes and conquers Qadesh. Meanwhile, troops of Hayaša (in Eastern Anatolia) made an incursion, so Muršili now ordered Nuwanza to take care of that danger. But this time Nuwanza wanted to be on the safe side, so he asked the king to consult the oracles for him. The king, still in Kizzuwatna, now first gives the reason why he himself does not march against Hayaša. In a broken passage the name Carchemish occurs, followed by the verb "defeated"; apparently Carchemish, which just had lost its king, was threatened by some enemy whose name is lost (Assur and Egypt have been suggested). Muršili argues like this: "Had I now marched against this foe (meaning, Hayaša), would not [the new enemy], if he heard it, have spoken thus: 'His father conquered Carchemish . . . His brother, whom he had made king in Carchemish, has died. But he (Muršili) did

33. Götze, *AM*, pp. 107–127.
34. For this reading of the name see W. F. Albright, *BASOR* 95 (1944), pp. 31f. The text has a clear *ma*, not *ba*. The same name also in a letter found by the British at Qadesh (Tell Nebi Mend) itself, as reported by A. R. Millard at the 23e Rencontre Assyriologique Internationale in Birmingham, 1976.

not go to Carchemish and did not put it in order, but rather went into another country.' When I had said so to myself, I did consult the oracles for Nuwanza, the general, and it was decided for him by the oracles in the affirmative."

The king now sent a special messenger to Nuwanza with a letter telling him the favorable outcome of the oracles and commanding him to proceed: "The Stormgod has already given you this Hayašaean enemy, so you will smite him!" The king himself then proceeded to Carchemish, with a detour via Aštata (Emar near Meskene)! When he arrived at Aštata, he built a citadel and stationed a garrison there. Now Kurunda brought Niqmaddu of Qadesh, who had killed his father Aitakama, before the king, who now accepted him as vassal. While on his way from Aštata to Carchemish, Muršili was met by the prince who had been sent to Nuwanza. He reported that Nuwanza had indeed defeated the Hayašaean army of 10,000 men and 700 chariots. After a gap we read that Muršili installed in Carchemish the son of his late brother. He then proceeded to Tegarama, where he was met by the successful Nuwanza and other lords. With another of those "I would have − but" constructions he writes: "I would even have marched against Hayaša, but the year had grown short. The lords, too, said to me: 'The year has grown short! Don't march against Hayaša, o lord! So I did not go to Hayaša but rather to Harran, where I met my troops."

The full text of the episode just summarized once covered two columns or 160 lines of a tablet. In all its complexity it gives a vivid picture of events which most probably really happened the way they are told here. The description of how the king had to make decisions in difficult situations has the ring of truth. You will ask: does the objectivity go as far as admitting defeat? The answer is that I do not remember any mention of a defeat of one of the king's own campaigns. Advances of an enemy are frequently mentioned, but always as preceding the king's successful countermeasures. But Muršili says on some occasions (of which we just saw examples) that he was unable to act, and why.

Finally there is one other aspect: the degree to which the narrative includes actions of the gods. Recognition of divine help is common to the historiography of many nations, so we can expect it also in that of the Hittites. We saw that Anitta ascribes the conquest of Hattusa to the action of his god, whose rescue from Zalpa he tells in an inserted account of antecedents, a device used by Muršili four hundred years later. Muršili invariably mentions the help of the gods whenever he reports a victory – it is almost a cliché.[35] More specific action of the gods also occurs. During the war against Arzawa a phenomenon called *kalmišana*, traditionally translated "thunderbolt", appeared in the sky and frightened the ruler of Arzawa so much that he became ill and unable to deal his troops against the Hittites. Another time, when Muršili successfully leads his troops in night marches, unnoticed by the enemy, it was the Stormgod who summoned the god Ḫašameli who then "hid" the army, that is, made it invisible.[36] While the "thunderbolt" may well be a real natural phenomenon, possibly a meteorite, the other instances are no more than the devout acknowledgment of divine help that we expect. They do not constitute the kind of active interference of the gods which are found in myths and epics. Nor is the mention of divine help comparable to biblical concept of divine guidance.*

35. For the frequent phrase "the gods helped me" (lit. "walked in front of me") see the references in Götze, *AM*, p. 287 s.v. *ḫuia*-with *piran*.
36. The two episodes are in Götze, *AM*, pp. 47–49 and 127, respectively. For this kind of divine help see M. Weinfeld's paper in the present volume.
* In the interim, a detailed treatment of the subject by H.A. Hoffner, "History and Historians of the Ancient Near East: The Hittites" has appeared in *Orientalia* 49 (1980), pp. 283–332.

AUTOBIOGRAPHICAL APOLOGY
IN THE ROYAL ASSYRIAN LITERATURE

HAYIM TADMOR

The Hebrew University of Jerusalem

I

Literary compositions by kings who assumed their office in an irregular fashion are not uncommon in the literature of the Ancient Near East. One may detect them in Egypt, among the Hittites, in ancient Syrian states, and in more explicit form in Assyria and Babylonia. These compositions are the only ones within the entire corpus of the Ancient Near Eastern royal literature to contain autobiographical elements. Furthermore, they are usually of an apologetic nature, explaining the irregular circumstances under which their royal authors, not being first in the line of succession, reached their thrones.[1]

The most eloquent specimen of the autobiographical genre belongs to Hattushili III, king of the Hittites – an apologetic account of his usurpation of the throne. The term "apology", given most fittingly to this composition by Sturtevant[2] and reaffirmed recently by

---

1. This genre should be set apart from the fictional or pseudo-autobiographies, such as those of Sargon and Naram-Sin, kings of Akkad, or Nebuchadnezzar I, king of Babylonia. Though similar in form to the apologetic autobiographies, they constitute an entirely different literary and ideological category. For the classification of this genre, often referred to as the "*narû*-literature" (H. G. Güterbock, *ZA* 42 1934, pp. 19–24), see now A. K Grayson, *Babylonian Historical Literary Texts*, Toronto and Buffalo, 1975, pp. 7–8 and nn. 10–11; and most recently: *idem, Orientalia* 49 (1980), pp. 187–188 and B. Lewis, *The Sargon Legend* (*ASOR* Dissertations Series 4), Cambridge, Mass., 1980, pp. 88–93. In this connection of special interest is the discussion of A. Momigliano on the apologetic biographies and pseudo-autobiographies in Greek literature: *The Development of Greek Biography*, Cambridge, Mass., 1971, pp. 58–60.

2. E. H. Sturtevant, and G. Bechtel, *A Hittite Chrestomathy*, Philadelphia, 1935, pp. 43–99; cf. also G. Furlani, *Saggi sulla civiltà degli Hittiti*, Udine, 1937–39, pp. 141–186; H. M. Wolf, *The Apology of Hattusilis Compared with Other Politi-*

Hoffner,[3] may be applied also to other similar autobiographical compositions, even when the apologetic section is only part of a longer royal inscription.

And indeed, the Assyrian apologetic documents – the main focus of the present study – all form the introductory section of longer royal *res gestae*, narrating the achievements of the king as a military-hero and as a pious master-builder.

Our present inquiry will not be concerned with the formal structure and the literary qualities of these and similar royal documents of self-justification – a topic which deserves a separate study and methodologically different approach – but with their specific historical *Sitz im Leben*. It is our contention that they were composed not so much in order to reflect apologetically upon the past but rather to serve certain imminent political aims in the present or some particular design for the future. Save for the few apologetic autobiographies which carry a date (e.g., Idrimi's of Alalakh, composed in his 30th year[4]), it has usually been assumed that these compositions stem from that psychological and political situation which confronted the usurper at the beginning of his reign. It was then that he was supposed to have made the literary effort to convince his audience gods, courtiers, and posterity of the legitimacy and the smooth order of his succession. However, an inquiry into the historical circumstances under which some of the Mesopotamian apologies were composed corroborates that assumption only in part. Whereas apologies written at the beginning of the reign seem to have been typical of the Chaldaean kings of Babylonia and their Achaemenid Persian successors, the extant apologies of the Assyrian kings were not put into writing until long after the accession. Their *raison d'être* could hardly have been the immediate need to conciliate opponents and allay complaints stemming from the irregular elevation to the throne. They were written, we shall attempt to show, in conjunction with the appointment of the successor – a crucial moment in the

cal Self-justifications of the Ancient Near East (University Microfilms), Ann-Arbor, 1967, pp. 12–13; A. Archi, *Studi Micenei ed Egeo-Anatolici* 14 (1971), p. 186; for new editions of the text see now: A. Ünal, *Hattušili III*, Heidelberg, 1974; H. Otten, *Die Apologie Hattusilis III* (*StBoT* 24), Wiesbaden, 1981.

3. H. A. Hoffner, Jr., "Propaganda and Political Justification in Hittite Historiography" in H. Goedicke and J. J. M. Roberts (eds.), *Unity and Diversity*, Baltimore, 1975, pp. 49–62; and now *idem*, *Orientalia* 49 (1980), pp. 315–317 (but cf. reservations of H. Cancik, *Grundzüge der hethitischen und alttestamentlichen Geschichtsschreibung*, Wiesbaden, 1976, p. 42; and Professor H. G. Güterbock's paper "Hittite Historiography" in the present volume).

4. See below, n. 66

life of every king and especially of those whose own coming to the
throne was not entirely in order. This can be exemplified by the autobiographical composition of Esarhaddon, designated henceforth as
"Esarhaddon's apology."

II

Esarhaddon's apology is not a self-sustained composition, but an introductory section to the longest of his historical prism inscriptions from
Nineveh,[5] Nin A according to Borger's classification.[6] Esarhaddon's installation in the royal office is described there in a fashion unparalleled
in any royal inscription as if an unusual literary form has been adopted
to express an equally unusual political situation. It was, as far as we
know, the first time in the history of Assyria, that an aging king
provided for his succession through an extraordinary state ceremony, in
which the courtiers, the royal family and the people were demanded to
swear a loyalty oath (=*adê*) to the heir apparent. As the introduction of
loyalty oaths in matters of royal succession was, as it seems, a novelty in
Assyria,[7] such a procedure would have been unusual even had that heir
been the first-born or elder son. It was certainly outstanding in this
particular case: Sennacherib's choice was not the eldest surviving son
but a younger prince, the beloved son of the dominant queen Naqi'a-
Zakutu.[8] And indeed, an actual fragment of such a loyalty oath – or one
of its drafts – was unearthed in Assur, but until recently remained
unidentified.[9] The far-reaching measures taken by Sennacherib to safeguard his succession should not surprise us. Sargon, his own father,
though a royal prince, usurped the throne, displacing the short-lived
branch of Tiglath-pileser III, who in turn was not the son of his predecessor, but a usurper, though also a prince of the royal family.

5. R. Campbell Thompson, *The Prisms of Esarhaddon and Ashurbanipal*, London
   1931, pp. 9ff.
6. R. Borger, *Die Inschriften Asarhaddons Königs von Assyrien* (*AfO* Beiheft 9),
   Graz, 1956, pp. 36ff. (Hereafter: Borger, *Asarhaddon*).
7. H. Tadmor, "Assyria and the West", in Goedicke-Roberts (above, n. 3), p. 43;
   idem, "The Aramaization of Assyria: Aspects of Western Impact" in H. Nissen
   and J. Renger (eds.), *Mesopotamien und seine Nachbarn* (*RAI* 25), Berlin, 1982,
   pp. 449–470; *idem,* "Treaty and Oath in the Ancient Near East" in G. M. Tucker
   and D. A. Knight (eds.), *Humanizing America's Iconic Book* (*SBL* Centennial
   Addresses 1980), Chico, Calif., 1982, pp. 128–155.
8. See H. Lewy, *JNES* 11 (1952), pp. 271–286; J. Nougayrol, *Syria* 33 (1957),
   pp. 156–158.
9. E. Ebeling, *Stiftungen und Vorschriften für Assyrische Tempel,* Berlin, 1954, p. 9,
   no. 2. See Tadmor, "Aramaization" (above, n. 7) n. 134.

Esarhaddon's apology begins with a *topos* well known from Mesopotamian royal literature – the motif of divine election. The king is said to have been chosen by the gods to rule over the country, while still in his childhood: Esarhaddon is the king "whose name Ashur, Shamash, Bel and Nabu, the Ishtar of Nineveh (and) the Ishtar of Arbela have pronounced (as destined) to reign over Assyria (ever) since he was a youngster (*ina ṣeherīšu*)" (Nin A, I, 5–7).

A similar statement was made by the royal scribe of Adad-nirari III, who like Esarhaddon benefitted from the protection of a powerful Queen-mother.[10] Yet, unlike his successor, who bore the presumptive name "Ashur the creator of an heir", Esarhaddon did not claim here that he had been predestined to rule Assyria while being "shaped in his mother's womb."[11] He could only assert that the gods had "pronounced his name" for kingship (*ibbû zikiršu*, a technical term for nomination) when still a youth. Royal rhetoric in this text had its limits.[12] Esarhaddon's argument is that his accession was well grounded in legal state-procedure. Though the youngest among his elder brothers, he was appointed as Sennacherib's heir with the approval of the gods, through a liver omen (I, 13–14): Shamash and Adad "answered by their affirmative yes" (*annu kēnu*) to the query about his nomination which Sennacherib put before them (I, 13). Moreover, the royal family, the court and the people of Assyria, rank and file, were assembled for the loyalty oath to the crown-prince (I, 15–19).[13] Esarhaddon was brought into the *bīt-ridūti*, the

10. "Whom Aššur, the king of the Igigi, had chosen (*uttûšu*), in his childhood (*ina* TUR-*šú*) and entrusted to him a rule without rival" IR 35 no. 1:1; no. 3:2. (add to *AHw*, p. 1087b, *ṣeḥēru* 2, b and *CAD* S p. 122).
11. So does Ashurbanipal, the Rassam Prism, I:5; Streck, *Assurbanipal und die letzen assyrischen Könige bis zum Untergange Ninevehs*, I–III, Leipzig, 1916, p. 2 (Hereafter: Streck, *Assurbanipal*). A similar statement is made by *Ashur-resh-ishi*, a king of the Middle Assyrian Period: *ša ... ina libbi agarinnišu kīniš iḫsuḫūšuma* = "whom (the great gods) truly chose (lit. desired), while he was (still) in his mother's womb", *CAD* A I, p. 146a.
12. However, in two other texts, unfortunately fragmentary, it is said that he had been "[created by, looked upon, with favour by] Ishtar, while still in his mother's womb" (*šassuru, agarinnu*): Borger, *Asarhaddon* §82, obv. 8; §101, obv. 12–13. This *topos* is attested once in an inscription of Sennacherib: D. D. Luckenbill, *The Annals of Sennacherib* (*OIP* 2), Chicago, 1924, p. 117:3.
13. Apparently, on that solemn occasion, Esarhaddon was given the new ceremonial name of *Aššur-etil-ilāni-mūkin-apli* – "Ashur the lord of gods is the establisher of an heir" – and the title of *mār-šarri rabû ša bīt-ridūti*, "the crown prince (lit. king's eldest son) of the Succession House." See Borger, *Asarhaddon*, §30:1 and *ABL*, 1432 rev. 1-3. In another document (*ibid.*, §95:1), Esarhaddon is called *aplu ašarēdu*, "the first and foremost heir," of Sennacherib.

House of Succession, where he received his training for kingship (I, 20–22).

The crisis came when the brothers, so Esarhaddon claims, estranged him from his father:

> They originated against me slander (*kī la libbi ilāni*, lit. "in a godless manner"), and constantly were spreading evil, incorrect and hostile (rumors) behind my back. (Thus) they alienated from me – against the will of the gods (*ša la ilāni*) – the warm heart (lit. "open") of my father, (though) in the bottom of his heart there was (always) love (for me) and his intentions were (always) that I should become king (Nin A, I, 26–33).[14]

Despite his assertion that "deep in his heart" Sennacherib continued to love him and did not want to change his original decision, the estrangement was acute enough to force Esarhaddon to seek refuge in a secret place (*ašar niṣirti*), probably a temple (I, 38–40), even before his father's tragic death.

The story of the struggle for the throne – "rebellion" (*sīḫu*), in Esarhaddon's terminology – then follows: "Thereafter my brothers went mad, doing everything that is wicked in the eyes of the gods and man, plotting evil" (I, 41–42). But the following sentence – *issiḫūma kakkē ina qirib Ninua balu ilāni ana epeš šarrūti ittakkipū lalā'iš...*", they rebelled and weapons, inside Nineveh, (. . .), godlessly, like goats they fought each other for kingship!" (I, 43–44) – has caused some difficulties. The word "weapons", *kakkē*, stands alone without subject or predicate. This *staccato*-like anacoluthon may reflect the excitement of its author – perhaps the king himself – or, perhaps a passage was omitted here, exactly at the point where the murder of Sennacherib should have been mentioned. (An implicit reference, however, may be detected in the passage describing Esarhaddon's excitement on being informed of the "evil deeds", *epšēti limnēti*, wrought by his brothers. Esarhaddon cries out 'Woe', rends his princely robe, and utters a lament: I, 55–57.)[15] It is this rather unaccountable omission of the tragic fate of the father and benefactor that has led scholars to

---

14. A. L. Oppenheim's translation in *ANET*, p. 289a.
15. The same *topos* is repeated in K 2671 (Borger, *Asarhaddon*, §71), a fragmentary text from the later part of Esarhaddon's reign. A rebellious king – no doubt Nabu-zer-kitti-lishir, the vassal-governor of the Sea-land (cf. below, pt. III) – is accused there of affronting Assyria by not expressing publicly his grief upon what must

suspect Esarhaddon of patricide, or at least of being a tacit collabora-
tor.[16] So too, the names of the rebelling brothers are not given and the
adversaries are grouped under the term "usurpers" – *hammā'u.*

In fact, 2 Kings 19 and Berossos supply us with the missing details:
the murderers were Adramelekh – identified most recently by Parpola
with *Arad-Mulissu* (Arad-Ninlil), Esarhaddon's older brother[17] – and
his accomplice *Šar'eṣer,* whose name survives only in the biblical
record (i.e. [god X]-*šar-uṣur*). In this context it should be noted that
both omission of details and vague language seem to be characteristic
of this apology. Thus the date of Esarhaddon's accession to the throne
is not stated, nor the date of the rebellion; the first date we encounter is
the 8th of Adar, when Esarhaddon joyfully enters Nineveh and assumes the throne (I, 87–11, 2). Everything prior to the accession is
blurred.

In spite of our suspicion regarding Esarhaddon's feeling of guilt
and possible involvement, however remote, in the patricide, it is not
the question of the murder of Sennacherib – discussed anew by
every generation of Assyriologists – which is the central motif of this
apology, but that of Esarhaddon's own succession. This question became especially acute in the course of Esarhaddon's 8th regnal year =
673/2, when Prism Nin A, which contains the apology, was conceived,
composed and "published".[18]

It was a difficult time for the empire. The attempt to conquer Egypt
had failed two years before and Esarhaddon's army was defeated in the
Delta. This unsuccessful attack on Egypt in the far west must have
promoted the reconciliation with Elam in the far east, Assyria's old
rival and bitter foe in Babylonian affairs. Very little is known about
Esarhaddon's unsuccessful war with Egypt. Our sole explicit source is
the laconic entry in the Babylonian Chronicle: "The seventh year, on
the 5th day of the month Adar, the army of Assyria was defeated in
Egypt" (IV, 16).[19] Was it an actual invasion of Egypt, like the one of

have been the news of Sennacherib's tragic death (obv., 2–3). For *epšēti limnēti* as
an oblique reference to the murder of Sennacherib see already Th. Bauer, *ZA* 42
(1934), p. 180.

16. B. Landsberger and Th. Bauer, *ZA* 37 (1927), p. 69; W. von Soden, *Herrscher im
alten Orient,* Berlin, 1954, p. 118.
17. S. Parpola, "The Murderer of Sennacherib" in B. Alster (ed.), *Death in Mesopotamia* (*RAI* 26=*Mesopotamia* 8), Copenhagen 1980, pp. 171–182.
18. Over 20 manuscripts of Nin A have survived (mostly from Nineveh, one from
Assur): see Borger, *Asarhaddon,* pp. 36–37.
19. A. K. Grayson, *Assyrian and Babylonian Chronicles* (*TCS* 5), Locust Valley,
1975, p. 84. (Hereafter: Grayson, *Chronicles*).

671 which succeeded, conducted through the coastal strip of Northern Sinai, or was the battle between the Assyrians and Taharqa, the Nubian Pharaoh of Egypt, fought somewhere in Southern Philistia, as in the days of Sargon? The presence of the Egyptian armies in the area of Ashkelon is evidenced by several queries to Shamash,[20] the lord of the oracles, prior to this ill-fated campaign of 674 or its precursor in 675 (planned but not carried out). Too little is known about the Assyrian-Egyptian rivalry in Philistia in the three decades between the Nubian intervention on behalf of the Philistine allies at Elteqeh (in 701) and Esarhaddon's conquest of lower Egypt in 671. Still, there can be little doubt that Esarhaddon gave urgent priority to the reconquest of Southern Philistia, as the Assyrian control over that distant Western tip of the empire was loosened or even lost during Sennacherib's last years.[21] So that already in his first campaign in 679, Esarhaddon marched as far as the Egyptian border, conquered the city of Arza,[22] thus reestablishing the Assyrian claim to entire Philistia.

Given this historical perspective, it would seem that the repercussions of the defeat in the spring of 673 had their effect not merely on the military-imperial level but also on the domestic scene. Every war of Assyria, led by her monarch – and in theory the high priest of Ashur – was on a theological as well as on a practical-cultic level a "holy war", ordered by Ashur and approved by oracles, celestial and terrestrial.[23] A defeat of "Assyria's (or Ashur's) mighty armies" – to use the ideological cliché of the period – was rendered in the traditional terms of theodicy: either the oracles must have been misinterpreted – and some astrologer or haruspex would pay dearly for that – or the king must have committed some cultic offence[24] to incur the divine wrath. How

20. J. A. Knudtzon, *Assyrische Gebete an den Sonnengott*, II, Leipzig 1893, no. 70; E. G. Klauber, *Politisch-religiöse Texte aus der Sargonidenzeit*, Leipzig 1913, No. 41.
21. For more details see: Tadmor, *Biblical Archaeologist* 29 (1966), pp. 97–100; A. Spalinger, *Orientalia* 43 (1974), pp. 298–302. Cf. Prof. I. Eph'al's paper in the present volume.
22. Nin A, III:39–46 and Esarhaddon's Chronicle I:7–8. (Grayson, *Chronicles*, p. 125).
23. Cf. A. L. Oppenheim's essay published posthumously in H. Lasswell, D. Lerner, H. Spier (eds.), *Propaganda and Communication in World History*, I, Honolulu, 1979, p. 121.
24. An extreme case is reported in K. 4730 (H. Winckler, *Sammlung von Keilschrifttexte, II*, Leipzig 1894, p. 52), a pseudo-autobiographical text from this period. Certain grave cultic offences of Sargon II (*ḫiṭāti ᵐŠarrukīn abīya*, obv., 16) led to his ignominious death in battle and to the spoliation of his corpse, so that he is "restless and not buried in his house" (obv., 20). More, in "The 'Sin of Sargon'", *Eretz Israel* 5 (1958), pp. 154-162.

else could Ashur's armies, headed by the king, an eternal victor, be overcome by the distant Nubians?

Fear of conspiracy and rebellion, denunciation and accusations of high treason are recurring topics in the letters addressed to the king by his various often-competing scholarly advisors: astrologers, haruspices, exorcists and physicians.[25] The opposition to the crown was not just a figment of Esarhaddon's imagination. Its existence is proven by the presence of Assyrian political fugitives in neighbouring countries. For example, in Shubria, north of Assyria, we find courtiers, provincial governors *pāhāti*, and other fugitive state functionaries referred to, in archaic style, as *akli, šāpiru, redû*.[26]

The case of Shubria is indeed instructive. An entire lengthy document[27] describes most vividly the humiliation of its king and the brutal punishment of his people. His plea for unconditional surrender and mercy was turned down. Esarhaddon was adamant: the rebellious vassal who harboured Esarhaddon's enemies should bear the full onus of his betrayal of the loyalty oaths. No wonder that the *Leitmotif* of this document – a letter to the god Assur, composed shortly after the fall of Shubria in the winter of 672 – is the validity of the *adê* and the severe punishments awaiting those who break it. As A. L. Oppenheim observed: "The stress placed on the sanctity of the oath of a vassal, the demand for absolute obedience to the king's commands . . . – all point to the same direction."[28] It was a warning that a similar fate awaits any person or community that does not respect the loyalty oath and openly defies the emperor.

The year 673/2 ended in a personal tragedy, the death of Esarhaddon's wife, which was considered a state affair significant enough to be entered in contemporary chronicles.[29] It was, I believe, against this particular historical background that Esarhaddon decided in the course of that very year – his eighth regnal year – on the question of his own succession. He intended to appoint his eldest son, Shamash-shum-ukin, as the incumbent king of Babylonia and the next-in-line (a twin brother?), Ashurbanipal, as the emperor of Assyria. It was a bold

25. See e.g. E. Weidner, *AfO* 17 (1954/6), pp. 5–8; S. Parpola, *Letters from Assyrian Scholars to the Kings Esarhaddon and Assurbanipal (AOAT* 5/1), Pt. I, Neukirchen-Vluyn, 1970, nos. 133; 247; 293 (Hereafter: Parpola, *LAS*); *idem, Iraq* 34 (1972), p. 31.
26. Borger, *Asarhaddon*, §68 I:3.
27. *Ibid.*, pp. 102–107.
28. Oppenheim (above, n. 23), p. 131.
29. Grayson, *Chronicles*, p. 85:22; p. 127:23.

decision, echoed in a contemporary letter from Adad-shum-uṣur, one
of the royal exorcists and astrologers:

> Good health (to the king), my lord. ... What has not been
> done in heaven, the king, my lord, has done upon earth and
> shown us: you have girded a son of yours with a diadem(?)
> and entrusted to him the kingship of Assyria: your eldest
> son you have put to the kingship of Babylon. You have
> placed the first on your right and the second on your left
> side! . . .[30]

The actual installation of the two heirs in office took place several
months later in 672, Esarhaddon's 9th year, when the royal family, the
court and state officials, the people of Assyria as well as the vassal
kings, swore the oath of allegiance.

The ceremony was now much more impressive and the legal means
much more effective. Letters from the Assyrian state archives report
the oath-taking ceremonies by court officials throughout Assyria, including scribes, haruspices, exorcists and augurs.[31] Very fortunately,
the actual text of the loyalty oaths was discovered in several copies in
the excavations at Nimrud which were published by D. J. Wiseman in
1958. These texts of major importance, customarily designated as "the
vassal-treaties of Esarhaddon,"[32] document the extent of the precautions taken by the king to ensure the stability of his succession in
Assyria and throughout the empire. Especially noteworthy is the concern shown regarding any involvement in a plot to slander the crown
prince designate before his father and so cause mutual hatred (ll.
336–352; also ll. 360–372). These precautions, as well as the repeated
references to insurrection or open rebellion (ll. 133, 148, 166, 254),
may echo the circumstances as reflected in Esarhaddon's apology.
They also seem to suggest that it was Esarhaddon's personal experience that shaped much of the content, if not the actual wording, of the
"vassal-treaties".

The turbulence of those days is reflected also in the queries put by
the king before Shamash. For example, Esarhaddon enquires whether
any of his courtiers, vassal kings and state functionnaries are planning

---

30. K. Deller, in W. Röllig (ed.), *lišan mithurti* (*Festschrift W. von Soden, AOAT* 1),
    Neukirchen-Vluyn, 1969, p. 57; Parpola, *LAS*, no. 129:3–13.
31. E.g. Parpola, *LAS*, nos. 1, 2.
32. D. J. Wiseman, *Iraq* 20 (1958), pp. 29ff. Translated anew by Erica Reiner in
    ANET [3], pp. 534–41.

to rebel; or whether certain, apparently high, officials to be appointed to their posts will be planning rebellion against the king and Ashurbanipal, the crown prince.[33] Of unusual interest is his query whether a son of his, Sin-nadin-apli, should be brought into the *bīt-ridūti*, an indication that, for a time, that prince was considered for Esarhaddon's successor.[34] The divine answer is not preserved, and we are left ignorant not only of the answer to this and all similar queries to Shamash, but also of the identity of the prince; George Smith surmised that he was no other than Ashurbanipal himself under his previous name, a conjecture not accepted by Knudtzon and Klauber.[35] In any event, though designated consistently in the "vassal-treaties" as *mār šarri rabû ša bīt ridūti*, Ashurbanipal was considered to be a younger son by Adad-shum-usur's circumstantial testimony. Shamash-shum-ukin's title in the "vassal-treaties" is Ashurbanipal's "'equal-brother' (*aḫu talīmu*) the crown prince of Babylon" (l:86). This title is also repeated later in Shamash-shum-ukin's royal inscriptions,[36] but in his legal records he refers to himself as *māru ašarēdu*,[37] the first and foremost son of Esarhaddon.

In summary, Esarhaddon's apology composed in the summer of 673/2 should be considered as an ideological *praeparatio* for the dramatic events of the early spring of 672 (Esarhaddon's 9th year). The procedure undertaken for his own succession to the throne, as described in the apology – became paradigmatic for his own acts. In both cases the first-born was by-passed: it was the will of the king and the gods that the younger prince– apparently better suited for the august office – should be preferred.

Esarhaddon's apology, however, cannot be discussed as a separate unit, as it forms an integral part of a larger document – the Prism Nin A. In order to grasp fully its specific character as a document of political-ideological intent, we have to examine it as a whole within the context of the entire body of Esarhaddon's historical records.

33. Knudtzon, (above, n. 20), nos. 108, 116–120.
34. *Ibid.*, no. 107.
35. See Klauber (above, n. 20), p. LXI, n.1.
36. C. F. Lehman, *Šamašumukin*, Leipzig, 1892, p. 10:12; 12:20; Streck, *Assurbanipal*, III, pp. 629–30; and cf. P. Koschaker, *ZA* 41 (1932), pp. 64–67.
37. L. A. King, *Babylonian Boundary Stones and Memorial Tablets at the British Museum*, London, 1912, No. X obv. 9; F. Steinmetzer, "Die Bestallungsurkunde des Königs Šamaš-šum-ukin von Babylon", in *Miscellanea Orientalia dedicata Antonio Deimel*, (*Analecta Orientalia* 12), Rome, 1935, p. 303:6. Cf. also n. 13, above.

III

New recensions of the historical prisms of Assyrian kings were usually motivated by a need to update the military achievements; followed by an account of a new building enterprise: the erection of a palace or the reconstruction of a temple. The first historical inscriptions recounting in retrospect Esarhaddon's military achievements (but not in chronological order) were composed in 676 in a brief form on cylinders[38] and in a longer form on a hexagonal prism. It was that latter document, the 'Heidel Prism',[39] henceforth "H" (Borger's Nin B[7]),[40] that became in 673/2 the basis for a new recension, Prism Nin A. This document was copied extensively: over 20 manuscripts from Nineveh and Ashur are known to date. Its author took over the historical parts of Prism H, but embellished them by introducing slight syntactical variations and occasional structural changes and expansions. In the building section, dedicated to the work done in the restoration of *ēkal-mašārti*, the arsenal of Nineveh, there are several detailed expansions, but in essence it is not a major departure from H.[41] Two entirely new compositions were introduced by the author of Nin A: the apology (I, 1–II, 11), followed by a list of laudatory epithets (II, 12–39) and a royal hymn, eulogizing in high poetic style Esarhaddon's imperial might (IV, 78–V 25), a tacit propagandistic response to the recent military debacle at the marches of Egypt. The hymn is followed by another laudatory appendix (V, 26–33) on a political theme: The Elamites and other proud highlanders ("*Qutū*", V, 26) – former enemies – now submitted to Assyria, acknowledged her supremacy and concluded a treaty of "peace and friendship (*tūbu u sulummû*)".[42]

Of special interest for the present topic is the longest divergence of Nin A from H: the case of Nabu-zer-kitti-lishir, son of Merodach-Baladan, the Chaldaean governor of the Sea-land in Southern Babylonia. Ten lines are devoted in H to that episode, the eighth in the geographical sequence of Esarhaddon's victories. He trusted Elam, took refuge there, but could not save himself; his brother came from Elam to Nineveh pleading submission and was appointed the new

38. Borger, *Asarhaddon*, §21; A. R. Millard, *Iraq* 20 (1961), pp. 176–78; P. Hulin, *Iraq* 34 (1962), pp. 116–118.
39. A. Heidel, *Sumer* 12 (1956), pp. 9–37.
40. Borger, *Asarhaddon*, p. 125; *idem*, *AfO* 18 (1958), p. 115.
41. Heidel (above, n. 39), p. 26, Col. IV, 32ff.
42. The treaty resulted in the return of the captured statues of the gods of Agade: Grayson, *Chronicles*, p. 84, IV, 12–18.

governor of the Sea-land (H II, 24–33). In Nin A this episode was placed as the first topic and it occupies twenty-five lines (II, 40–64), fifteen of them entirely new. The Nin A version relates in detail Nabu-zer-kitti-lishir's rebellion, stressing the fact that he did not keep the *adê* sworn to Sennacherib; in time of distress for Assyria (*dalihti māt Aššur*) – i.e. during the internal strife of 681/680 – he waged war on the governor of Ur, a faithful servant of Assyria; upon Esarhaddon's accession, "he did not send his messenger" to greet the new king and did not submit (II, 42–50). His punishment was that "the curse (*mamītu*) of the great gods was imposed upon him and he was killed in Elam with a sword" (II, 55–57).

The stress upon the *adê* and *mamītu* and the interest taken in the affairs of Babylonia in Nin A are hardly accidental. We take it that the author of that prism wrote under the impact of the new arrangements for Esarhaddon's succession when the elaborate text of the "vassal-treaties" (*tuppi adê*) was prepared for the ceremonies of the early spring of 672. The brief story of the Babylonian rebel in H, therefore, had been rewritten and adapted to carry a new and pertinent message: any transgressor of the loyalty oaths will similarly be punished by the great gods – a point elaborated in the lengthy maledictions of the "vassal treaties".

However, the extraordinary measures for the succession of 672, with the royal propaganda accompanying it, proved not to be sufficient. Upon Esarhaddon's death, the grandmother Naqi'a-Zakutu, imposed the *adê*-oaths once again upon the royal family, the courtiers and the state officials. They had to reiterate their loyalty to Ashurbanipal, and even Shamash-shum-ukin, "the equal brother", was now included among those who were obliged to take the loyalty oath.[43]

IV

Repeated acts of succession arrangements under the loyalty oaths of 672 and 669 have produced yet another document: Ashurbanipal's first autobiographical apology. As in Esarhaddon's Prism Nin A, it forms the introductory part of a longer text, K.3050+2694 – Streck's L,[44] which describes the transfer of Marduk's statue from the city of Ashur (Baltil) to Esagila, newly restored by Esarhaddon. In this text, inscribed on the king's statue placed before Marduk, Ashurbanipal

---

43. Harper, *ABL*, 1239; and cf. H. Lewy, *JNES* 11 (1952), p. 282.
44. Streck, *Assurbanipal*, II, pp. 252–71.

takes full credit for this act, though it was Shamash-shum-ukin, his *talīmu*-brother, who "held Marduk's hands" in that long procession from Ashur to Babylon.[45]

Over half of the text, the first part of the document, is devoted to Ashurbanipal's autobiography and the story of his succession. Unique among the Assyrian royal inscriptions, it relates the story of the king's education, praising both his military prowess — a traditional topic — and his scholarly achievements, an entirely new motif. From what we know of Ashurbanipal's literacy, this autobiography bears a highly personal imprint.

The section describing the education of the future king (Obv. Col. I, 13–26) is preceded by two traditional, though ideologically pregnant, motifs: first, Ashur, the father of the gods, chose and destined him for kingship, while he was still in his mother's womb (I, 5); second, the omens — apparently astral — had revealed that he should become king (I, 8–9). Remarkably, his elevation by Esarhaddon is linked to his education, not to divine predestination. Esarhaddon involved him, so he says, in state matters, in giving orders to the nobles and in appointment of governors and prefects (I, 28–29). Then, "at the command of the great gods," he conceived a great love for Ashurbanipal, selecting him among his brothers and obtained by praying to Ashur, Shamash, Adad, Marduk and Nabu, the divine approval for his succession (I, 30–35). Thus, Ashurbanipal was brought into the *bīt-ridūti* in the month of Ayaru — a date known also from Esarhaddon's inscriptions — and there he was raised above the other princes and named for kingship (II, 3–6).

The autobiographical apology ends with two additional topics: first, upon his accession to the throne (Esarhaddon's death is thus related obliquely) he was greeted by all the kings and vassals of the empire (I, 8–15); second, that peace and prosperity descended upon earth — there was no theft, no shedding of blood, no acts of violence; peace and perfect order of things prevailed everywhere (I, 19–23).

This "happy end" might well have been the end of Ashurbanipal's venture into the genre of Apology. And indeed, the theme of his accession to the throne is not found until 645. The introductory section

---

45. On the return of Marduk's statue to Babylon in the accession year of Shamash-shum-ukin (=Ashurbanipal's year 1) see: Grayson, *Chronicles*, p. 66: 34–36; cf. Knudtzon (above, n. 20), no. 179, and note especially the comment of B. Landsberger, *Brief des Bischofs von Esagila an König Asarhaddon* (*MKNAW*, N.R. 28 no. 6), Amsterdam, 1965, pp. 23–25.

of Prism B (649),[46] mentions only very briefly his divine nomination, his literacy, and expands upon the topic of miraculous prosperity (I, 27–38). In the next prism editions, K[47] and C,[48] written a year or two after the quelling of the Babylonian rebellion and the death of Shamash-shum-ukin, the lengthy introduction is devoted mainly to Ashurbanipal's pious deeds, the building and restoration of temples throughout Assyria and Babylonia. The stress on the cultic theme might echo another apologetic motif: though having committed sacrilege against Babylon and Esagila a year or two earlier,[49] Ashurbanipal asserts now that he has always been well disposed towards the holy shrines of Marduk and other Babylonian gods.

The change came in 645. In that year, the eponym-year of *Nabû-šar-aḫḫēšu*, a new recension of Ashurbanipal's *res gestae*, Prism F[50] was composed, with an entirely new introduction which includes an autobiographical apology. Ashurbanipal relates there how he, the crown-prince-designate of the *bīt-ridûti*, was installed in the office. Esarhaddon, his father, following the divine command, assembled the people of Assyria, "young and old" and imposed a loyalty oath upon them to safeguard his succession (I, 7–17). (Naturally, not a word is mentioned concerning the simultaneous appointment of Shamash-shum-ukin, his rebellious 'equal-brother', to the throne of Babylonia. By that time, he was, as Orwell would have it, a non-person.) The specific character of the *bīt-ridûti* where crown-princes are educated and trained for kingship, is extolled in this text (VI, 22–35) and no wonder: the building section is devoted to the restoration of the 'House of Succession' itself.

Another feature of this new autobiographical introduction is the claim of having been chosen by the gods a commonplace in royal titulary. It is reiterated here in a somewhat different fashion, which by itself is also not novel: Ashurbanipal's kingship, it is said, had been ordered by Sin "from days of yore" (*ultu umê ruqûti*), i.e., long before his birth (F, I, 3–4). This *topos* of royal ideology would be regarded by a modern reader as a traditional and hence not meaningful cliché. In

46. A. C. Piepkorn, *Historical Prism Inscriptions of Ashurbanipal* (*AS* 5), Chicago 1933, pp. 28ff.
47. M. Cogan and H. Tadmor, "Ashurbanipal's Conquest of Babylon: The First Offical Report – Prism K", *Orientalia* 50 (1981), pp. 229–240.
48. Th. Bauer, *Das Inschriftenwerk Ashurbanipals*, II, Leipzig, 1933, pp. 13–14; E. E. Knudsen, *Iraq* 29 (1967), p. 64.
49. Rassam Prism (see above, n. 11), Col. IV:42–91.
50. J. M. Aynard, *Le Prisme du Louvre AO 19.933*, Paris, 1957.

this particular case, though, it may well carry a new connotation, as it could be associated with the motif of 'old prophecy' which appears in several texts related to Prism T and composed in the very same year as Prism F (645).[51] There, the rebuilding of Ehulhul is justified by a prophecy of Sin, "from days of yore", Ashurbanipal has been created for the purpose of restoring the Moon god's temple in Harran (T, II, 29–35, a passage taken over from Prism C composed in the previous year). The motif of justification through an 'old prophecy' is found a second time in the same prism, an episode which bears even more closely on our present theme. It is stated there that the goddess Nana (=Inanna-Ishtar of Uruk) "who for 1635 years had been angry and gone to live in Elam, a place not fitting for her" (V, 9–13), had ordered Ashurbanipal when "she and the gods, her fathers" named him for kingship, that he should bring her forth from Elam and return her to Eanna, "her temple in Uruk" (V, 14–23). That divine utterance foretold "from days of yore" (*ultu umê ruqūti*) "was, now revealed to the later generation" (V, 26), and Ashurbanipal reverently executed the ancient divine command (V, 27–32). The very same episode – an 'old prophecy' and its fulfillment – appears in Prism F (V, 73–VI, 11), a postscript to the lengthy description of Elam's destruction.

Nowhere else in Assyrian royal inscriptions do we find a similar *vaticinium ex eventu*. It could therefore be regarded as yet another case of apology, though in a cultic setting, parallel to our dynastic apologies, and a product of the same period. This cultic apology is rooted in the sacrilegious acts of the preceding year (646) – vividly depicted in Prisms F and T – when Ashurbanipal conquered and destroyed Susa, Elam's sacred city, smashed the images of Elamite gods (F, IV, 67–V, 71), thus "appeasing the heart of the Lord of lords (=Ashur)" (T, VI, 2). It was in the very same manner and at about the same time that a court historian in Jerusalem justified by a similar and equally unique *vaticinium*,[52] the destruction of Beth-el's sanctuary by Josiah, king of Judah, during his cultic reforms. A prophet, addressing Jeroboam I, roughly two hundred years earlier has said: "O, altar, altar: Thus said the Lord: A son shall be born to the House of David, Josiah by name, and he shall slaughter upon you the priests of the shrine who bring offerings upon you and human bones shall be burned

---

51. Thompson (above, n. 6), pp. 29ff with the corrections of Piepkorn (above, n. 46), p. 4, n.17.

52. Cf. F. M. Cross, *Canaanite Myth and Hebrew Epic*, Cambridge, Mass., 1973, p. 279.

upon you." (I Kings 13: 2, New JPS). Here, too, a prophecy forms the apex of a retrospective series of historical narratives designed to serve the needs – religious and political – of a great monarch.

Though fresh and eloquent, the dynastic apology of Prism F was not the last one. Several (I believe two)[53] years later, Ashurbanipal's autobiography was rewritten once again in the introductory section of Prism A – the so-called "Rassam Prism".[54] There the text of F was expanded by a pious redactor.Wherever possible, a full list of gods supporting the king, or accepting his prayers, etc. was consistently added.[55] Also, a part of the *topos* of the king's military prowess was excised and clumsily replaced by a pious gloss:

> By the consent of the great gods, whose names I utter and whose glory I am proclaiming, (who) ordered that I should become king (and) entrusted to me (the task of) the care of their sanctuaries – they (are now) assailing on my behalf, my adversary, smiting my enemy . . .
> (Rassam Prism 1, 35–39)

In the concluding part of the Rassam Prism, the building account (X, 51 ff.), the succession-motif of the *bīt-ridūti* is introduced once again (X, 59 ff.). As in the case of Esarhaddon's Prism A, so here, the author of the Rassam Prism did not compose a new building account, but simply copied it from Prism F. The result is that like in F, the topic of succession becomes the ideological framework of the entire text, appearing both in the opening and the closing portions of this longest of Ashurbanipal's *res gestae*.

What then were the historical circumstances during 645–642, which motivated Ashurbanipal to elaborate in the recensions of Prisms F and Rassam on memories some twenty years old? We have very little knowledge – if any – of the Assyrian domestic politics during the latter part of Ashurbanipal's reign. Contemporary letters and historical prism inscriptions shed light only on the political scene and this, too, rather sparingly. Still, it is clear that by 645 Ashurbanipal had quelled the Babylonian rebellion, after four years of bitter war, led several campaigns to Elam and finally sacked Susa, demolishing its temples.

53. H. Tadmor in *Proceedings of the 25th International Congress of Orientalists*, I, Moscow, 1962, pp. 240–241.
54. Rassam Prism: Streck, *Assurbanipal*, II, pp. 2–91; Luckenbill, *ARAB*, II, pp. 290–323.
55. E.g. Rassam Prism I, 13–17, 41–44; and X, 118–119.

The king would have been in his late fifties. The question of succession, the cardinal problem of Assyrian monarchy from the middle of the 8th century onward, must have worried him. Hence, the autobiographical-apologetic motifs recollected retrospectively in these two recensions which more than any others retained popularity. The number of manuscripts of F and Rassam that have survived exceeds by far any other historical inscriptions of that great literary monarch of Assyria.[56]

Unfortunately, the arrangements made by Ashurbanipal for his own succession did not survive. His personal concern to renovate the *bīt-ridūtī* in Nineveh, the same palace in which he and his father had received their royal training, indicates that by 645 the question of succession had become real, though perhaps not yet acute.

But whatever might have been Ashurbanipal's arrangements for the throne of Assyria, we know that over a decade later his two sons – again "equal (or twin)-brothers", Ashur-etil-ilani and Sin-shar-ishkun – fought each other and the Empire was divided for a time.[57] In a land-grant from Nineveh,[58] Ashur-etil-ilani claims that it was the commander of the army, the chief eunuch, Sin-shum-lishir, who safeguarded him during his minority, finally installed him safely on the paternal throne and made the people of Assyria take the loyalty oaths.[59] Sin-shar-ishkun, on the other hand, states in his official record that he, Ashurbanipal's heir, was selected by the gods, his benefactors, from among the "(two) twins"[60] to rule over Assyria and that he owes his kingship solely to their divine assistance. Nevertheless, the historical circumstances of this civil war and of the chronological issue still remain unsolved, in spite of the various *ad hoc* solutions proposed in recent years.[61]

---

56. For manuscripts of the Rassam and F Prisms see: Streck, *Assurbanipal*, I, pp. XVII–XXI; Aynard (above, no. 50), pp. 10–11; M. Cogan, *JCS* 29 (1977), pp. 97–107.
57. W. von Soden, *WZKM* 53 (1957), pp. 316–319; *ZA* 58 (1967), pp. 241–255; Tadmor (above, n. 53), n. 53, p. 241.
58. J. N. Postgate, *Neo-Assyrian Royal Grants and Decrees*, Rome, 1969, nos. 13, 14.
59. *Ibid.*, no. 14:11 ...]*adê mamīt* [. . .]. One may then perhaps restore in no. 13:10 : [*adê ušazkiršūma*], "he made them take an oath" or the like. While no evidence of the loyalty oath sworn to Ashur-etil-ilani has survived, an actual fragment of a loyalty oath to Sin-shar-ishkun has been discovered in the excavations at Assur: E. Weidner, *AfO* 13 (1939/40), p. 215, n. 69.
60. *ina birit maššišu/ia*: R. Borger, *JCS* 19 (1965), p. 76:5; von Soden, *ZA* 58 (1967) p. 252.
61. Borger (above, n. 60), pp. 59–78; J. Oates, *Iraq* 28 (1965), pp. 135–159; von Soden (above, n. 60), pp. 241–255; J. Reade, *JCS* 23 (1970), pp. 1–16.

V

The third, though less pronounced autobiographical motif in a royal Assyrian inscription, which should (still) be discussed in this context, is the introductory section of the annals of Shamshi-Adad V (824–811), wherein he relates the circumstances of his own accession to the throne:[62]

> When Ashur-da'in-apli, in the time of Shalmaneser, his father, acted evilly, fomented rebellion and sedition, caused the country to rebel and prepared for battle, made the entire people of Assyria side with him, binding (them) by sworn oaths (of mutual obligations), incited the cities to rebel and set his face to begin hostilities; the cities of Nineveh, Adia, Shibaniba, Imgur-Bêl . . . Zaban, Lubdu, Arrapha, Arba-ilu, together with Amedi, Til-abnê, Hindanu, a total of 27 cities, along with their districts, which had rebelled against Shalmaneser, king of the four regions (of the world), my father, sided with Ashur-da'in-apli − (all these cities) I entirely subdued.

Unlike Esarhaddon, he does not admit that he was a younger son, but this is obvious: Ashur-da'in-apli, the rebel, by the very nature of his name, was probably the first-born of Shalmaneser III. Shamshi-Adad would be one of the younger princes. No doubt, Ashur-da'in-apli's revolt (to use Shamshi-Adad's terminology) was a major crisis in Assyrian history. The war between the brothers lasted six years and is referred to in the Eponym Chronicle as years of *siḫu* (=rebellion).[63] The circumstances of this civil war are entirely obscure and the only record of it is Shamshi-Adad's own statement; viz. that his brother was the rebel and that he restored the legal order. Such a situation is rather unusual, though not impossible (e.g., Absalom's rebellion against the aging David). Still, it would be oversimplified to accept Shamshi-Adad's record as objective history. Whatever might have happened, the autobiographic narration bears an apologetic tone, especially if we realize that the account − in both "manuscripts" (Calah stela and Ashur stela) − was composed rather late: the Calah stela not before his 10th year and the Ashur stela was written two years later, i.e., a year or so before his

---

62. L. Abel in *Keilinschriftliche Bibliothek*, Vol. I, 1889, p. 176: 39–53 (=Luckenbill, *ARAB*, I, §715) and E. Weidner, *AfO* 9 (1933/34), p. 91.
63. *RLA*, II, p. 433, years 827–822.

death.[64] It is true that we do not have any earlier historical records of Shamshi-Adad V, but I would suggest that also here the Assyrian king was describing his accession at a time he was about to appoint his successor. The latter, Adad-nirari III, to judge by his name, was hardly a first-born, and during his reign was dominated by his mother, Sammuramat (Semiramis).[65] Is it only accidental that in all the three cases discussed above, a powerful queen-mother seems to have meddled in the issue of succession and acted as co-regent: Naqi'a-Zakutu (Senacherib's wife) in the case of Esarhaddon and Ashurbanipal and Sammuramat in the case of Adad-nirari III? We can add to this list of "first ladies" Puduhepa, the wife of Hattushili III, and Bathsheba, David's wife, the mother of Solomon.

VI

Though our present argument has been devoted to the Neo-Assyrian apologies, the analogy between these and the similar historiographic documents from the 2nd millennium deserves a comment. It stands to reason that these documents, as well, were primarily aimed at ensuring the legitimacy of the successor and that like their Assyrian counterparts, they also were composed a considerable time after the ascent to the throne. This is rather obvious in the case of Idrimi's autobiography, written in his 30th year, in which the king of Alalakh, explicitly mentions his son Adad-nirari, intended, as it appears, to be Idrimi's successor.[66] The apology of Hattushili III appears also to have been

64. For the chronology of Shamshi-Adad's reign see now: A. K. Grayson, *Bib Or* 33 (1976), pp. 142–43; J. E. Reade, *ZA* 68 (1978), p. 258.
65. See the latest discussion by W. Schramm, *Historia* 21 (1972), pp. 513–521, (and the literature there, p. 513. n. 1)
66. S. Smith, *The Statue of Idri-mi*, London, 1949, p. 20:90–91; cf.the remarks of A. Goetze, *JCS* 4 (1950), p. 229; and more recently: E. I. Greenstein and D. Marcus, *JANES* 8 (1976), p. 92; and D. Collon, *The Seal Impression of Tell Atchana/Alalakh* (*AOAT* 27), Neukirchen-Vluyn, 1975, p. 167. n. 3. The reading "30-years" (MU 30! *KAM.MEŠ*, l. 102) of the *editio princeps* has now been confirmed by a collation: See G.H. Oler, *JCS*, 29 (1977), pp. 167–168. Whether Adad-nirari did actually reign for a short while and was replaced by Niqmepa, son of Idrimi, or died still during Idrimi's lifetime (i.e. after year 30) is irrelevant to the present issue. Obviously, Idrimi's mentioning of Adad-nirari and entrusting him with certain duties (even though, as some claim, only cultic ones), must mean that he intended Adad-nirari to succeed him. One also should not fail to note that the cultic duties mentioned there (88–89) involve ancestors cult, a point of significance for a usurper. [In this connection I should mention that M. Liverani has pointed out the folkloristic elements in Idrimi's inscription and its literary-ideological character: *VT* 24 (1974), pp. 438–453. Most recently, in a stimulating study which will surely

composed almost a decade after his accession.[67] As he mentions there (IV:76–78), his successor Tuthaliya IV, must have been considered his heir already during Hattushili's own lifetime.[68] The 'kernel' of that document, as observed by Gurney,[69] is the passage about Hattushili's nephew Urhi-Teshub, the legitimate king, whom he deposed and exiled. The main argument is new: Ishtar of Samuha, the goddess for whose temple the document was composed – as a *Stiftungsurkunde*[70] – preferred the older uncle. She stood by him from the time he was a governor under Urhi-Teshub and finally promised him kingship in an oracle to his wife, the influential princess Puduhepa (IV:7–15). Hattushili's piety and Ishtar's desire justified an obviously illegitimate act. Another factor which urged the composition of that autobiographical apology was that Urhi-Teshub, though exiled, was still considered a menace and was, as shown in the royal correspondence of that age, accused of constant scheming.[71] An effort was, therefore, made (by Hattushili) to discredit Urhi-Teshub and enhance his own divine election.

The apologetic motifs are present, as Hoffner pointed out, in yet another noted Hittite document, the edict of Telipinu, which stresses Telipinu's own legitimacy and arranges the order of the Hittite succession.[72] The edict may also have been composed, not at the very inception, but in the course of his reign or even towards its end.

provoke debate, Jack M. Sasson has argued that the text is a late pseudo- (or "simulated") autobiography with folkloristic embellishments, fabricated by Sharruwa, a court scribe, for his self-enhancement (note his colophon, ll. 129–143). The inscription, it is argued, should be dated to the last half of the thirteenth century (= Alalakh Level IA) rather than to the late sixteenth or early fifteenth centuries, as commonly held:"On Idrimi and Šarruwa, the Scribe," in M.A. Morrison and D.I. Owen (eds.), *Studies on the Civilization and Culture of Nuzi and the Hurrians in Honor of Ernest B. Lacheman*, Winona Lake, 1981, pp. 309–324. Contrast, however, the comments of N. Na'aman on the activities of Sharruwa in the archive of Alalakh IV: *Oriens Antiquus* 19 (1980), pp. 107–116).

67. This is the case, if we assume that the treaty with Egypt is referred to in IV:58: "(Those) who had been hostile in the days of my fathers and my forefathers made peace with me", and cf. recently H. Cancik, (above n. 3), p. 42.
68. Cf. H. Otten, "Puduhepa" in *Akademie der Wissenschaften und der Literatur*, Mainz, Abh. der Geistes- und Sozialwiss. Klasse, 1975, no. 1, p. 27.
69. O. R. Gurney, *The Hittites*, Hammondsworth, 1962, p. 176.
70. H. Cancik (above, n. 3), p. 43 (cf. also H. G. Güterbock's paper in the present volume).
71. For a full discussion of this question see P. H. J. Houwink Ten Cate in K. Bittel *et al.* (eds.), *Anatolian Studies Presented to H. G. Güterbock*, Istanbul, 1974, pp. 139–147. Cf. also A. Schulman, *The Journal of the Society for the Study of Egyptian Antiquities* 8 (1977–78), p. 119.
72. Hoffner (above, n. 3), pp. 53ff; on Telipinu's succession see S. R. Bin-Nun, *The Tawananna in the Hittite Kingdom*, Heidelberg, 1975, pp. 227ff.

And finally, though not a case of autobiography, one cannot fail to mention in this context the obvious apologetic nature of the Davidic and Solomonic succession-stories in 1 and 2 Samuel and 1 Kings 1–3. In spite of several current, though largely misguided, attempts to discredit their validity as contemporary records, I adhere to the belief that their only possible *Sitz im Leben* was the necessity to prove the legitimacy of these founders of the Judahite kingship.[73] It is very likely that the Davidic apology, which criticized King Saul and his successors, originates in David's lifetime, perhaps from the later part of his reign, when two rebellions shook his throne, and one of them put to trial the very legitimacy of his dynasty.[74] Also, the kernels of Solomon's apologetic narration could not have been written much later than the time when the Jerusalemite Royal-Dynastic Ideology[75] – the apotheosis of David and his dynasty – had already become an accepted *credo*.

The second millennium Hittite, North Syrian (or even Egyptian) "autobiographies", as well as the biblical apologetic accounts of the early first millennium, indicate that the genre of the apology was at home in the countries west of the Euphrates. The Neo-Assyrian samples of this genre were relatively novel in Mesopotamian historical writing and could be regarded as further evidence of the Western impact upon Assyria.[76] Such a genre was foreign to the rather rigid and formalistic traditions of Southern Mesopotamia. It appeared in Babylonia – though in a different guise – with the coming of the Chaldaean kings, Nabopolassar[77] and Nabonidus.[78] It was continued by the Persian conquerors of Babylonia and found its most masterful expression in the apology of Darius I.[79] These later manifestations of the genre of apology, however, merit a separate study.

73. On the history of David's rise to power and various suggestions as to the date of that narrative, see: A. Weiser, *VT* 16 (1966), pp. 325ff; T. N. D. Mettinger, *King and Messiah*, Lund, 1976, pp. 33–41; and most recently P. K. McCarter, Jr., *1 Samuel* (*Anchor Bible*), Garden City, 1980, pp. 27ff; idem, *JBL* 99 (1980), pp. 489–504.
74. Cf. Tadmor, *Journal of World History* 11 (1968), pp. 49–56.
75. Cf. T. Ishida, *The Royal Dynasties in Ancient Israel* (*BZAW* 142), Berlin–New York, 1977, pp. 81–117.
76. This Western impact on Assyria is elaborated on by the present writer in several forthcoming studies; see above, n. 8. On the "Western" origin of the autobiographical genre in Mesopotamian literature see most recently E. Reiner in W. Röllig (ed.), *Altorientalische Literatur*, Wiesbaden, 1978, p. 178.
77. S. Langdon, *Die Neubabylonischen Königsinschriften*, Leipzig, 1911, p. 66:4: *mār la mammānim anakūma*.
78. *Ibid.*, p. 280:47–48; C. J. Gadd, *Anatolian Studies* 8 (1958), p. 56:7–9: . . .*ša šarrūtu ina libbiya la bašû/tabšû*.
79. M. A. Dandamaev, *Persien unter der ersten Achämeniden*, Wiesbaden, 1976,

We shall conclude with the brief apology of Xerxes – the inscription XPf from the harem at Persepolis[80] – which, though the latest of that genre in cuneiform literature, exhibits the same typological elements we have observed in the autobiographical apologies of Hatti and Assyria.

Xerxes admits that he was not the first-born son – his father had older sons – but Darius made him "greatest after himself". It was Ahuramazda's desire that he become king (XPf §4). He also discloses that Darius himself had no right to the throne, since at the time of his accession Hystapes, Darius' father, and Arsames, his grand-father were still alive. But it was Ahuramazda's desire that none but the young Darius should "be made king of this earth" (XPf §3). Thus, we have here the element of irregular succession for both father and son, and the element of divine choice. Herodotus, commenting upon the choice of Xerxes as heir to Darius (VII, 3), adds yet another element familiar from the instances discussed above: the influential queen-mother. Atossa, the daughter of Cyrus and mother of Xerxes, thus joins our list of equally famed and highly influential queens from the West, like Bathsheba or Naqi'a-Zakutu, who obviously were not the only *grandes dames* in history, ancient or modern, to have imposed their favourite sons upon aging monarchs.

pp. 76ff, 118ff; and E. J. Bickerman and H. Tadmor, "Darius I, Pseudo-Smerdis, and the Magi", *Athenaeum*, nuova serie 56 (1978), pp. 239ff; E. J. Bickerman, *ibid.*, pp. 413–415.
80. R. G. Kent, *Old Persian: Grammar, Texts, Lexicon,* New Haven, 1950, p. 150, §3–4.

PRELIMINARY REMARKS ON THE HISTORICAL INSCRIPTIONS OF SENNACHERIB

Louis D. Levine

Royal Ontario Museum

The study of the neo-Assyrian royal inscriptions has become popular once again.* In the last twenty years, a series of books and articles have been published dealing with specific new texts, with historical problems related to the corpus as a whole and to parts thereof, with textual criticism and historiographic problems, and with re-translation.[1] All of

---

* This paper is partially reworked from a lecture originally delivered at the Colloquium held in Jerusalem on 9 May 1979. The research was undertaken during my year as a fellow at the Institute for Advanced Studies of the Hebrew University of Jerusalem. To the Institute and my colleagues there, no words can express my debt of gratitude. The paper is, as the title indicates, a preliminary statement based upon published material and catalogue entries, with only a few unpublished pieces collated kindness of E. Sollberger, C.F.B. Walker, A.K. Grayson and Penina Yisrael. I hope to be able to present a fuller discussion of the issues raised here after examining the unpublished texts.

1. It is obviously impossible to list here all of the works that have contributed to advancing the field over the last twenty years. What follows is a short, selected listing of some of the works to show the scope of the venture. One area, that of editions and translations, is dominated by two names. The first is R. Borger, who prepared the standard edition of Esarhaddon's texts, *Die Inschriften Asarhaddons, Königs von Assyrien* (*AfO* Beiheft 9), Graz, 1956, as well as a working edition of Sennacherib in his *Babylonisch-assyrische Lesestücke* (see below, n. 12). The second is A.K. Grayson, who has reached the earlier neo-Assyrian kings in his translation of the entire corpus, *Assyrian Royal Inscriptions*, Vol. 2, Wiesbaden, 1976. In the study of the history and historiography of the period, H. Tadmor's seminal article, "The Campaigns of Sargon II of Assyria," *JCS* 12 (1958), pp. 22–40 and 77–100, deserves special mention, as does his "Introductory Remarks to a New Edition of the Annals of Tiglath-pileser III," *Proceedings of the Israel Academy of Sciences and Humanities* 2, No. 9 (1967). The second volume of the *Einleitung in der assyrischen Königsinschriften,* by W. Schramm, marked a new benchmark in assembling the sources and commenting on them for the early neo-Assyrian inscriptions. Articles on selected aspects of the broad problem are too numerous to list here. Special mention should be made, however, of the work of Cogan, Tadmor, Tadmor and Cogan, Spalinger, Grayson, Na'aman, Reade,

this activity has appreciably advanced our understanding of the genre, and made it possible to ask yet further questions of the material. The present study is an attempt to take up where some of these other works have left off. In it, I have focused upon the military component in the inscriptions of Sennacherib and tried to set out some of the preliminary considerations that have to be dealt with in treating a corpus of neo-Assyrian royal texts.[2] The choice of Sennacherib was dictated by two factors. One is the size of the collection, which is large enough to present an adequate sample, but not so large as to make the task overwhelming. The second is the fact that a representative range of the texts has been published, and catalogue descriptions exist for a great many more of the texts.

In this article, I begin by presenting a brief review of the history of work on the inscriptions of Sennacherib. I then proceed to a description and classification of the sources, and this is followed by some methodological considerations and a section on procedures used in this work and proposed for future work on the subject. A final short statement places the work on Sennacherib in some perspective relative to other corpora of neo-Assyrian texts.

History of research

In the year 1878, A.H. Sayce edited and brought to press the manuscript of George Smith entitled *History of Sennacherib*. This volume represented the first attempt at preparing a critical edition of the

Levine, de Fillipi, and Paley. Finally, the publication of the *Second Supplement* to the *Catalogue of Cuneiform Tablets in the Kouyunjik Collection* by A.R. Millard and W. Lambert, London, 1968, made the later additions to this most important collection available in coherent form.

2. I use the term "military" rather than the more familiar "historical" at the suggestion of my colleague A.K. Grayson, who has properly pointed out that the "building" component of the inscriptions is fully as historical as are the campaign records.

I would also take this opportunity to point out that many of the phenomena dealt with in this paper are not restricted to the inscriptions of Sennacherib. I have limited my observations to this one corpus for what I believe are sound methodological considerations. It has yet to be demonstrated that the same processes were at work in the corpora of other neo-Assyrian kings. While there is little reason to doubt that at least some of these were operative, it is only by systematic and thorough review of each corpus separately that this will be proved. It would not have been difficult to point out similarities with other neo-Assyrian inscriptions, but it is unclear what these necessarily haphazard examples would demonstrate. I am aware that limiting myself in this way may mask certain processes that are clear in the records of other monarchs, but this is a small price to pay for the systematic results that I am attempting to achieve here.

inscriptions of this king. The book, based on thirteen different manuscripts,[3] devoted a separate chapter to every campaign, each such chapter presenting a number of versions of the campaign. When different manuscripts contained highly similar accounts, they were presented as a single text with variant readings. Where differences were great, the entire text of the variant version was published. As was so characteristic of Smith's work, the book was a model of careful scholarship, and is useful even now.

Smith did not, however, present an outline of how he understood the relationship between these manuscripts. From the book itself, it seems that he divided them according to the number of campaigns covered in each manuscript. But it is unclear to what extent he used duplicate manuscripts. Many of the complete and famous ones, including the Rassam cylinder and its duplicates, were not yet available to him.

Smith's effort was followed by that of Carl Bezold.[4] Work on the catalogue of the Kouyunjik collection afforded him access to many new manuscripts which he employed in re-editing the inscriptions.[5] He drew upon twenty-eight manuscripts, dividing them according to the form of the object on which they were written, prisms, cylinder, monumental bulls and tablets, but made no further division within these classes. But Bezold did present most variant readings, and with minimal effort one can disentangle his voluminous footnotes and use his publication. Whatever the rationale behind the edition of Smith, it is clear that Bezold was interested in producing a single useful text, and not in more complex questions of the relationship between manuscripts.

The next two decades saw no further basic work on Sennacherib's historical inscriptions. But in 1909, L.W. King started the process moving forward again with his publication of an almost complete new manuscript in *CT* 26. In his introduction to this volume, King broached the subject of the relationship between the various Sennacherib in-

---

3. I have chosen the term "manuscript" deliberately, although its use in connection with cuneiform documents is somewhat unusual. It means, self-evidently I believe, a single copy, complete or partial, of a "literary" work. This may be the only such copy extant, or one of many. It can be inscribed on any material, and that material can be in any shape. This use of the word is similar to that in classical textual criticism, but the manuscript is here not a book written on paper, papyrus or skin, but rather an inscription on clay or stone.
4. In *Keilinschriftliche Bibliothek*, (ed.) E. Schrader, II, Berlin, 1890, pp. 80–119.
5. "Die Thontafelsammlungen des British Museum," *Sitzungsberichte der König. preuss. Akad. der Wiss. zu Berlin*, Berlin, 1888, pp. 745–763.

scriptions known then (p. 7), but did not develop the inquiry. He, too, was basically interested in making a new text available. Four years later, King made yet another of Sennacherib's inscriptions available with his publication of the Judi Dagh rock reliefs.[6] The situation was radically altered with the appearance of A.T. Olmstead's seminal work, *Assyrian Historiography*.[7] For the first time, an Assyriologist and historian turned his attention to the question of the relationship between various manuscripts and to the historical worth of these documents. Olmstead's work encompassed the inscriptions of all of the neo-Assyrian kings, and in it he made a basic observation that the source closest to the events was probably the most reliable for historical reconstruction. He also introduced both the term "edition" and "recension" in describing the texts, and seems to have defined the term "edition" as being synonymous with a group of manuscripts written in a given year and containing a certain number of campaigns, but left the term "recension" undefined.

Olmstead also developed another concept in this publication that has left a lasting imprint on all subsequent work. Building upon F. Thureau-Dangin's publication of Sargon II's eighth campaign, and some laconic notes to that text,[8] Olmstead assumed that all campaigns were first presented in a full account, and that later editions simply cut the full account to accomodate the most recent events. He saw the famous letter to Assur recounting the events of Sargon II's eighth campaign as such a full account, but could point to no such text for Sennacherib's reign. Finally, he put forth the plea for a new critical publication of Sennacherib's inscriptions, which was very much needed at the time.

Before Olmstead's plea could be heeded, Sidney Smith published what seemed to be a confirmation of the "full account" theory.[9] In the tablet collection of the British Museum he found a manuscript which seemed to be a long account of the first campaign of that king. In his lengthy introduction to the monograph, Smith dealt briefly with the question of the relationship between his text and later accounts of the

---

6. "Studies of Some Rock-sculptures and Rock-inscriptions of Western Asia, I. Some Unpublished Rock-inscriptions of Sennacherib on the Jûdî Dâgh," *PSBA* 35 (1913), pp. 66–94.
7. *The University of Missouri Studies, Social Science Series*, 3.1, Columbia, Miss., 1916. pp 66–94.
8. *Une relation de la huitième campagne de Sargon* (*TCL* 3), Paris, 1912.
9. Sidney Smith, *The First Campaign of Sennacherib, King of Assyria, B.C. 705–681*, London, 1921.

Louis D. Levine

same campaign, but confined most of the discussion to historical questions. With Smith's publication, however, a clear pattern began to emerge. Each time a new text was discovered, the editor felt constrained to remark on the relationship of that text to others already known, but no thorough-going reanalysis of all the texts was undertaken. In 1924, D.D. Luckenbill took up Olmstead's challenge and published a new edition of all the Sennacherib texts.[10] This book has served since its release as the standard publication of these inscriptions. Luckenbill explicitly followed Olmstead's lead, grouping his manuscripts by the number of campaigns contained in each. He also gathered together the miscellaneous bits and pieces of Sennacherib inscriptions that had been published since Bezold's effort some thirty-five years prior. Unfortunately, the volume that he produced is marred by a number of serious flaws. He did not consult all of the manuscripts that were available to him, he sometimes equated texts that were not equal, and his assignment of manuscripts to a certain edition was imprecise.[11] Nonetheless, these faults went unobserved or unremarked, and no further serious work was done on the Sennacherib texts for almost forty years.

This interim period ended with the publication of R. Borger's *Lesestücke*.[12] Borger not only prepared a new transliteration of the longest of Sennacherib's inscriptions, the Chicago/Taylor prisms, he also combed the literature in his usually thorough manner and re-classified all the manuscripts (pp. 59–80). In this classification, the first criterion used was the shape of the object on which the inscription appeared, and within these groups, the number of campaigns appearing on each manuscript.

Borger relied for much of his information on catalogue descriptions, and apparently did not actually examine most of the manuscripts. This was done for part of the corpus by Julian Reade, in 1975.[13] Reade had available to him not only the manuscripts known to Borger, but also those identified by Millard in the second supplement to the catalogue

10. *The Annals of Sennacherib* (*OIP* 2), Chicago, 1924.
11. E.g., Luckenbill's list of manuscripts (pp. 20–22) does not even include those already published by Bezold (see note 4); he states that Rassam equals Chicago for the first three campaigns (p. 60), thereby omitting an important variant in the Rassam text (Bezold [above n. 4], p. 114, n. 6); he assigns both BM No. 103,000 and K. 1674 to one group, although the former has the first five campaigns plus the campaigns against Cilicia and Tilgarimmu while the latter has only the first four campaigns. Other such lapses could also be noted.
12. *Babylonisch-assyrische Lesestücke*, Rome 1963 (2nd rev. ed.; Rome, 1979).
13. "Sources for Sennacherib: The Prisms," *JCS* 27 (1975), pp. 189–196.

of the Kouyunjik collection.[14] After making a number of important joins, Reade was able to present a new list, refining and somewhat departing from the system of Olmstead, Luckenbill and Borger. He assigned manuscripts to "editions" according to the year in which they were written, rather than only using the number of campaigns each manuscript contained. This difference stemmed from a different focus of research. While all of the former scholars had been interested in political and military history, Reade's work was apparently preparatory to a series of articles on Sennacherib's building and irrigation projects.[15]

The first article by Reade not only contained a great deal of new and useful information, but also brought home a very important and previously unnoticed point. It demonstrated that on the prisms, one and the same military text was used with different building inscriptions. This can now be demonstrated not only for the prisms, but for other texts as well.

These observations suggest that the converse situation may also be true, and that different military inscriptions may be found with the same building inscriptions. Only a full investigation of all the manuscripts will serve to confirm this.

Finally, this third phase of activity on the Sennacherib inscriptions has seen the publication of two new important texts. The first is the Walter's Art Gallery Inscription, the second – the join of two long-known fragments thought to belong to Tiglath-pileser III and Sargon II, and now most probably assigned to Sennacherib.[16] Both of these significantly differ in one respect or another from previously known inscriptions in the corpus and are therefore of special interest.

Reade's observation that the two major component parts of many of the inscriptions, the military and the building, can have different histories, when taken with the newly published material, raises the question of what is meant by the terms "edition" and "recension" when they are used in the literature. This, in turn, implies a series of further questions about how the texts in the corpus relate to one another. One point that seems clear, however, is that to answer these questions, at

14. See above, n. 1.
15. "Studies in Assyrian Geography, Part I: Sennacherib and the Waters of Niniveh," *RA* 72 (1978), pp. 47–72 and 157–180.
16. A.K. Grayson, "The Walters Art Gallery Sennacherib Inscription," *AfO* 20 (1963), pp. 83–96; N. Na'aman, "Sennacherib's 'Letter to God' on his campaign to Judah," *BASOR* 214 (1974), pp. 25–39; *idem*, "Sennacherib's Campaign to Judah and the Date of the *LMLK* Stamps," *VT* 29 (1979), pp. 61–68.

the very least, it will be necessary to separate the building component of the inscriptions from the military component. The methodology for the study of the military component is discussed below, after we have examined the sources available.

The Sources

There exist references to approximately two hundred and fifty manuscripts which can be attributed with certainty to Sennacherib. Of these, some one hundred and fifty-seven contain either complete military inscriptions, or fragments thereof. The inscriptions are written on two media, clay and stone, and each of these can be further subdivided into the actual form of the object upon which the inscription is written. Thus, for the clay objects, we find barrel cylinders, on which the inscription runs the length of the barrel, six and eight-sided prisms, on which the text is inscribed in columns, one to a side, and clay tablets. The first group consists of sixty-eight pieces, the second of sixteen, the third of forty-nine, and the fourth of eleven. These figures represent many fragments, some of which probably stem from the same original object. On the other hand, manuscripts which had a military component that is now missing or in which the catalogue description is inadequate, are excluded from the count. Thus, it is immediately apparent that the cylinders and prisms, consisting of one hundred and thirty-three exemplars, make up the vast majority of the texts on clay, with the eleven tablets playing a relatively minor role.

The stone objects with military components can also be divided into sub-groups. These include inscriptions on stone slabs (six exemplars), on monumental bulls (four exemplars), on rock reliefs (two exemplars), and epigraphs on the reliefs (six exemplars). As can be seen, these stone-cut inscriptions make up a very small part of the total corpus, and their number is so limited as to render the relative occurrence of one type rather than another of little statistical significance. The paucity of inscriptions in this medium does not, however, bear on their importance to our study.

From the literary point of view, the inscriptions can be divided differently. Here five basic groups emerge, three of which are coherent, while the fourth serves as a catch-all for those relatively complete texts that are not easily classified. The groups are what I have called "annals", chronological summaries, epigraphs and special inscriptions. The fifth group contains texts which are fragmentary and thus difficult to assign, but these texts seem to differ sufficiently from those in the groups named above to make their inclusion in those groups difficult. The number of inscriptions that fall into each of these groups is harder to arrive at, given the sometimes laconic nature of the catalogue descriptions; but the impression that one gains is that the vast majority are annalistic, with the chronological summaries running a very distant second. All of the other inscriptions taken together probably do not total the number of summaries.

Annals are distinguished by being arranged according to *girru* or campaign. Normally, each campaign is introduced by the phrase *ina* n *girriya*, "on my nth. campaign", starting from the first. Two exceptions to this rule occur. In manuscripts from early in Sennacherib's reign, the first campaign is introduced by the phrase *ina rēš sarrūtiya,* "at the beginning of my reign", but even in these texts the second campaign, where present, is already marked by the normal *ina* 2 *girriya.* This system is abandoned once manuscripts containing three campaigns are composed. From this point forward, the first campaign is introduced as the others with the standard formula *ina maḫrê girriya,* "on my first campaign".

The other exception is the occurrence of the phrase *ina limmu* PN. This dating formula is a familiar one in Assyria, but after the early years of Shalmaneser III, it is rarely found in the body of neo-Assyrian royal inscriptions. Within the Sennacherib inscriptions, the phrase only occurs in connection with the two campaigns to Cilicia and Tilgarimmu, and follows a string of others which are dated with the standard formula.[17] Unlike the phrase *ina rēš šarrūtiya*, however, when this new phrase is abandoned, so too are the accounts of the campaign proper, at least in the annals group.

Chronological summaries differ from the annals in two important respects. First, they do not use the phrase *ina* n *girriya*, and second, they generally give a much abbreviated version of the events described in the annalistic texts. They do, however, generally follow the same chronological order as the annals in the presentation of events.

The epigraphs are hardly texts in the sense that we use the term here, as they present no connected narrative. Rather, they are captions to a pictorial narrative, that of the reliefs decorating the walls of Sennacherib's palace.

The fourth group bears no standard patterning, and is very small,

---

17. Luckenbill, (above, no. 10), pp. 61–63.

consisting of three examples. The first, the Judi Dagh inscription, is in reality a number of almost identical texts of the fifth campaign, all of which are only partially preserved. The pattern here differs from both the annals and the chronological summaries in that the campaign is introduced by the phrase *ina ūmešuma,* "at that time", but with no further specification of what time is meant. The second text, the Bavian inscription, also has an unusual dating formula. The events of the first campaign are described as starting *ina* MU.AN.NAᵘ-*ma,* "in that year", that is in the year that the canal mentioned in the first part of the inscription was dug. The second campaign recorded in this text contains the standard annalistic formula *ina* 2 *girriya,* but the campaign referred to is not the second of 702 B.C., but the campaign that resulted in the destruction of Babylon in 689 B.C. The third text in this group, the Walters Art Gallery inscription, uses yet a third formula. It speaks of four campaigns to Babylonia and three to Elam, but only treats the three to Elam. Furthermore, the first of these, the sixth of the annals, is disposed of in a single sentence, while the seventh and eighth are treated very fully. It is of interest that the sixth and seventh are treated as a long subordinate clause in the account of the eighth campaign, the latter being the occasion for which the inscription was created. It is also worth pointing out that the dating formula used is *ina tarṣi* RN, "in the reign of RN". The occurrence of this formula here is unique in the Sennacherib corpus and rare in the neo-Assyrian royal texts. Thus, the features that unite these three inscriptions are that each one uses a dating formula different from the ones regularly encountered, and that each deals with only part of the military activity of Sennacherib, rather than starting with the first campaign.

In the fifth group, the fragmentary texts, there are two that must be singled out. One is the document recently joined by N. Na'aman (see note 16). This is part of the account of a campaign to Palestine, presumably the third campaign, written in a very high prose. The second is the clay tablet K.2655, which carries an account of the eighth campaign on its reverse that is similar to, but not identical with, the accounts in the annals and on the Walters Art Gallery slab. On the obverse of this text, however, appear copies of three royal grants, one dating probably from the reign of Shamshi-Adad V, and the other two from the reign of Adad-nerari III.[18] Thus, it is clear what all of the previous campaigns were not recorded on this tablet. Unfor-

18. J.N. Postgate, *Neo-Assyrian Royal Grants and Decrees* (*Studia Pohl,* series maior 1), Rome, 1969, pp. 101–105.

tunately, both texts are fragmentary and cannot be assigned to any of the above groups.

There is one further aspect of the corpus of Sennacherib inscriptions that we should note. Virtually all of the manuscripts are part of the Kouyunjik collection, and thus, most probably stem from the site of ancient Nineveh. Unfortunately, in the vast majority of the cases, the find spot is unknown, and even when it is known, such as the texts from the Campbell Thompson excavations, the accompanying archaeological publication is of poor quality and adds little useful information.[19] A few of the manuscripts come from Ashur, although most of the Ashur documents did not contain a military component in the manuscript. Only three inscriptions do not stem from one of these two major Assyrian centres. These are the rock reliefs and the Walters Art Gallery text, or all of the examples from the special inscriptions group.[20]

When we take the two sets of data, physical and literary, and combine them, certain tendencies emerge. Annals, by far the most common among all of the historical inscriptions, are almost exclusively written on clay. Only one exception to this rule exists at present, the Large Bull inscription. Furthermore, as already noted, the vast majority of the annalistic texts occur on cylinders and prisms, with only a small percent inscribed on tablets. The function of the cylinders and prisms is known. They were included as foundation deposits in major constructions of the king; and Reade has demonstrated that certain shapes, hexagonal as opposed to octagonal prisms, for example, have specific archaeological proveniences.[21] The purpose of the tablets is less clear, and here the lack of a good archaeological provenience is especially to be regretted. It is possible to propose that they served as drafts for, and/or as archival copies of, the other texts, or as student exercise tablets.

The chronological summaries present a very different picture. Of the nine examples that we have, seven are written on stone. Four of these, those on the stone slabs, have a relatively limited surface, and this may well account for the shortness of the text when compared with

---

19. See Reade, (above, n. 13) and Millard & Lambert (above, n. 1) for references.
20. The Jerwan inscriptions also do not stem from one of the major centres, but the fragmentary nature of Inscription D, the only text with a military component, has placed it outside the present discussion. See T. Jacobsen and Seton Lloyd, *Sennacherib's Aqueduct at Jerwan* (*OIP* 24), Chicago, 1935.
21. Reade, (above, n. 13).

the annals.[22] But, the three small bulls had sufficient surface for a long text, and yet the shorter version was chosen. It should also be noted that of the two copies written on clay, one was on a tablet, and might, therefore, be considered as a draft or an archival copy, but the second is on a prism, and here again the argument citing lack of space does not fit.[23]

Methodological considerations

The broad categorization just presented, painted as it was with a very large brush, leaves many more questions unanswered than solved. Among these are questions of the sources used in the compilation of the royal inscriptions, the relationships between the various inscriptions and the compositional techniques employed by the scribe, and ultimately the bearing of these on the historical value of the accounts. Answers to these should also eventually lead to insights into the place of the royal inscriptions in the Assyrian view of the world, and to a deeper understanding of Assyria's world view.

Unfortunately, we lack any explicit description of the workings of the neo-Assyrian royal scribal establishment and of the factors motivating its operation. Thus, the only avenue open to us for conducting an investigation into the questions raised is a close comparison of the various manuscripts available, with the full realization that what we have probably represents only a partial picture of the ancient reality.

The problem that arises from this proposed procedure of close comparison between manuscripts is, however, not a simple one. The proper unit of analysis must first be defined. As was noted above, most people working on Sennacherib's inscriptions have grouped the manuscripts into editions, and compared these editions. But it is not necessary to postulate that the entire manuscript, or even the entire military component, is the proper unit of analysis. That such a procedure has been followed in the past stems from the hypothesis that later manuscripts simply add to earlier ones, without changing the former accounts except for abbreviating in the interest of saving space. But such an approach masks significant differences between accounts of the same set of events, and the hypothesis is in need of serious testing. To do so, it

22. See Borger (above, n. 12), II, p. 61, *sub* "Platteninschriften" for references, and add the Kestner-Museum piece referred to at the top of the same page.
23. For a different suggestion, see Reade, (above, n. 13), p. 194.

would seem that the individual campaign, and not the entire text, must serve as the basic unit of analysis. The complete text is but a chain of such campaign narratives that has links added to it from time to time, but each link is forged complete unto itself, and the manner in which each is forged may not be uniform. Furthermore, a close reading of the texts suggests that, at times, accounts of campaigns could be added to, or deleted from, and that the process is considerably more complex than the simple model of Olmstead.

This is not to say that all questions can be answered by using the campaign as the unit of analysis. On the one hand, the campaign itself is often composed of sub-units, which we call episodes, and for certain purposes we must use this sub-unit to understand compositional and historical questions. But the episodic unit is not always easily recoverable in the Sennacherib inscriptions, and this makes it difficult to build upon. Likewise, it is clear that the entire manuscript must eventually be examined. However, the questions put to this larger, composite unit are not those which can be put to the smaller unit of the campaign. For questions of sources and compositional technique, the episode and the campaign must serve. For questions of historical worth and historiographic intent, both the individual campaigns *and* the entire manuscript must be examined.

One further observation is necessary. While I advocate the campaign as the unit of analysis, it is also true that a sample of one campaign is not sufficient to draw wide-ranging conclusions. It is the repetition of patterns that must be observed as well as the deviation from these patterns. One campaign may be anomalous, and, thus, it is dangerous to use it as a basis for generalizations.

Procedure

From these methodological observations, it follows that the first step in our procedure must be to establish the total number of compositions that we have for each campaign, defining a composition as a text of an individual campaign which differs from a second text in any way other than orthography or copying error. The places wherein the compositions diverge must then be examined, and an explanation offered for the process by which each variation arose. This explanation may differ with different types of variations, or even for the same type of variation. After noting the differences and coming to some understanding of the process by which they arose, we can turn to the question of the

Louis D. Levine

relationship between compositions. It is only then possible to examine the way in which the campaign compositions are strung together to make up entire military inscriptions.

The procedure just described, that of assembling compositions, noting all variants, explaining these variants and then examining the entire manuscript, should ideally be done for all of the Sennacherib inscriptions before any statements are made. But to do this would involve examining as many of the unpublished manuscripts as possible, and would in any event result in a monograph rather than an article. Since neither of these options is presently available, I have chosen a sample of the published texts to test the procedure outlined.

The data base used was all of the published accounts of the first, sixth, seventh, and eighth campaigns of Sennacherib. All compositions were recorded and all differences noted. These differences were then arranged hierarchically, from simple to complex. The chart that follows is the result of this investigation:

Hierarchy of differences

1.0   Word level variation

    1.1   Inversion of word order
    1.2   Synonymity (prepositions, conjunctions, verbs, nouns)
    1.3   Expansion or deletion (prepositions, conjunctions, pronouns, nouns)
    1.4   Alteration
        1.4.1   Alteration of person or verb
        1.4.2   Alteration of numbers

2.0   Phrase level variation

    2.1   Displacement of phrase
    2.2   Synonymous phrases
    2.3   Expansion or deletion

3.0   Episode level variation

    3.1   Episode order
    3.2   Expansion or deletion of an episode
    3.3   Alteration of events

4.0   Composition level variation

    4.1   Combination of separate campaigns
    4.2   Division of events into campaigns

5.0   Manuscript level variation

    5.1   Scope of what is included and excluded in a manuscript

The list just presented is wholly descriptive in nature, and represents an attempt to make order out of what appears at first glance to be a welter of types of variations. What the list does not do is to provide any explanation of the reason for the variations. If we can divide the reasons into two general classes, which can be called intentional and unintentional, or conscious and subconscious, it is generally true that as we move towards the higher numbers on the list, the reasons for the change are more likely to be intentional and conscious. But even in the lower numbers, this may also be the case, as for example, the alteration in the person of the verb (1.4.1), or an even more banal example, the choice of an orthographic variant to fill out the remaining space in a line.

Within the intentional variants, there is probably also a range of factors contributing to the changes. These may include a misunderstanding on the part of the scribe of the source material available to him,[24] an aesthetic judgment as to what better fits the immediate context, or a conscious attempt at revisionism in the recording of the events. What is abundantly clear is that only at times is it possible to recover the motive. Often we are left with only a descriptive statement and can push the evidence no further.

Another observation must be made concerning the list, or rather about certain items on it. In categories 1, 2, and 3 we have items that are called "expansions" or "deletions". As long as one operated within the framework of Olmstead and those who followed him, all of these would be termed "deletions", on the assumption that the original account was the longest and most complete. But it can be clearly demonstrated that this was not always the case. In certain instances, we have "later" manuscripts which contain information that is not

24. See Levine, "The Second Campaign of Sennacherib," *JNES* 32, (1973), pp. 312–317.

Louis D. Levine

present in the longer and "more complete" early accounts. While the control which we exercise over the sources available to the scribe is minimal, such examples prove the process to be more complex than a simple model of copying combined with deletion would account for. With these strictures in mind, a few examples can be advanced, both to demonstrate the types of variation and to show some of the implications that can be drawn from them. Let us take, for a start, what on the face of it are simple differences. These range from inverted word order, as in *ālānišunu dannūti bīt dūrāni* versus *ālānišunu bīt dūrāni dannūti*, to synonymous words, such as, *qirib šadê* and *qabal šadê* or *šar Elamti* and *Elamû*, or *kašādu* and *ṣabātu*, to synonymous phrases such as *bušê bīt ilānišunu* versus *makkur ešrētišunu*. Each of these alternations occurs at the same point in the same episode of the same campaign. The frequency with which they occur indicates that the scribe exercised a freedom of action within certain bounds even when producing a so-called duplicate text. It would seem, therefore, that the idea of a canonical version, at least in the strict sense that the term is used in Biblical studies, was a concept foreign to the Assyrian scribe; and that certain parameters of variation were acceptable from the very beginnings of the transmission of the text. This phenomenon should be seriously considered when faced with similar problems in other ancient Near Eastern literary creations, including the question of the "original" text of the Bible.

We move now to a somewhat more complex type of difference, the "expansions" and "deletions" referred to above. In the earliest account of the first campaign, the manuscript lists four cities from which people were deported: Uruk, Nippur, Kish, and Harsagkalamma. Slightly later manuscripts add Kutha to this list, and later ones still, add Sippar as well. It is clear that what we have here is not a deletion, but rather the addition of information from sources unavailable to the writer of the first manuscript. In this case, I believe that I can show that the reason our first manuscript did not contain the two additional names is that the two cities had not yet been captured.[25] What I wish to stress here, however, is that the explanation of differences between manuscripts of different dates is a more complex process than simple excision, and, as I noted, expansion from independent sources must also be taken into account.

Before leaving this example, it is useful to underline two further

25. See my article, "Sennacherib's Southern Front: 704–689 B.C.", *JCS*, in press.

points that can be learned from it, and which have other independent confirmatory examples as well. The first is that a "campaign", as reported in the annals, does not necessarily end with the events described in the original document. Here, actions post-dating the first account of the first campaign were included in later manuscripts dealing with the "same" campaign. Indeed, for the first campaign, this phenomenon has important historical implications.[26] The second point worth making is that it was possible to produce an account of a campaign before that campaign had been completed. This can be shown not only for the first campaign, but for the sixth campaign as well. This latter campaign can also serve as our final and most complex example of yet another type of variation.

The events of the sixth and seventh campaigns, as related in the Chicago prism, can be summarized as follows. In the sixth campaign, Sennacherib attacked the coast of Elam, and on his return defeated Shuzubu the Babylonian and his Elamite allies in central Babylonia. In the following seventh campaign, he attacked northern Elam. The inscription on the Large Bull ends with the initial attack on Elam, and includes neither the second part of the sixth campaign, nor the seventh. Were this the totality of our information, we could suffice with the observation that the Large Bull was written before the sixth campaign ended. However, the situation is more complex. The events of the first part of the sixth campaign, the attack on the Elamite coast, are separated from those of the second part, the events in central Babylonia, by over a year. This second part of the sixth campaign and the seventh are separated by three months at the most. On the face of it, then, there is a principle operating in the "annals" composition that assigns events to a campaign on other than chronological grounds. But, the historical summaries apparently divide these same events differently. They, like the Large Bull, end the sixth campaign with the attack on the Elamite coast, and combine the defeat of Shuzubu the Babylonian mentioned in the second part of the sixth campaign with events of the seventh, the attack on northern Elam. It should be stressed that neither text is wrong. Rather, the historical summaries reflect different historiographic principles for the organization of a consecutive series of events than those operating in the Chicago/Taylor annals, even though both stem from the same royal court, at approximately the same time.

The three examples just presented are only illustrative of the range

---

26.   Note 11, above, and Levine, "Sennacherib's Southern Front" (above, n. 25).

of variations outlined in the chart above. They do not cover all types of variations, nor all the implications that can be derived from an examination of such variation. Any consideration of the totality of these would require more than a series of preliminary remarks. But the examples presented do indicate, I believe, the desirability of such a full study.

One of the results of such a study would be a clearer understanding of the quantitative difference between different texts. This would, in turn, allow a clearer definition of such terms as "edition" and "recension", and these would be based upon a consideration of all of the works of a king, rather than as generalizations from single, often unique texts. Without the resulting precision, both methodological and terminological, it is unlikely that we can make the kind of advances that will serve as building blocks for further research.

A second result of this kind of investigation will be the ability to see whether certain manuscripts exhibit tendencies that are consistent throughout the manuscript, regardless of the compositions used as the basis for the manuscript. If such tendencies are observable, they may well hold keys to understanding the purpose of these inscriptions that have not yet been noted, as well as insights into their method of composition.

Sennacherib and Neo-Assyrian Royal Inscriptions

It is apparent by this point that the procedure proposed for the investigation of the Sennacherib inscriptions is similar, at least in some of its formal aspects, to suggestions recently put forth for the study of other genres of cuneiform texts. Edzard recently argued that Sumerian literary compositions need to be dealt with in a similar manner, rather than trying to produce a composite text based upon the best judgement of the person preparing the edition.[27] Reiner has actually produced an edition which follows the system proposed by Edzard for a part of one of the omen series[28] Although the reasons advanced by these works are somewhat different than the reasons advanced here, and although the two procedures are not strictly comparable, the end result is not dissimilar. What we need are parallel texts presented in a

27. D.O. Edzard, "Zum sumerischen Hymne auf das Heiligtum Keš," *Orientalia* 43 (1974), pp. 105–107.
28. Erica Reiner with David Pingree, *The Venus Tablet of Ammiṣaduga* (*Bibliotheca Mesopotamica* 2.1), Malibu, 1975.

way that makes the range of variations between the texts immediately apparent. The level on which the text is presented, transcription or transliteration, will depend upon the questions addressed to the text. It is also apparent to all familiar with the corpus of neo-Assyrian royal inscriptions that Sennacherib holds no monopoly on the questions we are raising here. But his lack of monopolistic control over the questions does not mean that the answers derived from an investigation of this one group of texts will also hold true for the corpora of earlier or later neo-Assyrian kings. Each of these must be closely investigated, and we must free ourselves from the over-generalizations that have thus far characterized much of the work in the field. In details, we have long recognized significant differences between the inscriptions of the neo-Assyrian kings, but these have not led to the necessary doubts that should have been generated over general issues. It is time to start voicing such doubts, and to begin a close investigation of the texts involved. Only by freeing ourselves from the old models will it be possible to make the necessary breakthroughs to new levels of understanding in this rich and varied corpus of material.

Postscript

This article was completed in December 1979. Since then, the very important book edited by F.M. Fales, *Assyrian Royal Inscriptions: New Horizons in Literary, Ideological and Historical Analysis* (Orientis Antiqui Collectio - XVII, Rome, 1981) has appeared, and should be referred to in conjunction with this paper. See especially the remarks of M. Liverani in his article "Critique of Variants and the Titulary of Sennacherib."

OMENS AND IDEOLOGY IN THE BABYLON
INSCRIPTION OF ESARHADDON

MORDECHAI COGAN

Ben-Gurion University of the Negev

The 'Babylon Inscription' of Esarhaddon indeed resembles a well-plowed field. Students of Assyrian history have repeatedly worked this text in search of the key to understanding Esarhaddon's policy towards Babylon; for it is the Babylon text which provides the basic description of the king's projects of reconstruction within that city, as well as the rationale explaining its original destruction at the hands of Sennacherib. The masterly study, some fifteen years ago, by Benno Landsberger, in his *Brief des Bischofs von Esagila*,[1] represents the high water mark with regard to most questions concerning Esarhaddon and Babylon. Our return to this inscription was, therefore, limited to one small corner of this plowed field, that dealing with the composition of the text, in which further tilling produced an unexpected yield.

I

The text of the Babylon inscription is preserved on over a dozen manuscripts,[2] inscribed on clay, and once on stone, the famous Black Stone of Esarhaddon, now at the British Museum.[3] A comparison of these manuscripts led R. Borger to divide our text into forty-one episodes,

---

1. B. Landsberger, *Brief des Bischofs von Esagila an König Asarhaddon* (*MKNAW*, N.R. 28 no. 6), Amsterdam, 1965 (Hereafter, Landsberger, *Brief*).
2. See the text editions in R. Borger, *Die Inschriften Asarhaddons Königs von Assyrien* (*AfO* Beiheft 9), Graz, 1956, §11 (Hereafter, Borger, *Asarhaddon*).
3. Borger, *Asarhaddon*, §11, recension D. Landsberger, *Brief*, p. 19, thought that our Black Stone is the very one mentioned in Episode 27 – NA_4 *ṣalamti* – "found by chance at Nineveh."

delivered in one of three distinct versions, all of which have been edited in eight identifiable recensions.[4]

Following Borger's lead, we define an episode as a textual unit which describes a distinct stage in the history of Babylon's destruction and restoration. Consecutive numbering of these episodes, from 1–41, suggests a chronological sequence, so that, e.g., the molding of the first brick by the king himself-Ep. 21, naturally precedes the year-long production of bricks by the assembled workers-Ep. 22.

The story told in our text appears in one of three versions (or *fassungen*), a term used by Borger to indicate varying descriptions of the same event or episode. Thus, Episode 7, in version A, reports the raging flood of the Araḥtu canal which swept over Babylon and its cult centers; in version B, a single terse sentence states, quite colorlessly, that the city became an abandoned wasteland; a third version, C, details the effects of the flooding: newly formed marshland, swarming with wild-life. The term "recension" is used when refering to the complete inscription, as relates to its total number of episodes and their particular sequential arrangement. For example, in recension B, Ep. 34 precedes Ep. 27; recension E is distinguished by the absence of Episodes 2, 3, 4 and 6.

II

It is clear that many of the recensional differences in our inscription are on the whole, of minor significance; they represent abridgements in which questions of space and/or stylistics likely played a part. For example, recensions A, B and C present information on matters of construction on the temple Esagila and its buildings – details of the floor plans, material utilized, stonework and their finishings – in eight separate episode units.[5] Recensions D and E, on the other hand, simply summarize all this detail in a short paragraph.

---

4. We have adopted Borger's division of the text, as it has become standard within Assyriological circles. But some reservations concerning this division must be noted at the outset. Borger did not always rigorously apply the principles of division into episodes and versions noted above. For example, he states that "episode 18 is parallel to episode 19ff. in the other recensions," (Borger, *Asarhaddon*, p. 19 notes) yet these two episodes were not set out as synoptic, i.e., different versions of a single episode, but were presented as consecutive. Furthermore, recensions D and E summarize the work on the temple Esagila and its buildings (D, Episode 23; E, Episode 26 c); while the other recensions A, B and C provide construction details (Episodes 24, 25, 26, a, b, 27, 28, 29, 30 and 31). Here, too, we would have been better served with the texts presented in parallel fashion.

5. Borger, *Asarhaddon*, §11, Eps. 24, 25, 26a, 26b, 27, 28, 29, 30, 31.

> Esagila, the temple of the gods,
> and its shrines;
> Babylon, the privileged city,
> Imgur-Enlil, its wall,
> Nemet-Enlil, its ramparts—
> from their foundation to their pinnacle,
> I renewed, I made them greater,
> I raised higher, I besplendered
> (more then before).[6]

As the Black Stone has a limited surface – only four sides – recension D just may have condensed, for this reason, eight episodes into one.

At the same time, two particular features which mark recension E as distinct from the other recensions are of especial significance; they allow us, as it were, to peer over the shoulder of the royal scribes and to observe the process by which they edited the Babylon inscription. These two features of recension E will be discussed under the headings: omens and ideology.

Omens

Among the episodes missing from recension E are the complimentary Episodes 2 and 12. Episode 2 tells of evil omens (*idāti lemnēti*) observed during Sennacherib's reign, fortelling bad times in Sumer and Akkad. Episode 12 reports good omens (*idāt damiqtim*) during the accession year of Esarhaddon which meant that Babylon was to be restored. Several recensions (A, B and C) even record the specific astronomical configurations observed in the heavens which signaled the arrival of the propitious season, the time to begin the work of reconstruction of Babylon.

> The bright Jupiter ... came close in the
> month Simanu and stood in the place where
> the sun appears; it was shining brightly,
> and it's appearance was exceedingly great.[7]

This specification is most unusual, for, as a rule, the scribes used

6. Borger, *Asarhaddon*, §11, recension D, Ep. 23; recension E, Ep. 26c.
7. Borger, *Asarhaddon*, §11, Ep. 13. The omen is repeated in Borger, *Asarhaddon*, §53, Rs. 3–9a.

rather general phraseology in the historical inscriptions when referring to omens.[8]

In recension E, episodes 2 and 12 were omitted; to take their place, two new episodes were composed. In these, Babylon's dire fate came about because of the lord Marduk's anger, and it was only his subsequent pacification which permitted the city's pardon.

> Before my reign, Marduk, the great lord,
> was angry. He was wrought with the temple
> Esagila and with Babylon. His heart was
> agitated and he was enraged. Because of his
> anger and his violent mood . . .[9]

> Marduk, the great lord, was calm, his
> mood relaxed and he had compassion upon
> Esagila and Babylon, with which he had
> been angry.[10]

Thus, in recension E, there are no portending signs; even the famous omen concerning the seventy year period of devastation set by Marduk, which he later reversed into eleven years (*eliš ana šapliš ušbalkitma*), is not part of the E text.[11] Furthermore, recensions A, B and D depict a cautious Esarhaddon,[12] who, despite these signs of encouragement from on high, defers to yet other divinatory procedures, the tradition-honored science of extispicy and to lecanomancy.

> In the bowl of the diviners, trustworthy
> oracles were set for me. Concerning
> the reconstruction of Babylon and the

8. Considering the passage under discussion, the mention of ominous phenomena in Sargon's 'Letter to God' (F. Thureau-Dangin, *Une relation de la huitième campagne de Sargon* [*TCL 3*], Paris, 1912, pp. 317–318) is not as unique as A.L. Oppenheim originally thought. Cf. his remarks in *JNES* 19 (1960), p. 137 and n. 10.
9. Borger, *Asarhaddon*, §11, Ep. 5.
10. Borger, *Asarhaddon* §11, Ep. 11
11. This *crux criticorum* was first puzzled out by D.D. Luckenbill, *AJSL* 41 (1924), pp. 166–168. See Borger, *Asarhaddon*, §10; H. Hirsch, *AfO* 21 (1966) p. 34, and most recently A. Shaffer, *RA* 75 (1981), p. 188.
12. This would seem to be the proper description of the Assyrian king who, according to our available sources, was under continual bombardment by his scholarly advisors at court. Esarhaddon's occasional distrust of the omens may have stemmed from conflicting interpretations offered by different schools among these savants. Cf. A.L. Oppenheim, *Ancient Mesopotamia*, Chicago, 1964, p. 227; *Centaurus* 14 (1969), pp. 119–120; and the remarks of S. Parpola, *Letters from Assyrian Scholars*, Pt. IIA, Neukirchen-Vluyn, 1971, p. 23, and in particular pp. 46–47.

restoration of the temple Esagila, he
wrote in a liver oracle. I trusted in
their true "yes."[13]

This episode, too, is absent from recension E. E's authors dropped all reports of divination from their text. And, as if to underscore their obvious avoidance of all reference to divination – and to astrology in particular – they utilized a non-descript, neutral phrase which might bear several interpretations, and which is unique to recension E in this stage of the story:

> I was confident; I gave orders to begin
> work.[14]

Ideology
Further evidence for the distinctiveness of recension E may be derived from a comparison of the versions of the single episode, the subject of which is the work-gangs laboring at rebuilding Babylon.

Version One (recension G):

> adkēma gimir ummâni māt Karduniaš kalama . . .[15]
> I mobilized all the workers of the whole land
> of Babylonia.

Version Two (recensions A, B, C and D):

> adkēma gimir ummâniya u nišê māt Karduniaš
> ana siḥirtiša
> allu ušatrika ēmida tupšikki [16]
> I mobilized all my workmen and the people of
> Babylonia, round about. I had them handle
> the spade; I set the basket upon them.

Version Three (recension E):

> nišê mātāte kišitti qatēya upaḫḫirma
> allu tupšikku ušaššišunutima[17]
> I gathered people from the lands of my conquest.
> I had them bear the spade and the basket.

13. Borger, *Asarhaddon*, Ep. 17.
14. Borger, *Asarhaddon*, Ep. 15, fass. b.
15. Borger, *Asarhaddon*, Ep. 18. On the relationship between Episodes 18 and 19, see our comment in n. 4 above.
16. Borger, *Asarhaddon*, Ep. 19a and b.
17. Borger, *Asarhaddon*, Ep. 19c.

In version one, Babylonians were set to work on their own city's reconstruction; in version two, the Babylonians were said to have been joined by other workers under royal jurisdiction; in version three (recension E), captives from conquered territories labored alone on the Babylon project.

Now, more than mere semantics would seem to be involved in these alternate readings. The contrasting versions exhibit a sensitivity to the issue of state obligations imposed upon the citizenry of temple cities.[18] Thus, all recensions, again save recension E, report that Esarhaddon undertook to restore Babylon's abrogated *kidinnu*-rights, freeing it from certain imposts, as one of his concluding acts of grace towards the city.

> I established anew the freedom (*andurāru*) for the
> oppressed Babylonians, people of special
> privilege, freed by Anu and Enlil . . .
> Their privileges (*kidinnûtu*), which had been
> interrupted and disregarded, I set up again.
> I re-issued their exempt status (*zakûtu*).[19]

Recension E did not find it necessary to include this episode; it was as if the authors said: the rights of Babylonians were not restored, for they had not been violated to begin with. Moreover, according to E, it was foreign, not native, labor that rebuilt Babylon.

That indeed this was the issue here is learned from another Esarhaddon building inscription, this one dealing with constructions undertaken at Assur. As his first act in the ancient capital, Esarhaddon sealed anew its freedom (*šubarû*) and sacred privileges (*kidinnu*). Then, after the proper encouragement from the gods, he gathered captives from conquered lands to work on the restoration of the Assur temple.[20]

18. The privileged status of Babylonian cities is discussed by H. Tadmor, "Temple City and Royal City in Babylon and in Assyria," *The City and the Community* (Israel Historical Society), Jerusalem, 1968, pp. 189–196 (Hebrew). Cf., now, the comments of J.A. Brinkman in M.T. Larsen (ed.), *Power and Propaganda*, (*Mesopotamia* 7), Copenhagen, 1979, p. 228.
19. Borger, *Asarhaddon*, Ep. 37a, b.
20. Borger, *Asarhaddon*, §2, II, 42- III, 15; IV, 7–15. The rehearsal of these events in another Esarhaddon inscription (Borger, *Asarhaddon*, §53) combines phraseology from both versions one and two (Rs. 44–45). In addition, the restoration of the city's rights is also claimed there by the Assyrian king (Obs. 41–43). Our analysis of the literary elements in the Babylon Inscription is thus confirmed by an outside witness.

III

We have seen that the authors of recension E were selective in their choice of episodes included in the E text. Who, then, were these authors of recension E, whose anti-divinatory position found expression in E? Which circles at Esarhaddon's court would have concerned itself with the question of Babylonian rights? We must state at the outset that clear-cut answers are not immediately suggestable. Even in well-plowed fields such as ours, one can come up against formidable boulders; but the challenge of moving them still must be taken up. Our Babylon inscription casts the court astrologers in a prominent role; in most recensions, their omen reports are central to Esarhaddon's decisions concerning the city. If we follow Oppenheim and trace "the entire practice of reporting to the ruler on ominous celestial events" to a basically "Babylonian institution, adapted and perhaps expanded by the Assyrian kings,"[21] then it was indeed most appropriate to include such reports in a Babylon-oriented text such as the Babylon inscription. And, if we may be allowed to speculate a bit further, these reports might even be an indication of Babylonian inspiration and/or authorship of our text.[22]

One of these ancient scholarly reports is relevant to our discussion;[23] a certain Bēl-ušezib, who seems to have been a Babylonian scholar/scribe in the service of Esarhaddon.[24] In his report, Bēl-ušezib interprets the evil signs of an eclipse (*idāti annātu ša lumnu!*) as reference to Babylonian nobles who had been appointed by Sennacherib and who are seen as responsible for the ruin of the city. [25] The writer urges

21. A.L. Oppenheim, "Divination and Celestial Observation in the Last Assyrian Empire," *Centuarus* 14 (1969), p. 122.
22. This suggestion was originally put forward in M. Cogan, *Imperialism and Religion*, (SBLMS 19), Missoula, 1974, pp. 12–13. Cf. now the seconding remarks of P.D. Miller and J.J.M. Roberts, *The Hand of the Lord*, Baltimore, 1977, pp. 14–15.
23. R.C. Thompson, *Reports of the Magicians and Astrologers of Nineveh and Babylon*, London, 1900, I, p. 272 (Hereafter, *RMA*).
24. The exact whereabouts of Bēl-ušezib has been disputed. Oppenheim, (above, n. 21), pp. 104–105, located him in Sippar, a calculation based upon his invocation of that city's god, Shamash. But Parpola, *LAS* (above, n. 12), p. 2*, n. 1, shows that according to *ABL* 895, Bēl-ušezib resided in Nineveh, "in the capital, the city where the king lives." (URU BAL URU *ša šarri ina libbi ašbu*, obv. 4–5).
25. The text of *RMA* 272 reads at this point:
    rubê ša Babili ša šarri abūka iškuna
    Babili iḫtepû u bušê ša Babili ittašû
    ana muḫḫi idāti annātu ša lumnu! illikāni
    (rev. 13ff.)

Esarhaddon to replace them in all due haste. The tenor of Bēl-ušezib's warning recalls the description of the social decay within Babylon depicted in the Babylon Inscription.[26] If these assumptions concerning the Babylonian inspiration of our text are correct, then recension E's statement could be representative of a pro-Assyrian position. Avoidance of reference to omens is not accidental. The Assyrians behind recension E might have been opposed to the importation of what was basically a Babylonian science into the Assyrian court.[27] But, contrariwise, if ductus is any indicator of identity and/ or affiliation, we must note that copies of recension E were written in both Old Babylonian (2 mss.) as well as Neo-Assyrian (1 ms.) scripts.[28] An alternate hypothesis would be to classify the authors of E as "rationalists," out of step with the predominant belief in omens and fortune-telling as vital to decision-making in those diffident times.

How does the Assyrian background we have suggested for the composition of recension E line up with the question of Babylon's privileged status, also at issue in recension E? It is well known that the see-saw battle for influence in Babylon often centered around the city's *kidinnûtu*. Sargonid kings, before and after Esarhaddon, wrestled with this question. The violation by Merodach-baladan of Babylon's *kidinnu* became a point in favor of Sargon II's invited rule in Babylonia. A half-century later, the citizens of Babylon wrote a letter to King Ashurbanipal, in which they reminded him that:

26. Borger, *Asarhaddon*, §11, Eps. 3 and 4.
   In the communication *ABL* 1216, whose writer may have been Bēl-ušezib, an omen from the astrological series *Enuma Anu Enlil* is appparently referred to in lines 14–15, as alluding to the circumstances surrounding Esarhaddon's rise to the throne and his restoration of temples. On *ABL* 1216, see R. Labat, "Asarhaddon et la ville de Zaqqap," *RA* 53 (1959), pp. 113–118.
27. With reference to liver divination, J. Aro proffered "that Esarhaddon introduced fresh experts from Babylonia, who gradually taught the native Assyrian scribes" the art; an idea he based on an examination of the script and language of the omen documents. See Aro, "Remarks on the Practice of Extispicy in the Time of Esarhaddon and Ashurbanipal," *La Divination en Mésopotamie Ancienne*, Paris, 1966, p. 112. Just how important every bit of information garnered from these celestial observations was considered, may be seen in the seemingly routine communication to Esarhaddon from his son Shamash-shum-ukin. The king is informed of two reluctant diviners in Babylon who have been unmasked. See S. Parpola, *Iraq* 34 (1972), pp. 21–34.
28. The manuscripts in OB are E¹ (88-5-12,80), E³ (88-5-12,101 + AO 7736); in NA script - E² (88-5- 12, 103). Landsberger noted (*Brief*, 19) that no copies of our inscription were excavated in Babylon itself. But contrast the remarks of J. Nougayrol, *AfO* 18 (1957/8), p. 314.

the former kings who had sat on the
throne (of Assyria) had set their mind to
establish our privileged status and to make
us happy.[29]

Recension E of the Babylon Inscription, unlike the other recensions, did not mention Babylon's *kidinnu*. The Assyrian orientation of its authors was expressed in their disregard of this sensitive issue. Too much attention may have been given to this issue for E's tastes. While others might refer to Babylon as *āl kidinni*, privileged city,[30] E's authors chose to call her *ālum masnaqti ilāni*, the city, from where the gods control the world.[31] Respect for Babylon, yes; privileged status, no comment.

IV

Before closing, I wish to append a general word on recensional matters.

This study of recension E of the Babylon Inscription has suggested that the variations in the E text were not random. The shortenings and/ or lengthenings, and the phraseological substitutions were found to be expressions of a distinct ideological point of view in the debate over Babylon at Esarhaddon's court. By paying attention to what at first seemed chance alterations, and by listening for the particular message of each recension, we believe we have recovered several lines of that debate, which now seems more complex than even Landsberger imagined. Many groups vied for the king's ear; their ideological platforms were presented in literary compositions, such as the Babylon Inscription.

Now we have all assumed that the Assyrian royal inscriptions were more than neutral literary productions. That some were political, propagandistic works comes as no surprise. Our problem has been rather the development of the analytical tools with the help of which we can recover the messages imbedded in these texts. For example, Tadmor showed that by comparing the various god lists in the inscriptions of Sennacherib, the ups and downs of imperial policy towards Babylon

29. *ABL* 878, obv. 2–3.
30. Borger, *Asarhaddon*, §11, Ep. 23 (recension D only).
31. A.R. Millard, "Some Esarhaddon Fragments Relating to the Restoration of Babylon," *AfO* 24 (1973), p. 118.

could be traced.[32] Recensional variations of the kind examined here may prove to be another tracer in our quest to understanding the royal inscription.

32. See H. Tadmor, "The Sin of Sargon," *Eretz Israel* 5 (1958), pp. 150–154 (Hebrew).

Appendix

The date and the recensional order of the Babylon Inscription

The date of our inscription as inscribed in the extant colophon of all recensions reads:

MU.SAG. NAM. LUGAL. LA *Aššur-ahu-iddina šar māt Aššur*
The accession year of Esarhaddon, King of Assyria.[1]

Now, as it seems likely, Esarhaddon's accession year (*rêš šarrūti*) began on 8 Adar 680 B.C. and lasted all of 20 days.[2] Besides being a particularly short period of time, during which the complete restoration of Babylon as described in the text was hardly achievable, this *rêš šarrūti* date is openly contradicted by certain items within the narrative itself.

1. Episode 22, in all recensions, relates that the start of the work began with the preparation of brick molds made of ivory and precious woods and was followed by the year-long making of bricks. To be sure, we are dealing with stock phraseology in which we should not seek precision.[3] But just when did the task begin? And how long did the brick-making last?

2. Recensions C and F, Episode 36, report that divine images, taken as spoil in the past, were returned to their native cult centers from their places of exile in Assyria and Elam. But chronicle texts from Esarhaddon's seventh year, 674/3 B.C. tell us that it was not until that year

1. See Borger, *Asarhaddon*, §11, p. 29, and Nougayrol, *AfO* 18 (1957/8), p. 318.
2. A.K. Grayson, *Assyrian and Babylonian Chronicles* (*TCS* 5), Locust Valley, 1975, Chronicle 1, III, 38, now reads: UD [x (?)] XVIII[kám] and notes: "There is room for an extra winkelhaken in the break. Thus the number may be either 28 or 18."
3. The phrase is used in other Esarhaddon inscriptions with reference to constructions at Assur. Cf., e.g., Borger, *Asarhaddon*, §2, IV, 23–26; V, 1–2.

that "Ishtar of Agade and the other gods of Agade" were returned from Elam.[4]

Now in addition to the inherent improbability that much of this activity actually took place during the *rêš šarrūti* of Esarhaddon, it should be noted that recension G is the least problematic of the recensions as regards its date. Half the text of recension G is lost, but from the extant portions it can be determined that G was the shortest of the eight recensions,[5] and seems to have been the earliest composed. This supposition as to the earliness of G derives from a consideration of episode 18, unique to this recension. Ep. 18 reports that the work at Babylon began with the diversion of the Euphrates back to its original channel, a necessary first step in land reclamation. Little, if any, information on the succeeding steps was recorded in G. Other recensions, A and C in particular, omit Ep. 18, inserting in its place full descriptions of the materials and dimensions of the buildings, towers and walls restored and newly constructed. It is this concentration on a preparatory stage of the project and the apparent ignorance of latter activities which suggests the chronological priority of recension G.[6]

B. Landsberger was the last to discuss the intricate question of the date *rêš šarrūti*. He rightly saw in it a purposeful pseudo-dating. Yet in his criticism, Landsberger did not move far from the start of Esarhaddon's reign as the single point in time for the composition of all recensions.[7] Our suggestion, on the other hand, would be to arrange the eight recensions of the Babylon inscription in a broad chronological sequence, the criteria for early or late placement within the sequence being the amount of information each recension contains. Certainly few would remain in the slot: 20-day *rêš šarrūti*. Some may have been edited as late as year 7. The editorial process by which our text grew is relatively simple to reconstruct. An early text, e.g., G, was re-edited as plans developed and work progressed

4. Grayson, (above, n. 2) Chronicle 1, IV, 17–18; Chronicle 14, 21–22.
5. Only one copy of recension G is extant, 1904-10-9,1 (*CT* 34, 1f.), the bottom half of a pentagon upon which as many as 21 lines of a single column (col. IV) are preserved. Calculating on the basis of the other recensions where the introduction to the inscription contains approximately 20 lines, we possess fifty-percent of the G text. But G's introduction could also have been shorter. The break at the top of col. II in G, which separates the end of Ep. 3 from Ep. 5, might mean that at most only 10 lines are missing.
6. Cf. Borger's notes to Ep. 18 on p. 19.
7. Landsberger, *Brief*, pp. 18–20.

at Babylon. The original date, despite its blatant inaccuracy and, what seems to us, inappropriateness, was preserved in all recensions. It served as an exhibit of royal piety, for the *rêš šarrūti* dating was taken to mean: From his very first days on the throne, Esarhaddon turned to the affairs of Babylon, and with due deliberateness, rapidly completed its reconstruction. Obviously, this literary convention of ante-dating was thought to have propoganda value, if not with the Babylonians themselves – who must have known what actually had been accomplished in the field – then with the gods.[8]

8. And, indeed, H. Tadmor has shown that under not dissimilar circumstances, Nabonidus used *rêš šarrūti* in a "general, non-calendric sense" to indicate the early years of his reign. See Tadmor, "The Inscriptions of Nabunaid: Historical Arrangement," in *Studies in Honor of Benno Landsberger*, (*AS* 16), Chicago 1965, pp. 351–353. The author of the biblical book of Chronicles, in like fashion, employed the term "in the first year" to indicate the early piety of king Hezekiah. For a full discussion, see M. Cogan, "Tendentious Chronology in the Book of Chronicles," *Zion* 45 (1980), pp. 165–172 (Hebrew).

ON WARFARE AND MILITARY CONTROL
IN THE ANCIENT NEAR EASTERN EMPIRES:
A RESEARCH OUTLINE

ISRAEL EPH'AL

Tel Aviv University

> "Historians refer constantly to war without really knowing or seeking to know its true nature – or natures. We are as ignorant about war as the physicist is of the true nature of matter. We talk about it because we have to: it has never ceased to trouble the lives of men".
>
> F. Braudel, *The Mediterranean and the Mediterranean World in the Age of Philip II*, vol. II, New York, 1973, 836.

The Ancient Near Eastern empires to be dealt with in this survey are the Assyrian, Chaldaean and Achaemenid which existed in the 9th–4th centuries B.C. One basic characteristic they had in common was that they were large political divisions extending over most of the Fertile Crescent and sometimes even beyond it. Each came under the central authority of a king assisted by a social class which was relatively small in comparison both with the population of that empire, which consisted of various nationalities, and with the size of the territories under its control.[1] I refrain from referring here to other political

1. This basic characteristic does not provide an exhaustive definition for all the socio-political systems which have existed through the ages under various historical circumstances and to which the term "empire" is applied. As a matter of fact, it is difficult to offer such a comprehensive and exhaustive definition. Most sociological and politico-historical studies turn directly to the various types of empires avoiding a thorough discussion of the general term and its consequences (for such a tendency cf., for example, S.N. Eisenstadt, *The Political Systems of Empires*, New York, 1963; idem (ed.), *The Decline of Empires*, Englewood Cliffs, N.J., 1967; and recently M.T. Larsen (ed.), *Power and Propaganda*, A Symposium on Ancient Empires, Copenhagen, 1979). Nevertheless, since this outline concerns only warfare and military control, and not the complex of socio-political and administrative

bodies which dominated various parts of that region (such as the Hittite and Egyptian kingdoms) because I doubt whether the numerical proportion between the rulers and those under their control, and even more so, the proportion between the ruling group and the size of the territory controlled by it, would enable us to include them in the same category as the empires which we are discussing. Most of the following examples refer to the Assyrian empire since this is the best documented; however, various features dealt with below were common, in one way or another, to all three of the empires under discussion.

Military activity is one of the ways in which political bodies typically relate to each other. Much of our historical information refers to wars and related events (including an outcome terminating in the surrender of one of the parties, or in peace between them). Since historiography – ancient and modern alike – focuses mainly upon this subject, it is therefore natural that details about wars, their courses and consequences have become milestones in historical surveys, including those on the Ancient Near East.

Interest in the military history of ancient Near Eastern empires has yielded studies in various fields, of which the most significant are those dealing with the titles of Assyrian officers,[2] typology and technical development of weapons,[3] as well as the interpretation of reliefs[4] and the characterization of their various elements.[5] Likewise, descriptions of special campaigns (such as Sargon's eighth campaign,[6] as well as of

aspects related to the rise, structure and existence of empires, the somewhat over-simple characterization given here seems sufficient for our purposes.

2. See in particular W. Manitius, *ZA* 24 (1910), pp. 97-149, 185–224; E.G. Klauber, *Assyrische Beamtentum nach Briefen aus der Sargonidenzeit*, Leipzig, 1910.

3. Y. Yadin, *The Art of Warfare in Biblical Lands*, I–II, New York, 1963 (including detailed bibliography); E. Salonen, *Die Waffen der alten Mesopotamier*, Helsinki, 1965; A. Salonen, *Hippologica Accadica*, Helsinki, 1956; cf. also idem. *Die Landfahrzeuge des Alten Mesopotamien*, Helsinki, 1951.

4. See Yadin (above, n. 3). Among the various works of R.D. Barnett on this subject see especially *Sculptures from the North Palace of Ashurbanipal at Nineveh (668-627 B.C.)*, London, 1974; R.D. Barnett and M. Falkner, *The Sculptures of Aššur-naṣir-apli II, Tiglath-pileser III and Esarhaddon from the Central and South-West Palaces at Nimrud*, London, 1962.

5. T. Madhlum, *The Chronology of Neo-Assyrian Art*, London, 1970; M. Wäfler, *Nicht-Assyrer neuassyrischer Darstellungen*, Neukirchen-Vluyn, 1975; cf. also E.J. Reade, *Iraq* 34 (1972), pp. 87-112.

6. L.D. Levine, in L.D. Levine and T.C. Young (eds.), *Mountains and Lowlands: Essays in the Archaeology of Greater Mesopotamia (Bibliotheca Mesopotamica 7)*, Malibu, 1977, pp. 134–151 (including bibliography on previous studies on this campaign).

a series of campaigns of certain kings[7]), have been published. Details – sometimes quite incidental – relating to military affairs have also been incorporated in general studies on the Assyrian and Chaldaean empires.[8] To sum up this survey, it may be said that even those studies which deviate from very specific matters are basically limited to itinerarian observation. Thus, ancient Near Eastern military activity, its entire data, problems and implications for historical research remains almost untouched.[8a]

Over the last 25 years, research tools for the period under discussion have been improved with the impressive progress in publication of the Akkadian dictionaries (*CAD* and *AHw*), which today cover almost the whole alphabet; with the appearance of R. Borger's *Handbuch der Keilschriftliteratur*; with the comprehensive introductions of R. Borger and W. Schramm to the Assyrian royal inscriptions up to Tiglath-pileser III; with the progress in relief interpretation and in onomastical investigation; and with the publication of the Neo-Assyrian toponym list by S. Parpola. During the same period, numerous sources were published – for the purposes of this paper I shall refer only to groups of sources relevant to the present subject – such as new fragments of Babylonian chronicles (by D.J. Wiseman and A.R. Millard) as well as a comprehensive edition of the Assyrian and Babylonian chronicles (by A.K. Grayson); letters, "Wine Lists" and other documents from Nimrud; comprehensive editions of royal inscriptions such as those of Aššurnaṣirpal, Shalmaneser III and Esarhaddon; complete editions of the reliefs from the palaces of Tiglath-pileser III and Ashurbanipal; and the Arad inscriptions (including those from the Persian period). The availability of these sources and tools, along with the natural development of research, has extended and deepened our

---

7. See, e.g., on the Egyptian campaigns of Esarhaddon and Ashurbanipal A. Spalinger, *Orientalia* 43 (1974), pp. 295–326 and *JAOS* 94 (1974), pp. 316–328, respectively. Surveys of the entire campaigns of Aššurnaṣirpal and Shalmaneser III see A.T. Olmstead, *JAOS* 38 (1918), pp. 209–263; 41 (1921), pp. 345–382, respectively.

8. See, e.g., B. Meissner, *Babylonien und Assyrien*, I, Heidelberg, 1920, pp. 80–114; G. Contenau, *Everyday Life in Babylon and Assyria*, London, 1954, pp. 141–157; W. von Soden, *Iraq* 25 (1963), pp. 131–144; H.W.F. Saggs, *Iraq* 25 (1963), pp. 145–154; R.A. Henshaw, *Palaeologia* 16 (1969), pp. 1–24 (the latter paper deals with various matters of the structure, size and typology of the Assyrian army. A considerable portion of the data in it, however, suffers from non-systematic treatment).

8a. Close to the arrival of the final galleys of this paper the study of Fl. Malbran-Labat, *L'Armée et l'organisation militaire de l'Assyrie*, Genève – Paris 1982, appeared. It is a significant contribution to various issues dealt with in this paper.

knowledge considerably. Research has not only been enriched with basic data, but it has become possible to develop new fields of study and to compass a more comprehensive and clearer view of a wide range of fields, such as taxation systems and various aspects of agrarian regime, economic relations between various lands, typology of treaties and aspects of international relations, mass deportation as an implement of imperial policy and its significance for the ethnic and cultural structure of ancient Near Eastern empires.[9] This impressive development indicates that it may be possible to work toward a parallel advance in a comprehensive study of military activity, moving beyond mere discussion of details, in order to improve our understanding of the basic factors involved and the military problems which the ancient empires faced, to clarify their significance for the ruling peoples and countries and for the people and countries under their control, and to sharpen our perception of the ancient control and warfare systems in order to obtain a clearer idea of the military element, which plays a major role in political reality.

In this paper I shall confine myself to dealing with but a few points, just to demonstrate what can be achieved by a comprehensive perception. Most of the notes are restricted to the minimal necessary referential data; however in a few cases, where methodology marking seems significant, more space has been devoted to the notes.

I.   Let us start with a description of the main forms of warfare. The pitched, open field, battle is a continuous and intensive form of encounter, a physical match between armies in which a victory is gained within hours, while both parties use offensive tactics and manoeuvre, if possible. The siege, on the other hand, is by nature a static and longer contest, because the defender is supported by fortifications which considerably reduce the advantages of quantitative and qualitative superiority, as well as the maneuvering ability of the offender. (This form of battle enables an easy disconnection between the parties, if they have any physical contact, thus reducing the strain of fighting and

9.   We confine ourselves, for the purposes of this survey, to monographs only, each of which contains a comprehensive bibliography on the subject dealt with: J. Zabłocka, *Stosunki agrarne w państwie Sargonidów*, Poznań, 1971 (Polish); J.N. Postgate, *Taxation and Conscription in the Assyrian Empire*, Rome, 1974; M. Cogan, *Imperialism and Religion: Assyria, Judah and Israel in the Eighth and Seventh Centuries B.C.E.* (*SBLMS* 19), Missoula, Mont., 1974; M. Elat, *Economic Relations in the Lands of the Bible, c. 1000–539 B.C.*, Jerusalem, 1977 (Hebrew); B. Oded, *Mass Deportation and Deportees in the Neo-Assyrian Empire*, Wiesbaden, 1979.

prolonging the struggle.) It is therefore likely that considerably inferior armies would prefer the second method of warfare. This implies that an army will fight a pitched battle only if it can match swords with the opposing force in conditions of dynamic warfare and estimates that it will have a reasonable chance of success. If there is no such chance, it will avoid a direct confrontation on the battlefield and will compel the adversary to wage war in another way.

Application of this observation to the ancient Near Eastern empires illuminates a fundamental feature of their military and political history. At the beginning of their development, when their military superiority had not yet been established, we find among their wars of expansion (until the reign of Tiglath-pileser III and in the early consolidation stages of the Chaldaean empire) cases of encounter in pitched battles. Especially to be noted is Shalmaneser III whose inscriptions show that he fought in more pitched battles – not always successfully – than any other Assyrian king.[10] From this it appears that his opponents considered his army to be of more or less equal strength, especially when they confronted the Assyrian army with their combined forces as they did in Shalmaneser's campaigns in northern and southern Syria.[11] (Incidentally, it is noteworthy that the inscriptions of Aššurnaṣirpal mention only one field battle – against the people of Suḫu, Laqê and Ḫindanu – and the extent of his victory in this battle is somewhat dubious.[12]) The inscriptions of Aššurnaṣirpal and Shalmaneser III indicate that the military activity of these two archcombatants of the 9th century B.C., by means of which they extended their territory and brought to Assyria myriads of exiles as well as abundant spoils and tribute, concentrated largely upon the conquest of dozens of fortified cities and hundreds of

10. On the campaigns of Shalmaneser III see A.T. Olmstead, *JAOS* 41 (1921), pp. 345-382. For a list of his inscriptions, including classified references relating to military motifs, see W. Schramm, *Einleitung in die assyrischen Königsinschriften*, zweiter Teil (934-722 v. Chr.), Leiden/Köln, 1973, pp. 71 ff., esp. 100-102.
11. Cf. M. Elat, *IEJ* 25 (1975), pp. 25-32. Although Elat's opinion is acceptable, it does not mean that the numbers of horses and chariots given in the inscriptions of Shalmaneser should be taken without reservation; see also on this matter N. Na'aman, *Tel Aviv* 3 (1976), pp. 97–102.
12. On this battle see E.A.W. Budge–L.W. King, *Annals of the Kings of Assyria*, London, 1902, pp. 355–356 (hereafter: *AKA*) (=A.K. Grayson, *Assyrian Royal Inscriptions* [= *ARI*], II, Wiesbaden, 1973, § 579); cf. A.T. Olmstead, *JAOS* 38 (1918), p. 244; and also J.A. Brinkman, *A Political History of Post-Kassite Babylonia*, Roma 1968 [Hereafter: Brinkman, *PKB*], pp. 185–187. Beside this battle the Annals of Aššurnaṣirpal refer to some other minor field operations (ambush, skirmish etc.) cf. *AKA* 303–304 ii 24–29; 309 ii 45; 319–320 ii 70–71; 357–358 iii 38–40 (= Grayson, *ARI*, II, § 554, 558, 563, 579 respectively).

minor settlements. As far as we know from the inscriptions of Tiglath-pileser III, who renewed the expansion policy of the Assyrian empire, his army, too, seems to have been engaged in only a few field battles. This set-up whereby countries were subdued by conquering cities in them was typical of most of the Assyrian wars within the Fertile Crescent and in parts of the eastern and northern mountainous regions for over a hundred years, until close to the decline of the Assyrian empire. The exceptional cases, all of which were against enemies from outside the imperial boundaries, are dealt with below.

From these observations we may deduce the following:

The massive offensive activity of the Assyrian army, and to a certain degree, also of its successors, was directed towards subduing the enemy by conquest of cities, largely within imperial boundaries but partly also beyond them. After Assyria gained control over a certain region, the imbalance of power between the Assyrian army and the entity under its control was so great that the latter, whether a vassal kingdom or a province, was never able to match the Assyrian army in a field battle if a revolt occured. The impressive achievements of the attacking armies, i.e. the conquest of many cities within a short time, indicates (even if we consider the Assyrian royal inscriptions tendentious and affected by exaggeration) that in most cases the cities were not overcome by famine, which demanded a long siege, often lasting over a year, but rather by breaching their walls. We may conclude that the Assyrian army had developed the means – manpower, instruments of warfare and fighting methods – appropriate to breaching city walls. If this is true, it means that generally the fortification systems could not resist the aggressors' power and fighting methods.

The Assyrian reliefs depict many details relating to fighting over cities. Likewise, we possess a considerable number of technical terms relating to this subject. What is still needed, however, is a systematic study of these terms and a coordination of the linguistic material with the visual sources. Such a study will deepen our understanding of the fighting method most frequently used by the empires under discussion.

This matter gives rise to the question of the purpose of chariotry in the Assyrian army. Numerous written sources point to the importance attached to chariots, whose maintenance and upkeep demanded heavy expenditure. If, indeed, warfare, in most cases, meant fighting against cities, it is difficult to see how chariots could swing the balance of the battle or even provide support in such a system of warfare. It seems, then, that the use of chariots was limited to those pitched battles which though few were of great military and political significance. The pitched battles were waged against enemies from outside the empire, whom we shall discuss below. It should be noted, however, that even in some of these battles the chariots were not the decisive force, since they were sometimes opposed by trained infantry. This happened, for example, in confrontations between the Persian army and Greek warriors in whose country chariots had long since ceased to be used.[13]

Pitched battles and the assault of cities were not the exclusive methods of war. Records of long sieges, such as Nebuchadnezzar's on Jerusalem,[14] Shalmaneser V's and Nebuchadnezzar's on Tyre[15] and Ashurbanipal's on Babylon, indicate that occasionally a city was starved out. This method was rarely used because it involved tying up considerable forces for a long time, and it was adopted only when it was impossible to breach the city walls. Legal documents indicate that Ashurbanipal's siege of Babylon lasted about two years;[16] Sennacherib besieged it for over 15 months;[17] and Nabopolasar's siege of Uruk lasted at least 16 months.[18] Prolonged siege activity also included cutting off of traffic between the enemy towns. So, for example, in letters from the time of Ashurbanipal's struggle with Šamaš-šum-ukin in Babylonia, the Assyrian king is advised to send soldiers to cut off the

13. Cf. F.E. Adcock, *The Greek and Macedonian Art of War*, Berkeley–Los Angeles, 1957, p. 47. Observations on the purposes of chariotry operating in the Neo-Assyrian army, see now W. Mayer, *Ugarit Forschungen* 10 (1978), pp. 175–186.

14. Cf. 2 Kings 25:1–2; Jer. 39:1–2; 52:4–7. On the various interpretations of these data according to which the siege of Jerusalem lasted 19 or 31 months see A. Malamat, *IEJ* 18 (1968) pp. 150–155.

15. Cf. Josephus, *Ant.* IX, iv, 2 (§ 284–287), and Ezek. 29:18 (cf. *Ant.* X, xi, 1 [§ 228]) respectively.

16. The earliest attested date for this siege is 13 VII, year 18 of Šamaš-šum-ukin; the latest 29 II, year 20 of the same king; see M. San Nicolò, *Babylonische Rechtsurkunden des ausgehenden 8. und 7. Jahrhunderts v. Chr.*, München, 1951, nos. 19–20. Additional data refering to the length of the battle on Babylon and the severe famine in the city during that period see A.L. Oppenheim, *Iraq* 17 (1955), pp. 76–77; A.R. Millard, *Iraq* 26 (1964), pp. 28–29; E.E. Knudsen, *Iraq* 29 (1967), pp. 55–56.

17. See J.A. Brinkman, *JCS* 25 (1973), pp. 93–94.

18. Regarding the siege of Uruk cf. legal documents dated in a regnal year of Sin-šar-iškun with the additional phrase *ina edel bābi*, "during (the time when) the (city) gate was locked", H. Hunger, *Bagh Mitt* 5 (1970), p. 219, No. 12 (16 VI, year 6); M. San Nicolò, *ibid.*, No. 71 (12 X, year 7). Some documents from the Nabû-ušallim archive from Nippur, published by Hunger (*ibid.*, pp. 193 ff.) containing the phrase *ina edel bābi* are dated "year 4" and "year 5" with no royal name (Nos. 9, 16, 21, 22). If these year-numbers refer to Sin-šar-iškun's reign, then the length of the siege reaches 38 months at least.

traffic between Babylon and Borsippa, and to establish a camp at Dilbat in order to intercept every caravan passing there.[19]

A limited but significant and, apparently planned, activity were raids in frontier regions which took place when the imperial army could not get there. Letters from the reign of Ashurbanipal report that during the tension between Assyria and Elam both parties operated bands of 250–500 warriors in deep raids. In one such operation the raiders advanced until they were four days distance from Susa, the capital of Elam, killed over 200 men and captured 150. In another raid 500–600 head of cattle were killed.[20] Although the purpose of raids was not to assault the enemy's army, their moral and political influence was considerable. The raiders were mainly from among the frontier population who found in the hostile actions between the central political bodies an opportunity to settle accounts with neighbors beyond the border. Such, apparently, was the nature of the "bands of the Chaldaeans and the bands of Edomites (גדודי אדם ; MT: Aramaeans, גדודי ארם) and the bands of the Moabites and the bands of the Ammonites" whom Nebuchadnezzar sent against Judah when he could not send his army against the rebellious Jehoiakim (II Kings 24:2). Cf. also the warning against an Edomite incursion in Arad Letter 24.[21]

Some of the Assyrian and Babylonian campaigns were conducted against enemies who could not have been subdued by siege or conquest of cities because they had no permanent settlements. Such were all the Arabs in the deserts bordering the Fertile Crescent, some of the Chaldaeans in the marshes of Babylonia and some of the eastern and northern mountain people. The main difficulty in fighting against them did not stem from their strength but from the fact that they avoided contact with any army approaching them. Operations against them demanded special techniques of approach rather than a large army. In Babylonia the aggressors used reed craft to advance in shallow waters and screened swamped ground, partly covered with thick vegetation;[22] in desert regions they approached under the cover of darkness, often on horses and even on chariots, attacking the nomads'

---

19. *ABL* 326 rev. 13–14; 804 rev. 8–16.
20. See, e.g., *ABL* 280; 1000.
21. On this letter and its historical background see Y. Aharoni, *BASOR* 197 (1970), pp. 16–28.
22. Cf. A. Paterson, *Assyrian Sculptures: Palace of Sinacherib*, The Hague, 1915, Pls. 51, 92, 93.

camp before the latter could discover them and escape into the desert.[23] In mountainous country, where critical blocks were expected, surprise could be achieved by deep maneuvering of cavalry corps, cf. Sargon's attack on Muṣaṣir[24].

In summary, the above mentioned examples indicate the rareness of pitched, open field, battles and the variety of fighting methods in use among the armies of the ancient empires. It seems reasonable to suppose that these facts, in addition to the fact that the armies under discussion were engaged in large-scale military operations almost every year, had an influence on their organisation and operation.

II. As stated above, an immanent feature of empires was the fact that the ruling class constituted a small minority as compared with the extent of the population and areas under its control. Let us look into some aspects of this feature and into their applications for warfare and military control in the ancient Near East. We shall start with the factor of time and space.

Hundreds of examples, throughout all the period under discussion, point to the above mentioned conclusion about the frequent success of intensive fighting of the great armies against cities within the empires. Nevertheless, in the history of the ancient Near Eastern empires we know of a considerable number of revolts in various regions. From what we have seen, these revolts were condemned *prima facie* to failure in view of the strength of the imperial armies. It should be stressed, however, that rebellions arising only from desperation, i.e. whose planners realised in advance that they had no chance of success, are very rare. There are, therefore, grounds to enquire what the rebels had in mind when they took a step whose consequences could be disastrous in case of failure.

The answer can be found in the recognition that even a great power's ability to react was restricted because of the difficulty of operating a relatively small army in extensive areas. There was a large number of missions imposed on such an army, often at a rate of a campaign *per annum* and this compelled it to postpone reacting in regions of secondary importance because of the need to carry out missions in high priority regions. Such a situation is reflected, for example, in the postponement of Sennacherib's reaction in Palestine until 701 B.C.

23. Cf. Ashurbanipal, *VAB* IV, 74, ix, 12–18. On the use of horses, and even chariots, in attacks on Arab camps cf. R.D. Barnett and M. Falkner, (above n. 4), Pls. XIII–XVI; Barnett, (above, n. 4), Pls. XXXII–XXXIII.
24. Cf. *TCL* 3, lines 314-332 (=Luckenbill, *ARAB*, II, § 170).

because of his need to pacify Babylonia first. If the rebels were able to hold out longer than the time which the imperial army could allocate for action against them, there was a reasonable chance that the emperor would either not send his army against them or that he would have to stop fighting against them because the action extended beyond its allocated time. This situation arose due to the limitations of the imperial army, stemming from the combination of time and space factors, in the light of its obligations and missions throughout the empire and on its borders. (Enemy action across the border cannot always be predicted.) The time factor had, then, a crucial effect on the operation methods of both parties. The rebels' purpose was to gain time which they did by increasing the ability of the fortified cities to resist. It was not necessary for them to resist for a particularly long period! All that was necessary was to hold out a short time longer than the time available to the aggressors (cf. 2 Chr. 32:2–5; Isa. 22:8–11). On the other hand, it was in the interests of the imperial army to break the rebels' power and morale quickly and this demanded the operation of a great army, fighting intensively and simultaneously over several cities. The army would ruin the economic potential of the rebellious country by destroying unfortified settlements, cutting down plantations and devastating fields.[25] It became possible to split the aggressor's army for simultaneous operation against several cities since he was rid of the need to concentrate his forces against a strong opponent in a pitched battle. The distance of the rebellious region from the center of the empire affected, of course, the empire's ability to react and thus played a role in the revolt's chances of success.

A different situation existed in the case of war between two major powers, whose kings bore the title "great king" *(šarru rābu)*: Similar considerations led both parties to attempt to achieve a quick victory, i.e. to wage war in a pitched battle. In these battles, which were few but famous in ancient historiography by virtue of their scale and political consequences, great armies, frequently including considerable forces of chariotry, were put into action. The two types of battle – the pitched battle and the siege – obviously demanded different composition and sizes of the participating armies. Converting an army which was

---

25. Cf., e.g., Shalmaneser III: *BAs* 6 (1909), 135 iv 4–5; *WO* 1 (1949), 265–266: 15–16; 2 (1959), 414:4; Tiglath-pileser III: P. Rost, *Die Keilschrifttexte Tiglath-pilesers III*, Leipzig 1893, p. 34:204. A.G. Lie, *The Inscriptions of Sargon II, The Annals*, Paris 1929, p. 62:10; p. 49, n. 5 lines 9–10; Sennacherib: *OIP* II, p. 54:51, 53. For biblical references cf. Deut. 20:19–20; 2 Kings 3:19, 25.

designed to quell a revolt, and reorganizing it for an open field battle against an enemy advancing in full force, demanded a cessation of every operation against cities and building up a concentration of the army as quickly as possible. Such an event took place when Sennacherib and Nebuchadnezzar ceased their operations against Judaean cities upon the receipt of information about the advance of the Egyptian army towards the Shephelah (cf. 2 Kings 19:8 ff. = Isa. 37:8 ff.; Jer. 37:5 ff.).

The distance between the war arena and the center of the empire was also significant from this same point of view of time and space. While reinforcement from Assyria could be hastened in time to the forces operating against the Chaldaeans in Babylonia as information about the advance of the Elamite army arrived, a Mesopotamian commander operating in Palestine had to count only on the forces at hand with no chance for reinforcement to arrive in time. This may explain the relatively modest description of the results of the battle of Eltekeh against the Egyptian army in the Annals of Sennacherib (*ARAB* II, §240), lacking details which usually appear in descriptions of victories. Sennacherib's real achievement in this battle was his very ability to resist!

The memory of Sennacherib's bitter surprise upon the arrival of the Egyptian army during his campaign in southern Palestine apparently is echoed in Esarhaddon's letters to Shamash, the oracle god, inquiring about the possibility of waging war against the Egyptian army in the vicinity of Ashkelon.[26] Instead of the common interpretation, associating this letter with one of Esarhaddon's campaigns against Egypt, it seems preferable to connect it to his preparations for the campaign in South Philistia during the course of which the city of Arṣâ, near the Brook-of-Egypt (*Naḥal Muṣur*) was captured, some years before his attack on Egypt proper. If this document really refers to the preparations of an Egyptian campaign, Esarhaddon's fear seems incomprehensible since it would be preferable, as far he was concerned, to encounter his enemy in Palestine rather than to enter into battle at the approaches to Egypt, immediately after a strenuous march along northern Sinai. If our assumption is correct, we may consider Esarhad-

---

26. J.A. Knudtzon, *Assyrische Gebete an den Sonnengott*, Leipzig 1893, nos. 70–71; E.G. Klauber, *Politisch-religiöse Texte aus der Sargonidenzeit*, Leipzig, 1913, no. 41. Cf. H. Tadmor, *Biblical Archaeologist* 29 (1966), p. 100; I. Eph'al in A. Malamat (ed.), *The World History of the Jewish People*, IV/1: *The Age of the Monarchies: Political History*, Jerusalem, 1979, 279-280.

don's letter a request for advice from the god concerning what kind of army should be prepared for the campaign in South Philistia: an army for a limited operation such as the conquest of Arṣâ and other settlements in its environs, or a great army, able to match the Egyptians in a pitched battle if they come to assist South Philistia.

Another aspect of the time and space factor which should be taken into consideration is the length and duration of military campaigns. The more remote the arenas of war were from the imperial centers, so the duration of campaigns lengthened. Some figures will demonstrate the marching time needed by armies. To this should be added the time required for the various military actions, such as fighting, siege, negotiations, looting, and so on:

		Number of marching days at a rate of an average:	
		25 km daily	30 km daily
Babylon–South Palestine	3500 km to and fro	140	117
Nineveh–Memphis	3700 km to and fro	148	124
Susa–Sardis	4300 km to and fro	172	143

(Note: this calculation does not include days of rest which were obviously needed on long campaigns!)

Some conclusions and problems arising from these data follow:

The time and space of campaigns should be examined whenever possible. The real picture of a campaign emerging from such an examination differs sometimes from that of the historiographical records which are liable to be misleading.

These data may offer one explanation for the determination of imperial boundaries: the border of an empire was sometimes determined not by the existence of another great power in its neighborhood but by the limits of its ability to maintain effective control in view of the time and space factor.[27]

Thus it becomes apparent that organization of the empire into administrative sub-divisions – i.e. provinces – whose governors had command of military units able to cope with local problems within their boundaries or in neighboring regions without bothering the central army, was a need stemming from the very existence of the empires. The military forces under the command of Assyrian province-governors have been discussed by H.W.F. Saggs.[28] There is no need to say

27. Cf., for example, the extent of Assyrian control in western Anatolia and in the eastern mountainous region.
28. *Iraq* 25 (1963), pp. 145 f.

Israel Eph'al

more about the armies of the satraps in the Achaemenid empire. Historiographical sources and letters indicate that the kings participated in many campaigns – actually in most of them. This means that they were absent from their capitals for long periods.[29] The signifi-

29. The royal inscription, mostly written in first person singular, may sometimes mislead by attributing military achievements to the king when his personal participation in them is doubtful; cf., for example, Sennacherib's Bull Inscription and his Nebi Yunus Inscription (*ARAB*, II, §329, 349), which ascribe to him the achievements of the military expeditions against Ḫilakku and Til-garimmu conducted by his generals (cf. *ARAB*, II, §286–288, 290–292); similarly, Ashurbanipal's early prisms record that Ammuladi(n) king of Qedar had been defeated by Kamashalta king of Moab (B viii 39 ff.; C x 36–43), while the later inscriptions ascribe the event to Ashurbanipal himself ("Letter to Aššur", K 2802 v 15–25; Rm. viii 15–23; *AfO* 8 (1932–1933), p. 200, No. 79). We shall, therefore, refrain from using royal inscriptions as references for the participation of kings in military campaigns, confining ourselves to evidence from undisputable sources:
  a) The following kings found their death in battle or *en route* in military campaigns:
      Sargon fell in battle against Ešpai the Kullumaean, 705 B.C., (II R 69:9–10 = *RLA*, II, 435:8–10; cf. H. Tadmor, *JCS* 12 [1958], p. 97).
      Esarhaddon died on his way to Egypt, 669 B.C. (Grayson, *TCS* 5, Chron. 1, iv 30–31; Chron. 14 rev. 5–6).
      Cyrus fell in battle against the Massagetae, 530 B.C. (Herodotus I, 214).
      Cambyses died in Ecbatana in Syria on his way from Egypt, 522 B.C. (Herodotus III, 62–66).
  b) *ABL* 276:5–7 and 923:10 ff. refer to Esarhaddon's campaign to Egypt; on the latter reference cf. A Spalinger, *BASOR* 223 (1976), pp. 64–67.
  c) There is evidence that kings, while being absent from the capital and the country, used to appoint their grown sons to be in charge of various matters of state administration and control:
Among the Nimrud and Kouyunjik Letters we find such in which, following the common form of address "To the king my lord, your servant PN", comes the formula: "It is well in the land of Assyria, it is well with the temples, it is well with all the fortresses of the king. Let the heart of the king my lord be very glad" (*šulmu ana* ᵐᵃᵗ*Aššur šulmu ana ekurrāte šulmu ana birāti ša šarri gabbu libbu ša šarri bēliya lū ṭāb*). This formula is exclusively used by two addressers: Sennacherib (*ABL* 196–199, ⌈568⌉, 730, 731, 1083[?]) and Ululayu (NL 31, [46], 50, 51, 53. On the possible identification of the addresser of these letters with Shalmaneser V when he was crown prince see Brinkman, *PKB*, note 1564). A similar formula: "It is well with (the temple) Ešarra, it is well with the (other) temples, it is well with the city of Aššur, it is well with the land of Assyria. May it be well with the king my lord", occurs in letters of Tab-ṣil-Ešarra, the eponym of 716 B.C., who was governor of Aššur. It stands to reason that reports of the sons of Sargon and Tiglath-pileser III to their fathers about the well-being of Assyria were sent to the kings while they were outside Assyria proper; cf. especially NL 53 (H.W.F. Saggs, *Iraq* 21 [1959], p. 163) whose entire contents is nothing but the above mentioned formula. The letters contain reports on political and military matters (NL 46 [*Iraq* 20, 1958, p. 198]; *ABL* 197, 198, 730, 1083), on floods in a certain region (*ABL* 731), and details about taxes from vassal states and their arrival in Assyria (NL 46, 50, 51 [*Iraq* 21, 1959, pp. 159–160]; *ABL* 196, 568). It could be argued, *prima facie*, that all the letters were dispatched to the king

cance of this fact for the administrative structure and central control of the empires requires further study.

The fact that the arenas of war spread over vast areas also demands consideration of logistics, i.e. the art of moving and supplying armies. This subject, despite its crucial importance, is almost entirely neglected in the study of military history of all periods (because no glory is attached to it). In so far as we are concerned with ancient Near Eastern empires this is a difficult subject to deal with because documentation is scarce. For illustration, I shall content myself with one problem:

Royal inscriptions and archaeological excavations attest to the existence of a great arsenal *(ekal māšarti)* in Nineveh, as well as in other Assyrian capitals, in which battle equipment (including weapons, chariots and other vehicles) as well as horses and pack-animals were kept.[30] We have no evidence for the existence of such arsenals outside Assyria proper. In view of the remoteness of the arenas of war from the center and the change of military objective every year, however, we should ask how the great armies solved the problem of supplying unit equipment.

Thus, for example, the Assyrian army undertook five campaigns against Egypt within 11 years (673–663 B.C.), in three of which it was engaged with the Egyptian army in open field battles, which means that it had to arrive there in full force together with chariotry and with supporting troops from all the western vassals. Was all the equipment transported from Nineveh to Egypt five times or, were there rather

who was in the capital while the crown prince was travelling in Assyria (the content of most letters even supports such an argument). In this case, however, we would have to explain the *raison d'être* of some letters containing detailed reports about taxes and the behaviour of emissaries from vassal states in the capital (cf. *ABL* 196, 568). If – at least some of – the letters were indeed sent to the king while he was absent from the capital and the country, a survey of the issues reported in them can give us an idea about the extent to which the king was kept in the picture and of the administrative staff which accompanied him on campaigns.

An example of giving authority to the crown prince occurs in a letter from the reign of Nabopolasar king of Babylonia (*TCL* 9, 99 = Ebeling, *Neubabylonische Briefe aus Uruk*, Berlin, 1934, no. 324) in which Nebuchadnezzar announced three people, among whom were the ^{lú}qēpu and the ^{lú}šatammu of the Eanna temple, that "the king has left for Harran, a great Median army went with him. Whoever loves the king and loves me, father and son... (rest broken)"; on this letter and its historical background see P. Schnabel, *ZA* 36 NF 2 (1924/25), pp. 316–318; F. Thureau-Dangin, *RA* 22 (1925), pp. 27–29; D.J. Wiseman, *Chronicles of Chaldean Kings*, London, 1956, pp. 15–18; on the identity of the first two addressees – referred to only in their names, without titles – cf. H. Hunger, *Bagh Mitt* 5 (1970), p. 242, no. 29.

30. G. Turner, *Iraq* 32 (1970), pp. 68–85; M. E. L. Mallowan, *Nimrud and its Remains*, II, London, 1966, chap. XVI: Fort Shalmaneser, pp. 369–490; *CAD* M/I, pp. 358–359 s.v. *māšartu, ekal māšarti*.

stores at key points in various regions of the empire which enabled the army to move more conveniently and to prevent chariots and other war machines from wearing out quickly in marches of thousands of kilometres on unpaved roads? There is no explicit evidence for the second possibility. Perhaps, however, a hint can be found in the inscriptions of Aššurnaṣirpal reporting the settlement of Assyrians in ree key-towns in areas which were just annexed to Assyria and the gathering of barley and straw there.[31] These towns can be regarded as "logistic bases" for chariots and horses which were stationed there or passed through in a military campaign. For a similar system cf. 1 Kings 5:6–8 (Eng. version 4:26–28): "And Solomon had 40,000 teams of horses[32] for his chariotry and 12,000 horsemen. And these prefects used to supply provisions for King Solomon... And the barley and straw for the horses and the swift steeds they brought to the place where it was required, each according to his charge".

Another aspect of the time and space factor concerns intelligence and communication, which constitute the nervous system of the empire. The effective operation of this system is vital for the reaction and fighting ability of a broad political body whose activity is based on one great army.[33] Before moving such an army the central authority has to define what the main objective is in a given situation and to assess its urgency.

The Nineveh and Nimrud letter archives provide important details on the Assyrian intelligence activity, especially with regard to the Elamite and Urartian borders. These letters reflect an information collecting system consisting of governors and officers in the border

31. These towns were Tušḫa in the land of Nairi, Atlila > Dūr Aššur in the land of Zamua, and Aribua in the land of Patina (near the land of Luḫuti); see *AKA* 298–299 ii 8–9; 325–326 ii 84–86; 341–342 ii 117–118; 371–372 iii 81–83 (=Grayson, *ARI*, II, 550, 566, 573, 585).

32. On the term אר(י)ות meaning "teams", *Gespanne* (cf. Akkadian *urāte*), not "stalls", as in the common translations, see S. Parpola, *JSS* 23 (1976), p. 172; cf. K. Deller, *Orientalia* 27 (1958), pp. 312–313.

33. From the evidence of numerous Assyrian and Babylonian sources it becomes certain that the ancient Near Eastern empires employed central armies. Such an arrangement was significantly effective not only in field battles (which demanded, as mentioned above, large forces), but also in territories which were to be subdued quickly, by simultaneous attacks on cities. It should be noted, nevertheless that employment of a central army was not imperative in *every* empire. Thus, for example, considerations of time and space (i.e. the very same factor dealt with here!) prevented the Roman empire from operating its army by such a system. There was no sense in forming a "general reserve" in this empire because, due to the geographical deployment of the empire, there was no chance that such a reserve could arrive in time to the battle field. These conditions led to different strategy; see E.N. Luttwak, *The Grand Strategy of the Roman Empire*, Baltimore and London, 1976.

regions who operated the fortresses along the border, the tribal chieftains, and, in the border areas, when special information was necessary, even sent people beyond the border to get it. In certain cases the crown prince (Sennacherib and perhaps also Ashurbanipal, cf. *ABL* 1026) was dispatched to examine the situation closely and report it to the capital. Special attention was given to information which could be extracted from defectors (^{lú}*maqtūti*) and captives (lit. "tongues", *lišanātu*), and orders were given to deliver them to the capital for investigation. There is some evidence that in a certain case, when information was particularly important, there was a special scribe/ interpreter ready to go and question them in their own language in the site where they were being held.[34]

The information in the letters includes details about the position and movements of the enemy's army, the activity of its king and commanders and the mood of the population in the border regions. The letters refer to the source from which the information was obtained, and thus enable correct evaluation of the various pieces of information. Some letters contain reports from three different sources, referring to each of them and quoting it separately.[35] A preliminary survey of the Assyrian intelligence system regarding the Urartian border was done by R. Follet;[36] however, this subject demands a more profound examination on a greater scale (including the Elamite sector) in order to define the system of data collecting and the methods of analysis. Such an examination, following the principles of intelligence work, can shed light upon various aspects of an instrument of central control of the Assyrian empire.

Dealing with imperial communication systems, through which news and orders were dispatched to and from the capital, recalls the description of Herodotus (VIII, 98; see also V, 52–53) of the Persian communication system which stretched from Susa to Sardis, divided into 111 sections, at the end of each of which was a station with men and horses ready to deliver orders, like in a relay race, day and night, in all weather conditions. It also recalls the reference in the book of Esther about the "mounted couriers riding on swift horses that were used in the king's service, bred from the royal stud", who "rode out in haste, urged by the king's command" (8:10,14).

34. Cf. *ABL* 434 = A.L. Oppenheim, *Letters from Mesopotamia*, Chicago, 1967, No. 119.
35. E.g., *ABL* 197–198 (these are Sennacherib's reports concerning the Urartian border).
36. *Revista degli Studi Orientali*, 32 (1957), 61–81.

A. Alt attempted to show that there was an imperial communication system in Syro-Palestine during the Assyrian period.[37] Although most of his evidence has turned out to be irrelevant, the existence of such a system in other parts of the empire is obvious. Some of the evidence for it has been discussed by J.V. Kinnier Wilson,[38] but we can go further. The Assyrian letters use such terms as *bīt mardīti* for the station at the end of a road section, and the titles ^{lú}*kallû*, ^{lú}*rab kallê*, ^{lú}*raksūti*, ^{lú}*rab raksi*, ^{lú}*kallābu*, ^{lú}*kallāb šipirti*, ^{lú}*rab kallabāni*, and just *mār šipri* concerning letter delivery and escort within this station system. They reflect an organized procedure for delivering official letters; in one letter, *ABL* 1021, the signatory complains that his letters to the king were held up in certain stations, whose names are stated, and returned to him. It also appears that important news was dispatched to the center by the swift post system for initial warning and report and at the same time people (officials, officers, captives and informers) were sent at regular speed to complete the report and for de-briefing.

III. Let us turn to another factor – manpower – and survey some of its military aspects:

The elite groups ruling the Assyrian, Babylonian and Persian empires could not supply all the manpower needed for the achievement of all their military missions. We shall discuss here two main methods which were used for maintaining military control under the condition of quantitative inferiority:

Sources relating to the Persian empire (e.g. the Elephantine Papyri, and Herodotus VII, 61–79 on Xerxes' campaign against Greece) attest to the great number of non-Persians in the army. As to the armies of earlier empires, the evidence has not yet been systematically collected and its full significance not evaluated.

Assyrian royal inscriptions from the 9th century B.C. on abound in reports about the deportation of many thousands of soldiers in the course of the conquest of various lands. Only in a relatively few cases, however, do they tell that the deported warriors were incorporated into the Assyrian army and informal administrative documents give almost no figures on this issue.[39] These foreigners may be traced and some idea obtained about their significance in the army by using onomastical and other methods of inquiry. Non-Assyrian names are to be found

37. *ZDPV* 67 (1945), pp. 147–159.
38. *The Nimrud Wine Lists*, London, 1972, pp. 57–62.
39. See B. Oded, (above, n. 9) pp. 48-54.

among ordinary soldiers (including $^{lú}kiṣir\ šarri$, $^{lú}mukīl\ appāte$, $^{lú}bēl$ *narkabti* and $^{lú}tašlīšu$), low and high-ranking officers and attendants (such as $^{lú}rab\ ḫanšē$, $^{lú}rab\ kiṣir$, $^{lú}qurbūtu$ and even $^{lú}turtānu$), and even governors of provinces ($^{lú}šaknu$, $^{lú}bēl\ pīḫāti$), who had reached the top in the military and administrative system.[40] Additional evidence for non-Assyrians in the army is found in reliefs,[41] as well as in various foreign, mainly Aramaic, military terms whose introduction into Neo-Assyrian is explained as the consequence of incorporation of foreign soldiers into the Assyrian army.[42]

A group of considerable significance during the Persian period which seems, however, to emerge earlier in the Near East were the Greek mercenaries. Hints of them during the second half of the 7th century B.C. appear in Herodotus' report about the army of Psammeticus king of Egypt, in the Carchemish excavations and in a poem of Alcaeus on his brother who participated in the conquest of Ashkelon by Nebuchadnezzar in 604 B.C.[43] In this context, it should be asked who were the Kittim *(ktym)* of the Arad ostraca and perhaps also the soldiers garrisoned at Meṣad Ḥashaviahu.[44] If indeed Greek mercenaries appeared already in the 7th century, we should consider their role in the fighting methods from that period on.

Another way to handle problems of imperial security were political arrangements some of which are specified below:

Some of the deported soldiers were settled in border regions and at key places in conquered and vassal countries.[45]

Bedouin tribes supervised the Egyptian border and the Syrian frontier, receiving in exchange permission to graze in the settled land and an official recognition of their chieftains which was connected with benefits vis-a-vis the Assyrian authorities. Similarly, influential

40. See Oded, *ibid.*, pp. 105–109.
41. See J.E. Reade, *Iraq* 34 (1972), pp. 101–108.
42. See H. Tadmor, "The Aramaization of Assyria: Aspects of Western Impact", *25ᵉ RAI*, Berlin, 1982, pp. 449–470.
43. On Ionian and Carian mercenaries of Psammetichus I cf. Herodotus II, 152, 154. On a Greek bronze shield discovered at Carchemish in Building D, where stamps with the cartouches of Psammeticus I and Necho II were also found and which appears to have been destroyed in 605 B.C., see C.L. Woolley, *Carchemish, II: The Town Defences*, London, 1921, pp. 123–129. On the fragment of Alcaeus see J.D. Quinn, *BASOR* 164 (1961), pp. 19–20.
44. See Y. Aharoni, *Arad Inscriptions*, Jerusalem, 1975, p. 163 s.v. כתים. כתי, and the discussion on pp. 12–13. On Meṣad Ḥashaviahu see J. Naveh, *IEJ* 12 (1962), pp. 97–99.
45. See B. Oded, (above, n. 9), pp. 62-67.

Chaldaean chieftains on the border of Elam enjoyed the support of the Assyrian authorities for their loyalty.

We should also examine the extent of the contribution of the vassal states to the imperial security systems. They maintained the administration and the current security within their boundaries with local manpower. (Vassal kings and their armies also participated in campaigns of the imperial armies in their neighborhood.[46])

All these political arrangements enabled the mobility of the relatively small Assyrian army to be maintained and ensured that it could be assigned for substantial fighting.

IV. The study of warfare and military control, only some aspects of which have been demonstrated here, demands, then, a comprehensive view of the subject, beyond the individual events with which research has contented itself so far. Recognition of the existence of constants whose significance for military history has not changed through the ages – such as topographical and climatic conditions and, to a certain degree, also logistic data, as long as they were not affected by technological innovations – enables us to use analogy as a means for sharpening the definition of various aspects of military reality. Thus, for example, the detailed figures about water supply for Napoleon's army on its march through Sinai (1799) and for the Turkish expedition to the Suez canal (late 1915) help us to establish the problems faced by Esarhaddon and Cambyses in their preparations for their campaigns against Egypt.[47] Analogy, thus, helps us to understand the basic factors; but it is doubtful whether we can adopt it for the reconstruction of a particular battle. In most cases we lack precise geographical, and particularly topographical data; data on the course of the battle are too general; and, above all, we are limited because of the considerable dependence of warfare on a huge variety of unpredictable human, technical and other factors which cannot be assessed.

In conclusion, this outline demonstrates what should and can be done in order to gain a better understanding of military reality and its applications for the ancient Near Eastern empires. A systematic and comprehensive study will not only improve our familiarity with the basic factors of war which, according to Braudel, "never ceased to trouble the lives of men", but may promote the acquaintance with the nature of the ancient empires, of which our concepts are but too vague.

46. Cf., e.g., *KAI* 215:12 ff. campaign of Tiglath-pileser III; *VAB* VII 8 (Rm. i 68–74); 138–140 (Cyl. C i 23–51), campaign of Ashurbanipal.
47. See I. Eph'al, *The Ancient Arabs*, Jerusalem-Leiden, 1982, pp. 137–142.

BIBLICAL HISTORICISM

JACOB LICHT

Tel Aviv University

This paper tries to answer the old, plain but confusing question: what kind of history writing – if any – do we have in the Old Testament? The problem[1] touches many interesting subjects, and requires some detailed investigations and discussion of various scholarly positions; all these are tempting sidelines which cannot be accomodated in the space of a single paper. I have found myself forced to cut off many branches to keep my argument down to a manageable shape and size; I hope that the remaining scars won't bother the reader too much.

An Illustration

The account of Saul's elevation to kingship is, to the critically minded, rather unconvincing as a statement of fact. Literary analysis reveals that it is a tangle of textual elements. Yet I do find it rather impressive as a suggested solution to a typical historian's problem. Greek historians (e.g. Herodotus, or Plutarchus) frequently quote several accounts of a single event, remarking in between that 'others tell the following story'. A modern historian presents his own view of 'what must have actually happened', giving his divergent sources in footnotes. In the Book of Samuel we find three stories telling how Saul was made king,[2]

1. The circumstance which made me think about the subject in earnest was the symposium held in 1979 by the Old Testament and Near East group at the Institute for Advanced Studies at the Hebrew University on Mount Scopus. I have also made full use of the opportunity to discuss my ideas about the subject with my colleagues at the Institute, during the academic year 1978–79; I thank them all very much for their patience.
2. The suggestion that 'much in OT historiography might be explained by the absence of footnotes' (which make the accommodation of divergent bits of information easier) is Yair Hofmann's (in various conversations).

Jacob Licht

with some ideological discourses presented in speeches (1 Sam. 8–12). The stories are combined in a single narrative, on the assumption that they need not be really contradictory. First Samuel anointed Saul at Ramah in secret (1 Sam. 10:1–10, 16), since the presence of the Philistines (10:5) made caution necessary. Then, after a period of careful preparation, the Lord's choice was made public at Mitzpah (19:17–25). General recognition came only after the new king's victory over Ammon was ratified by a 'renewal of the kingship' at Gilgal (11, 14–15). The speeches conveying the significance of these events are neatly placed as a prologue (ch. 8) and epilogue (ch. 12). The whole pericope thus combines several sources about a single event into a plausible reconstruction of a political process. Its author, however, did not impose his reconstruction on his material, spelling out his views directly, taking care to underpin the weak points and radically rewriting his sources. He evidently used them more or less as he found them, suggesting his solution by the narrative itself, and leaving plenty of contradictions and loose ends in the story. The reader is thus shown the evidence in the hope that he will agree with the author's interpretation. This gentlemanly procedure has made the author look like a fool to his less civilized critics. They are happily busy in tearing his edifice apart, and trying to rearrange the pieces, caring nothing for the author's historical reconstruction.

Historiography

Such reconstructions are rather common in biblical historiography, and often enough noticed by scholars. I have chosen this rather transparent example because it shows clearly the problem-solving aspect of the ancient historians' work.[3] Reconstructing history means to narrate it, therefore I might have argued simply that the richness of biblical narrative about the past is by itself sufficient proof of genuine historical activity. This, however, might be taken for an overstatement of my case, because of the deceptive plainness of the narration. This is why I prefer to point out the problem-solving aspect; it shows that the historians of ancient Israel did what all historians are basically doing: finding out as much as possible about past events and showing how they make sense. Their occasional failures and awkward faithfulness to their

3.   H. Pirenne, "What are Historians Trying to Do?", in H. Meyerhoff (ed.), *Philosophy of History in our Time, an Anthology*, New York, 1959, p. 94.

sources show that the job was not as easy and 'primitive' as it seems. It was indeed quite an achievement to impose a more or less coherent single line of narrative on such a lot of events, beginning with the Creation and ending with the renewal of hope under Nehemiah. The solutions inherent in the job still determine much of our thinking,[4] though we are doing our best to replace them.

In the cultural context of the ancient Near East Israel was, as far as we know, the only local branch to produce a historiography. What is usually called ancient Mesopotamian historiography consists mainly, though not exclusively, of records of recent events;[5] and does not contain any extensive narratives about the actual (not mythical) but distant past.[6] Yet it seems that the intellectuals of ancient Mesopotamia were fully aware of their past, and quite knowledgeable about it, too.[7] They had all the equipment necessary for a historiography, but evidently felt no need for it. Seen in this light Old Testament historiography becomes more significant than a mere achievement, or than an art at which our ancestors excelled. It betrays a peculiar attitude to life.

Historicism

It is demonstrably true that my existence is largely determined by whatever has happened to my people in the past, but I need not be aware of this truth. As an individual, I might start any day with a feverish search for 'roots'; I might also blissfully ignore the past and find myself another cure for my existential discomfort. Similarly, communities develop preoccupations with their past, to legitimate political claims or for other reasons, but they need not do so. Human existence is rather confusing, and seeing how one thing led to another is only one – possibly not the best – way of dealing with the confusion.

A somewhat unorthodox use of the term historicism might be conveniently introduced at this point: Let it denote the existential attitude

4.   E.g. "the period of Judges".
5.   Such as royal inscriptions, annals, preambles to treaties. For a survey and evaluation of this material see A.L. Oppenheim, *Ancient Mesopotamia*, 1964, pp. 144–150. For a survey of the Hittite material see Güterbock's contribution to this volume on Hittite historiography.
6.   The point is made authoritatively by W.G. Lambert, ("Destiny and Divine Intervention in Babylon and Israel," *OTS* 17 [1971], pp. 65–72) who also considers possible exceptions.
7.   See Oppenheim, (above, n. 5), pp. 150–151.

just described, which seeks answers in the actual (not mythical) past. Or, in other words, it is an intellectual habit of finding the past interesting and significant. By this definition, there are many historicisms; the belief in progress, e.g., is a historicism, but whatever makes a modern historian tick is usually another historicism. I obviously cannot afford to list them all, still less to describe them, but I hope that my meaning is clear enough. So should be my point that Biblical Judaism is *a* historicism.

The Divine in History

These considerations should be of some help in the fairly recent debate about "the Divine in History". All ancient Near Eastern deities of some standing interfere in the affairs of their peoples. Victories, defeats and much else are quite regularly explained in the literature of the region as manifestations of divine benevolence and wrath. It has been argued[8] that this "experience of Divine in History" was simply shared by ancient Israel; so that the unique qualities of Israel's religion must be sought elsewhere. This argument is valuable as a debunking exercise and quite right as far as it goes. The only thing wrong with it is a misuse of the term 'history', or perhaps its confusion with 'destiny'. Chemosh being angry with his land[9] is a pious explanation of a defeat, not a historical reflection. Seen as an item in a chain of *past* events, which are supposed to make some sense, the defeat and the pious comment may become historically significant; they are not, however, presented in such a light on the Moabite Stone. The same comment can be applied to practically any remark about divine action determining human events, including many pious comments in the Old Testament.[10] "The only type of Old Testament statement about divine intervention which cannot be matched by some quotation from ancient Mesopotamian literature is the sort of thing which we have in Gen. 15:13–16";[11] i.e. contemplations of divine action through several

8. H.W. Saggs, *The Encounter with the Divine in Mesopotamia and Israel*, London, 1978, pp. 64–92; B. Albrektson, *History and the Gods (Coniectanea Biblica, Old Testament Series 1)*, Lund, 1967. For reactions to Albrektson see Lambert, "History and the Gods: A Review Article", *Orientalia* 39 (1970), pp. 170–177, and the literature quoted there.

9. King Mesha's Inscription, so called Moabite Stone, line 5 (no. 181 apud Donner-Röllig, *KAI* I, p. 33.; *ANET*, p. 320). King Mesha refers to the past, but only as far as it concerns his own deeds.

10. E.g. Num. 14:22; 21:3; Josh. 11:20; 1 Sam. 7:10; 2 Kings 9:6–9; 14:26–27.

11. I am quoting what Prof. Güterbock told me, from memory.

generations. Joshua 24, and other instances of von Rad's 'historical credo'[12] might serve as better examples. It follows that Israel was unique in the ancient Near East in its true 'experience of the Divine in History', and not only in current affairs. Or, other gods react to human behaviour; so does the God of Israel, but He also pursues a deliberate long-term policy. In other words: Israel's culture is historicist, Mesopotamian culture is non-historicist.[13]

Biblical historicism is not confined to the historical books of the Old Testament. Prophets occasionally remind the people of their past (e.g. Micah 6:5); psalmists spell out the lessons of history in long reviews (Pss. 78; 105; 106) and refer to it in prayer (e.g. Ps. 44:2–4). Historicism is indeed a basic component of the OT attitude to human existence.

General Features of OT Historiography

Its foremost manifestation is, of course, the historians' work at reconstructing the past. Its general features are somewhat difficult to recognize, first because we are too familiar with them to take notice, second because we tend to overvalue either the quality of the religious thought involved, or the 'historicity' (=factual reliability) of some accounts. The third, and objective, reason for our difficulty is that no two subjects are treated in the same way. The problem-solving activity must have encountered too many variables for the development of a standard procedure. These were: the quantity and quality of the available material, the discrepancies in the sources, the elements calling for various treatments on the story-telling level, the significance of each event with the need for its particular theological interpretation. I shall nevertheless attempt a series of generalizations. They may seem banal and even cavalier, but I hope that they will reveal the basic attitudes of biblical historicism.

The large part of OT historiography dealing with events from Joshua to Nehemiah is mostly about wars for territory, political dominance or independence, personal power struggles and (less explicitly) social tensions. These are what we have become accustomed to regard as the

---

12. G. von Rad, *Gesammelte Schriften,* 1961, pp. 11–15.
13. The point is made by Lambert, (above, n. 8). Saggs (above, n. 8, p. 91) is aware of the difference between the recording of recent events and retrospective writing about the past, but does not realise its significance.
   The Hittites were apparently more interested in the past than the Babylonians and Assyrians; see Prof. Güterbock's contribution to this volume.

ordinary stuff of history. Their treatment is relatively free of mystifications and ideological distortions: it displays a grasp of geographical, social and political realities, and an ability to point them out. The historians of the OT may be less sharply analytical (or long-winded) in their appreciation of geopolitics than their Greek and modern colleagues, but they are nobody's fools. Neither miracles, nor obviously false (i.e. factually unreliable) reconstructions of events, such as Samuel's victory over the Philistines (1 Sam. 7), prevent the functioning of this feeling for geopolitics; a story may look improbable to the critically-minded, but it will make some sense geopolitically.

In other words, we are always shown how one thing led to another, on the human level. The question why it did so is invariably answered by the assertion that it was the Lord's just and reasonable decision. The historian always finds an explanation using the terms of reward, punishment, or mercy. A general theory of theodicy has been developed in the process into a very subtle and flexible tool, which is effectively used to solve all kinds of problems. Its result is to make Divine initiative rather rare and marginal. God has sent Samuel to anoint David. The choice was entirely His own and rather surprising in human eyes (1 Sam. 16). It was, however, the outcome of the Lord's decision to reject Saul, a decision based on Saul's disobedience. It is man who sets Divine theodicy in motion by his behaviour, deserving reward or punishment, it is not God's business to push him along. So we cannot truly say that God acts in history; He reacts in most cases, though neither automatically nor arbitrarily: He takes His time, and pursues His policy. Nevertheless, if it were not for Israel's sins they would be secure in the enjoyment of their land, living in a perfect society based on the Lord's laws and commandments. Such contemplations, however, are not the ancient historians' concern. They reconstruct what has actually happened in the past, in terms of geopolitics, and they explain it by theodicy.

A different set of generalizations is necessary for the treatment of Israel's early history, from Abraham to Joshua. Only small bits in it belong to the ordinary stuff of history. The patriarchs are shown as seminomads, gradually gaining wealth and respectability. Such a group of seminomads is as geopolitically real as any other social unit, yet it does not belong to the ordinary stuff of conventional histroy, which does not bother with the fortunes of a single peaceful family. This is one of the several reasons for the ordinary empirical historian's difficulty to get a real grasp on the Patriarchs: they may be real enough but they are not his sort of subject. Another, and more profound, reason is that the ancient historian shows the realities of the Patriarchs' existence only incidentally; for him they are first of all the carriers of a blessing and of a promise, though he also sees them as real persons with real problems. To speak about them in terms of geopolitics means a translation of the biblical account into another 'universe of discourse'; while no such translation is necessary for any subject later than Joshua, the translation becomes even more "violent" when applied to the Wandering in the Wilderness: for us it is a hazy rememberance of the nomadic stage of Israel's existence, for the biblical account something entirely different. I have excellent reasons to believe that the Exodus was an actual event,[14] but I can not find much useful geopolitical information about it in the Bible. The initiative in the early stage of Israel's history is entirely the Lord's. He brought Abraham to Canaan from a distant place, promised him the inheritance of the Land, and then worked in wondrous ways to fulfill His promise. He decided that the time has come to redeem His people from Egypt, He brought them to Sinai and imposed on them His Covenant, He led them through the Wilderness. Theodicy is occasionally employed by the narrators,[15] but only to justify God's ways in the margin of the argument. The tale as a whole is about the twin themes of the Election and the Covenant, which remain entirely unjustified, because they are due to His Sovereign Will. They are of course theological rather than historical themes, and the problem-solving activity in the Pentateuch is consequently concerned with theological precisions. We are not shown how one thing led to another, but rather how God made things happen to carry out His policy.

Heilsgeschichte is a history

Now it may be argued that this juxtaposition can only serve to illustrate the trite truth that the early history in the Bible is no history at all. One can call it a legend overburdened with theological speculation, or a peculiar kind of myth,[16] or, using von Rad's term,

14. These, however, are only considerations of a general nature, such as that it is extremely unlikely for a people to invent a story about its past servitude, which is not a thing to be proud of.
15. Such as the rather lame justification of God's ways in Gen. 15:13–16.
16. Using the term 'myth' in the sense of 'a story about the origin of things and institutions, with some god in it', or in the sense of 'something which is supposed to have happened in the past and which is very important for the present'. Even by

Heilsgeschichte.[17] The last term is preferable. It characterizes the phenomenon as an expression of the religious experience of the people by the means of historical narration. This implies that it need not contain any actual history.[18] The conclusion is, again, that we need not bother with it under the heading of the historical thought in the OT. I do not think so. *Heilsgeschichte* is built on very ancient material and concerned with some close meetings between God and men, so it cannot be quite ordinary history. Its events, however, are as real to the narrators as anything else, and we have no grounds to doubt the actual occurence of these events on the human level. It provides a down-to-earth background for its sublime subject, presenting it as realistically as possible. The most important thing about it is that it tries to solve theological (or existential) problems by the methods of historical narration; this alone makes it a rather emphatic (if one may use the term) sort of history.

The Lord's Policy

We are thus faced with two modes of OT historiography. One, dealing with Israel's origins, is slightly deterministic and not geopolitical; the other dealing with the people's subsequent existence, is geopolitical and adeterministic. I have juxtaposed them above. The dichotomy is due to the subject matter: in the period of its origins Israel is not seen as a geopolitical entity, so it cannot be treated geopolitically: such a treatment begins as soon as the historiography passes over to a description of Israel's 'normal' existence. Israel's origins are conceived as entirely due to God's mighty deeds, so the deterministic view dominates in their description. A major theme in the story of the origins is the covenant; during their subsequent existence Israel are expected to live up to it: the

these definitions the type of subject discussed does not look quite like the kind of myth to most observers; which is why some prefer to use the term 'broken myth'. I suggest that in the context of the present discussion the term myth should be reserved for stories about the very distant past, in which most things were not as they are; their origins were caused, according to such stories, by various actions and adventures of the gods, though some men and animals also appear. This definition fits all stories normally called myths (in Greek, Mesopotamian and similar contexts); and makes a neat separation of myth and history in the OT itself possible. Myth passes into history as soon as the stories are mostly about the actions of men and things happening to them, with the world around them mostly as we know it.

17. I am not using the term quite exactly in von Rad's sense, (above, n. 12), p. 20.
18. The realization of this conclusion has caused some theological trouble to von Rad's school, though unnecessarily; see A. Soggin in *ThLZ* 89 (1964), pp. 722–736.

initiative is theirs, so the historians' treatment becomes adeterministic. By this simplification we can focus our attention to the purpose of OT historical thought. It explains Israel's existence in the terms of Election and Covenant,[19] which are conceived as historians' notions: *First* the Lord has made us His people, *then* he dealt with us accordingly, and so He does even now. Israel has developed a historiography because it was conscious of its Lord's policy throughout the ages. The policy is simple: To establish and to maintain Israel as His people.

Establishment

Heilsgeschichte can be described as a grand historians' construct, showing the process of Israel's establishment in its present status. The stages of the process are the major themes of the Pentateuch: The election of the Patriarchs, the sojourn in Egypt, the Exodus, the covenant at Sinai, the wandering in the Wilderness and the Settlement in the Land. The main texts, however, which tell us about these events, do not present them as stages of a process. Each is told by its own independent (and rather complex) bunch of stories, developing a theme different from the others. Only occasional bits of reflection or comment indicate God's policy behind the chain of events (Gen. 15:13–14; Exod. 6:8; etc.). The *process* of Israel's establishment emerges from the telling only as the whole narrative line from Abraham to Joshua evolves in its loose coherence; it is a consequence of the chain of events in general, not a *leitmotif* in the detailed telling of the events themselves.[20]

On the other hand, one may discern a shadowy presence of the notion of an individual *act of establishment* in most major themes of Israel's early history. Bringing Abraham from his native land the Lord has established the genealogical beginnings of Israel. To realize that the Exodus conveys the notion one has to visualize the event in one's

19. I am using these terms in a very general sense, not implying any opposition between them (nor do I think that they should be opposed). Election in the strict sense is only in those places where the Lord's rule over all nations is expressly mentioned, mainly in Deuteronomy, as Prof. R. Rendtorff argued before the Seventh World Congress of Jewish Studies (1977) in Jerusalem. Here, however, I am concerned with the general idea. The Covenant notion has also several variations in the OT, which need not be considered in the present context.
20. To be more precise, one should distinguish between the grand themes about the main and decisive events (the call to Abraham, the covenant with Abraham, the Exodus and the Sinai events) on the one hand, and the developments in between (the story of the Patriarchs, the notion that Israel multiplied in Egypt, becoming quantitatively 'a people') on the other hand.

Jacob Licht

mind: what has been only yesterday a shapeless mass of slaves, hardly conscious of their collective identity is now marching through the desert as a social body. The Sinai covenant, in its various formulations, has the quality of a constitutive act. The additional covenant in the Plains of Moab, as formulated by Deuteronomy spells out the constitutive aspect (see below). These themes convey the notion of an act of establishment in various indirect ways: I do not argue that the notion is really there as a full-fledged and properly formulated idea, but that it is a-crystallizing through various themes. Consequently there is some overlapping and even a mild competition between the ways in which the feeling that Israel came into being by an act of its Lord is finding its expression.

The grand historical construct of Israel's establishment by a process, or a series of significant events, is derived from a number of primary historical constructs, which interpreted several ancient narrative themes as constitutive or establishing acts. OT historians knew that Israel was more or less a nation like any other, placeable in the large genealogical scheme which explained the existence of many nations and their degrees of similarity or dissimilarity (Gen. 10). As they saw it, each nation had its god,[21] and lived in its country, though there was some wandering about with conquests and expulsions. All this was to them the given, or natural, condition of mankind. They refused[22] to accept it for Israel. Neither its very existence, nor its relationship with its Lord could be taken for granted, because Israel should live by the terms of its special situation. This situation (=the election, the covenant, the obligations and hopes inherent in such notions) could not have been just there to a historicist mind. It must have been established by a decisive great act of God. Or, since such an act could be observed in several very ancient events, by a series of constitutive acts. The great historical reconstruction based on these feelings is not quite spelled out in the OT. I suggest that it is there mainly *in nuce*, in the various formulations of the themes of election

21. See 2 Kings 17:29; Jonah 1:5; Micah 4:5; etc.
22. Amos 9:7 is spoken against this refusal: the Lord directs the destinies of all nations, the fact that He has brought Israel from Egypt does not indicate a special relationship. The Chronicler seems to be opposed to the notion that Israel was established by an historical act, or series of acts, see S. Japhet, *The Ideology of the Book of Chronicles and its Place in Biblical Thought*, Jerusalem, 1977, pp. 322–333 (Hebrew). To my mind these indications of a disagreement with the basic notion with the main school of OT historiography within the OT itself shows indirectly that the notion must have been alive.

and covenant, and in the underlying claim that Israel was established
as a people unto its Lord.

Formulations of the Establishment Claim

All this is, of course, an interpreter's construct, even a rather bold one.
I would not feel free to come forward with it,[23] if it were not for a single
verse which puts the claim of establishment into almost explicit language. It makes Moses declare: "Listen and hear Israel, this day you
have become a people unto the Lord your God" (Deut. 27:9). This is a
rhetorical exaggeration, even a paradox, for Israel did not really become a people unto its Lord on the day of the covenant in the Plains of
Moab, according to the general context of Deuteronomy. The exaggeration, however, betrays the orator's wish to see things as if they were so.
He claims the act of establishment for the Deuteronomic covenant,
perhaps for the sake of theological clarity. He would not be able to do
so in an ideological vacuum. His formulation of the claim is only
slightly (though decisively) more explicit than some related deuteronomic phrases;[24] Deuteronomy is again (on this subject) only slightly
clearer in its formulations than other expressions of the establishment
claim.[25]

Biblical Historicism Defined

I can now attempt a general definition of OT historicism. It is, of
course, closely linked with some major aspects of the religion of Israel,

23. In a rather longish Hebrew article on "The Establishment Claim", *Shnaton* 4
    (1980), I have tried to demonstrate the phenomenon by detailed analysis of texts
    and phraseology. I have also compared the OT consciousness of a historical begin-
    ning (or claim that there was such a sharply marked beginning) with various
    cultural phenomena in imperial Rome, ancient Greece, and some other times and
    places. Here I give only the main points about the phenomenon itself, because I try
    to put it into a broader context.
24. Deut. 4:34 is true *as a claim*: as far as I could find out, no similar claim is made on
    behalf of any other god; it is a typical OT notion that Israel's God 'took out for
    himself' His people from Egypt, heightened by deuteronomic rhetoric. The distinc-
    tive sign of our phenomenon is the phrase *". . . a people unto your God, a God unto
    you . . ."* which appears in various combinations and forms in Deut. 4:20; 26:16–19;
    29:13; *et al.* It denotes the relationship itself, rather than its more elaborate
    definition as a covenant, or an obligation, an oath, etc. The context says always that
    this or that was done, or is being done, so that this relationship might be estab-
    lished, but the date of establishment is not clearly spelled out. Only Deut. 27:9
    claims clearly and unequivocally that Israel has actually become a people unto its
    God on 'this day'; the other formulations are softer.
25. Gen. 17:7; Exod. 6:7 (which I think is the key text); Lev. 26:45; Num. 15:41;

but I do not think that the preoccupation with the past can be logically derived from the religion. One might say that it is the other way round, that a feeling for the significance of the past has determined the shape of Israel's religiosity. We have no way to decide which formulation is preferable: they are merely two rather artificial descriptions of a single phenomenon.

No reference to eschatology, explicit or implicit, is needed to explain this phenomenon. In the OT eschatology is strictly a prophetic concern, it does not affect the historiography. The past explains the present, it does not indicate the future; God is supposed to pursue a policy (see above), He has no plan by which He guides the chain of events towards some preconceived future purpose. The notion of such a plan has been evolved from OT elements by post-biblical Jewish apocalyptic;[26] to postulate it for the OT itself is a wholly unwarranted telescoping of the whole Christian Bible (plus some Church-Fathers) into a single theological statement.[27] OT eschatology itself contains only some hazy or rudimentary ideas of a plan oriented historicism.[28] Occasionally, however, it relies on God's policy in the past (to establish and maintain Israel as His people) for its future hopes: since the first covenant did not achieve its purpose, it shall be

---

1 Sam. 12:22; *et al.*

26. Mainly conveyed by the typical apocalyptic *Gattung* of a 'preview' of history (Ten Weeks Apocalypse in 1 Enoch. ch. 93 and 91:12–17 [reconstruction of correct sequence confirmed by fragments from Qumran publisched by Milik]; Sheep Apocalypse 1 Enoch. chs. 85–90; the book Assumption of Moses; Apocalypse of Bright and Dark Waters in Syriac Baruch ch. 53 *et. seq;* etc.) Charles wrote in 1899: "Determinism thus became a leading characteristic of Jewish apocalyptic; and accordingly its conception of history, as distinguished from that of prophecy, was often mechanical rather than organic" (*Eschatology*, 1969 reprint, p. 206). The historical determinism of apocalyptic has been since recognized by every writer on the subject; it reappears in a special form at Qumran. I have tried to work out Charles' point that this is a definite way of seeing history in "Time and Eschatology in Apocalyptic Literature and in Qumran", *JJS* 16 (1965), pp. 177–182. The apocalyptic view of history reappears in various secular ideologies of the 19th and 20th centuries; most lucid about this is K. Löwith, *Meaning in History,* 1949.

27. I did not come across this mistake in the writings of OT specialists, but it is rather common among those attempting a general 'epistemology' of history. See H. Meyerhoff, *The Philosophy of History in our Time,* 1959, p. 2; also the article "Historiography and Historical Methodology" in *Encyclopaedia Britanica* (1974 edition) "Macropaedia" Vol. VIII, pp. 947–8. Lambert (above, n. 6) also adopts this view of OT historiography, because of the need to explain somehow the phenomenon of OT historicism. My point is that the thing does not need this sort of explanation.

28. Isa. 44:6–7; 46:8–10; 66:2.

renewed in the future, only then shall Israel truly become a people unto its Lord.[29]

A Difficulty

We are historicists ourselves, by the definition suggested in this paper. One should, however, distinguish between the blend of historicist attitudes inherent in our culture generally and the particular scholarly historicism which determines a great part of the work in the humanities. This historicism is based on the demonstrable truth that everything becomes at least partially comprehensible when measured on the twin scales of chronology and development. It also (perhaps consequently) makes history the Queen of Humanities. Nowadays it is less dominant[30] and vigorous than it was at the time when the 'critical' scholarship of the OT was young. In those days 'peoples with no history' was the definition of miserable savages. An ancient and primitive *Kulturvolk* was expected (by definition) to produce a poor and rudimentary kind of history writing. Consequently there was nothing remarkable about OT historiography: both its existence and its shortcomings were taken for granted. The task of OT scholarship was to utilize the texts and their faults for a reconstruction of a true history of ancient Israel. Everything else was a necessary *Vorarbeit*. *Prolegomena zur Geschichte Israels* was more than a title of a book; it was the program of a discipline. Reading the classic works of the period, one occasionally notices an intuitive recognition of the ancient writers' work as historians; it is, however, treated as a nuisance, to be cleared away, so that truth might become apparent. The attitude was hardly conducive to a contemplation of ancient Israel's preoccupation with its past.

Much has changed since the old days. We know more than our teachers' teachers, and are less simple-minded: a whole range of subjects has become respectable. It is mainly the theological dimension of

29. Jer. 31:30–33; Ezek. 20:34–38; Hos. 2:25.
30. The ancient Art of Poetics has become *Literaturgeschichte*, Theology became secularized as *Religionsgeschichte*, and Grammar was made scientific by the comparative study of languages in their development (dealing mainly with *Lautverschiebungen* and reconstructions of *Urindogermanisch and Ursemitisch*). Since the middle of the twentieth century these are being replaced by Comparative Literature, Study of Religion, and various modern trends in Linguistics. All these recognize the 'historical' or 'diachronic' aspect of things, but put the emphasis elsewhere. The movement has not made much headway in OT and Near Eastern studies, which are as strictly historicist in outlook as ever.

the OT historiography which has gained scholarly appreciation. The intellectual dimension of the thing remains largely unnoticed. We know that the great work of OT history writing was an unusual achievement, we occasionally let on that we are rather proud of it, but we do not know what to do about it, for it is almost impossible to discuss something which one cannot quite identify. The difficulty lies in the circumstance that the ancient writers were as curious about the past as we are. Noting down a list of the kings of Edom (Gen. 36:31–43) just for the record, without any other apparent reason, is rather strange behaviour by any logical standard; to us it is obviously a part of the historian's job. One does not describe court politics in detail, in most cultures, unless one needs the matter for some special pleading, or moralizing. To us and to the ancient narrators the events at David's and Solomon's court are fascinating in themselves, the lessons to be drawn should be indicated briefly and discreetly. Such examples show that the two historicisms overlap, with the result that most modern scholars are as unable to see the basic preoccupation with the past (which is a characteristic of the text) as the nose in their faces. The thing becomes noticeable only when there is something wrong with it, e.g. a contradiction in detail. There are, however, cases in which the two historicisms produce radically different results; in such cases it is difficult for the modern scholar to identify a basic historian's posture beneath the ancient writer's elaboration of legends and pursuit of religious themes. He is actually reconstructing the origins of Israel, or the introduction of kingship, or some other typical historian's subject, by his own methods; but it is difficult for us to recognize his endeavour, because we need (for our satisfaction) quite different solutions of the same problems.

The barrier to understanding has become deeper and subtler than it was in the old days, but it is still there, because OT scholarship and neighbouring disciplines are even nowadays strongly historicist. Another kind of historicism is bewildering to us: we should be able to see how it works in details, but we cannot, the thing itself is too ellusive for us. All that I can suggest at present is to point it out; to call it a name which might help to exorcise it in the future.

DIVINE INTERVENTION IN WAR IN ANCIENT ISRAEL AND IN THE ANCIENT NEAR EAST

MOSHE WEINFELD

The Hebrew University of Jerusalem

Scholars have recently begun to realize that the image of the fighting god who hastens to the aid of his people was widespread in the Ancient Near East and is not necessarily unique to Israel.[1] The descriptions of the god, riding on a cherub and on the wings of the winds, thundering and scattering lightning and sending his arrows against the enemy, like those which we find in Ps. 18:11–18 and others similar to it, are rooted in the tradition of the storm god (Adad/Hadad), lord of thunder, lightning and rain.[2] The same applies to the accounts of the changes of nature which follow the appearance of the Storm god, known not only from Mesopotamian tradition[3] but also from Canaanite, Egyptian, and even Greek tradition (see below). It is important to observe that the language in which the change of nature is formulated is identical in all these sources: *the voice (=thunder) of the god shakes heaven and earth.*

So for example **in Akkadian**: (a) "which at the sound of his voice the

1. See in particular M. Weippert, "Heiliger Krieg in Israel und Assyrien," *ZAW* 84 (1972), pp. 460 ff. However, his discussion, as shown by the title of the article, is limited to Israel and Assyria only.
2. See M. Weinfeld, *Th. Gaster Festschrift* (=*JANES* 5, [1973], pp. 421 ff.), and also in *Beth Mikra* 57 (1974), pp. 145–146 (Hebrew). On the deity riding on "the wings of the wind" in battle compare the hymn to Inanna: 'lady mounted on a beast . . . you are lent wings by the storm . . . you fly about in the nation . . . in the van of battle everything is struck down by you . . . with a roaring storm you roar, ' W.W. Hallo and J.J.A. van Dijk, *The Exaltation of Inanna* (*Yale Near Eastern Researches 3*), 1968, p. 16, 11. 14ff.
3. On the Mesopotamian motif and its parallels in the Bible see S.E. Loewenstamm, 'The Quaking of the Earth at the Appearance of the Lord,' *Oz leDavid* (D. Ben-Gurion Anniversary Volume), 1964, pp. 508–520 (Hebrew); J. Jeremias, *Theophanie, Die Geschichte einer alttestamentlichen Gattung*, 1965.

heavens shake, the earth quakes, the mountains tremble;"[4] (b) "who set his voice in the heavens like Adad, and all the earth trembles[5] at his voice."[6]

In the Bible: "And the Lord will roar from Zion, and from Jerusalem will give His voice, and the heavens and the earth will shake" (Joel 4:16; compare Amos 1:2); and in reversed order (first the quaking and then the voice): "The earth shook and quaked . . . and the Lord thundered in the heavens, the Most High uttered His voice" (Ps. 18: 8–14).

Likewise, Psalm 29, which entirely revolves around the *voice of God* which shakes and "makes dance" the whole earth, and whose connection with the world of Canaanite imagery was first dealt with by H.L. Ginsberg.[6a]

In Ugarit: Ba[al gives] forth his holy voice . . . earth's high places reel (*ANET*, p. 135).[7]

In Egypt: "The earth trembles when (Amon) sends forth his voice".[8]

In Greece: "Zeus, whose voice is borne afar,[9] himself sat upon his throne of gold, and beneath his feet great Olympus quaked" (Iliad VIII, 442–443);[10] "the high mountains trembled and the woodland

4. *ša ina zikir pīšu šamû irūbū, erṣetu inerrutu, itarraru ḫuršāni*, E. Ebeling, *Akkadische Gebetserie "Handerhebung,"* 1953, p. 104:8–9 (Hereafter: Ebeling, *AGH*). Cf. also: *kīma ᵈAddi ana šagimmešu itarraru šadû* in the Tukulti Ninurta Epic: W.L. Lambert, *AfO* 18 [1957–58], p. 50:6).

5. *tar-gu-ub*; the verb *ragābu* is apparently West-Semitic (see *AHw*, p. 941), compare *rgb* in Ugaritic, examined recently by J.C. de Moor, *UF* 1 (1968), p. 188.

6. *ša iddin rigmašu ina šamê kīma Adad u targub gabbi māti ištu rigmišu* (J.A. Knudtzon, *Die El-Amarna-Tafeln*, no. 147:14–15).

6a. Cf. H. L. Ginsberg, 'A Phoenician Hymn in the Psalter', *Atti del XIX Congresso Internazionale del Orientalisti*, 1935, pp. 472–276; idem, אוגרית כתבי, 1936, pp. 129–131; idem, 'The Rebellion and Death of Ba'lu', *Orientalia* 5 (1936), pp. 180–181. See most recently a thorough analysis of this Psalm by Y. Avishur, "Psalm 29 – Canaanite or Hebrew," *B.Z. Luria Anniversary Volume*, 1979, pp. 247–274 (Hebrew).

7. *qlh. qdš* [.] *b['l. y]tn . . . bmt. 'a[rṣ] tttn.* (*CTA* 4 VII: 29–35). For a discussion see recently L. Fisher, *Ras Shamra Parallels*, 1972, pp. 26–27. Compare Psalm 99:1: "The Lord, enthroned on cherubim, is king, peoples tremble, the earth quakes (תנוט)".

8. A. Gardiner, *ZÄS* 42 (1905), p. 25, III, 5: *t3 ḥr ktkt wḏi.f ḥrw.f.* This attribute is taken over from Canaanite Baal and was transferred to Seth, compare in the story of Wenamun: 'lo, Amun could make a thunder in the heaven and appoint Seth for his time'. (II,19), see recently the analysis of H. Goedicke, *The Report of Wenamun*, 1975, pp. 82–83.

9. The meaning of ευρύοπα is "seen from afar" and also "sounding from afar". (Compare Exod. 20:18 "and all the people saw the thunder and lightning".) For the expression see *LSJ*, s.v.

10. αὐτὸς δὲ Χρύσειον ἐπὶ θρόνον εὐρύοπα Ζεὺς ἕζετο, τῷ δ'ὑπὸ ποσσὶ μέγας πελεμίζετ' Ὄλυμπος.

beneath the immortal feet of Poseidon as he went" (Iliad XIII, 18f.)[11]

The excitation of heavens and earth, sea and the deep, mountain and forest at the appearance of the deity which is found in all these sources is very prominent in the Psalmodic literature:

> Let the heavens rejoice and the earth exult,
> let the sea and all within it thunder,
> the fields and everything in them exult;
> then shall all the trees of the forest shout for joy
> at the presence of the Lord, for he is coming.
> (Ps. 96:11ff)

> Let the sea and all within it thunder,
> the world and its inhabitants;
> let the rivers clap their hands,
> the mountains sing joyously together
> at the presence of the Lord.
> (Ps. 98:7–8)

Compare also Isaiah 44:23 and 49:13.[12]

11. Compare the idiom in the Iliad VIII, 443 quoted above and see also *Theogony* of Hesiod 11. 442 f. In the *Theogony* we also find the quaking of the underworld (line 850): 'Hades, the ruler of the dead below, trembled', a motif also found in the Iliad XX, 57f:
> 'from beneath did Poseidon cause the vast earth to quake . . . and seized with fear in the world below was Aidoneus, lord of the shades, and in fear leapt he from his throne and cried aloud.'

These descriptions should be compared to Isaiah 14:9f.:
> 'The underworld below trembled...
> rousing for you the shades...
> raising from the thrones
> all the kings of the nations.'

The personage at whom the kings in the underworld quake is the one who imagines himself 'the most high' who 'mounts the back of the cloud' and 'shakes the earth' (v. 13–16), a personage whose characteristics are comparable to those of Zeus and Poseidon. The title 'shaker of the earth' ἐνοσίχθων is, to be sure, one of Poseidon's regular titles, however he embodies in this characteristic an aspect of Zeus (see A.B. Cook, *Zeus*, III, 1940, pp. 20 ff.). The anxiety of the king of the underworld from the 'shaker of the earth' is nicely materialized on a bronze medallion from the period of Valerianus. There we see Zeus with Poseidon at his right who shakes the earth with his trident and to his left Hades who leaps from his throne in terror with his sceptre in his hand. See the discussion of Cook, pp. 6 ff. It has already been pointed out that the source of these concepts is in the East. See M.L. West (ed.) Hesiod, *Theogony*, 1971 (in his note on line 850 and on the parallel section from the Iliad XX, 57 ff., quoted by him): "The motif is Near Eastern" (p. 391). Moreover, the concept "shaking" in context with "shades" is found in Phoenician funerary inscriptions, see *KAI* 9A:5; 13:4, 6, 7, 8. (*rgz...rp'm*).

2. See on this issue E. Lipiński, *Biblica* 48 (1967), pp. 191ff.

That the excitation of nature on the occasion of the appearance of the god can also be out of joy, as in these passages, can be learned from the Hymn to Adad.[13] There, after the epithets "carrier of lightning" and "ruling heavens, mountains and seas" we find: "At your voice mountains rejoice . . . fields exult."[14]

However, the main point of this paper is to discuss the concrete descriptions of war in which the intervention of heavenly factors is prominent: the stars, the pillars of cloud and fire, etc. These Biblical descriptions relate to the War of God with Egypt (Exod. 14:15–25) and the wars of Canaan (Judg. 5:20), and are paralleled in Egyptian and Hittite descriptions of war from the 2nd millenium and likewise in the Homeric Epic. Therefore, there is no place for the claim that these accounts reflect in particular the Ancient Israelite faith before its contact with the Canaanite traditions, as G. von Rad has claimed.[15] On the contrary – these accounts are identical to those known to us from the vicinity, except that they underwent an Israelite interpretation. We shall begin with the fighting stars in Judg. 5:20–22.

I. The Stars Fighting from Heaven (Judg. 5:20–22)

The stars fought from heaven, from their courses
they fought against Sisera. The torrent Kishon swept
them away, the raging torrent, the torrent Kishon . . .
then the heels of the horses were battered by the
gallop galloping of his steeds.

It has not been noticed up to now that the three motifs combined here[16] – 1) the heavenly factors who wage battle on the enemy, 2) the torrent which sweeps away the enemy and 3) the destruction of the enemy's chariotry[17] – appear in Exod. 14:19ff., in connection with the

---

13. Ebeling, *AGH*, p. 104.
14. *ina rigme[ka] ḫadû šamê...rîšu ugarû* (lines 33–34).
15. G. Von Rad, *Der heilige Krieg im alten Israel*, 1951, pp. 32–33.
16. The three factors in the destruction of the Canaanites: the heavenly bodies, the torrent of Kishon, and the injured horses were seen by Y. Kaufmann in his commentary to *Judges*, p. 142 (Hebrew), but he did not notice the parallels of Exod. 14.
17. The most reasonable explanation of סוס עקבי הלמו אז is that of Kimḥi, and others, who take הלם here as intransitive (see Ibn Janāh, *Sepher Haschoraschim*, [ed. Bacher], p. 120) and what is meant is the putting the horses out of action which can be understood also from the prose account of Judg. 4:15, and may be learned from the parallels in Exod. 14 and Psalm 76, and also from the Egyptian text and the Homeric Epic (see below). Version A of the Septuagint translates "the horses

defeat of the Egyptians in the sea:[18] 1) the pillar of fire and cloud which causes panic in the Egyptian camp (vs. 24), 2) the hurling of the Egyptians in the midst of the sea (vs. 27), and 3) the dismantlement of the chariotry (vs. 25). The 'sea' in the Exodus stories, and the 'torrent' in the story of the defeat of Sisera's army (and the same holds for 'the Jordan' in the accounts of the crossing of the river in Joshua 3–4) derive from the mythological war of God against 'sea' and 'river'[19] and their development is particular to Israel's epic. On the other hand, the pillar of cloud and fire and the war waging heavenly bodies constitute, as we shall see, a motif found in Egyptian descriptions of battle, and in Hittite and Greek descriptions as well.

In the Gebel Barkal stela of Thutmose III in which are related the exploits of his warriors in Mitanni,[20] we read in the speech of the king:[21] 'Hear you, O people of the South who are at the holy mount . . . so that you may know the wonderful deed (of Amon-Ra) . . . (the guards) were about to take up (their watchposts) in order to meet at night and carry out the watch command. It was in the second hour (=in the second watch)[22] and a star came from the south of them. Never had the like occured. It flashed[23] against them from its position (*m 'k3.f*).[24] Not one withstood before it . . . with fire for their faces. No one among them found his hand nor looked back. Their chariotry/horses were not more . . .'

hooves were cut off (ἀπεκόπησαν)", whereas version B: "were fettered (ἐνεποδίσ-θησαν)". Targum translates in the same vein as the Sages: אשתלפא טופרי סוסוותהון 'the hooves slipped' (see the following note), and the Syriac is similar to this. This is to be compared to Exod. 14:25, where the Samaritan Pentateuch, the Septuagint and the Syriac read "He bound (ויאסר) (the wheels of their chariots)" in place of "took off (ויסר)". Thus, all the readings point to the decapacitating of the horses and chariotry.

18. The Rabbis referred to the hooves of the Egyptian horses which slipped, on the basis of Judg. 5:25 (*Mechilta*, Tractate Beshallah, Sec. 5, [ed.] Horowitz, p. 108) and also saw in the sweeping away by the torrent Kishon the completion to the drowning in the Sea of Reeds (TB *Pesahim* 118b).
19. See on the whole issue S.E. Loewenstamm, *The Tradition of the Exodus in its Development*, 1965, pp. 101ff. (Hebrew); F.M. Cross, *Canaanite Myth and Hebrew Epic*, 1973, pp. 135ff.
20. G.A. Reisner and M.B. Reisner, *ZÄS* 69 (1933), pp. 24–39. 11. 33ff. (Urk. *IV* 1238, 2ff.). See translation of the inscription by W. Helck, *Urkunden der 18. Dynastie*, 1961, No. 365, pp. 5–12.
21. Ll. 33ff.
22. Read: *iw wn wnwt sp 2* (see Helck, above n. 20), p. 10, n. 6. On the second watch compare the account of the deliverance by Gideon: "Gideon arrived . . . at the beginning of the middle watch, just after the sentries were posted" (Judg. 7:19).
23. Egyptian *wdi* is connected with Semitic ידה and also means "to shoot."
24. Translation of Helck (above, n. 20), after Pap. Harris I 75, 3.

In the beginning of the stela in the eulogy in which the glory of the king is described, we find similar references to a flashing star in battle, except that there the star is personified: it represents the king:

> A hero whose hand is outstretched in battle ... who flashes between the two arches [of heaven] like a star crossing the sky,[25] who comes within a great multitude, his glowing breath[26] against them like fire, devastating them, weltering in their blood. It is his diadem[27] which subjugates them to him, his flame[28] which vanquishes his enemies. The great army of Mitanni was overthrown in one hour, disappeared like those who have never existed (1229, 20–1230, 6).

The shooting star motif is also found in the poetic stela of Thutmose III (line 15): 'I cause them to see thy majesty as a shooting/flashing star' (*ANET* [2], p. 374).[29]

25. The star to which the king is likened is apparently Resheph, who sends forth his arrows against the enemy. See below.
26. *hh* appears with the determinative of wind (see Erman-Grapow, *Wörterbuch*, s.v.), compare Psalm 21:10: "The Lord with the blast of his nostrils (באפו) destroys them; fire consumes them." Compare also Exod. 15:8, 10; 2 Sam. 22:16: "At the blast of the breath of His nostrils." (=Psalm 18:16), see below, p. 137.
27. *3ḥt* 'serpent-diadem' is parallel to Akkadian *melammu* (=halo, brilliance), which is also connected with the crown around the head; see the article by A.L. Oppenheim, *JAOS* 63 (1943), p. 31, and recently the material collected by W.H. Ph. Roemer, *Bib Or* 32 (1975), p. 308; *CAD* M II, pp. 9–12. Cf. also the effulgence of Achilles' helmet (Illiad XVI, 70; XVIII, 205 ff.) Akkadian *melammu* plays an important part in the defeating of enemies (the most common formula is *melam šarrūtiya ishupšunūti* = the brilliance of my kingdom overthrew them) and so also the *3ḥt* in our Egyptian inscription (the causative conjugation of *3ḥ*, *3ḥt* means to glorify, to bless and to honor); compare in the poetic stela of Thutmose III (Urk. VI 615:9): 'My serpent-diadem (*3ḥt.i*) which is upon thy head consumes them' *ANET*, p. 374).
28. The flame (*nsrt*) here is the divine fire, the source of the brilliance and the splendor (*3ḥt*) Cf. the poetic stele of Thutmose III (see preceding note): She (Uraeus = *3ḥt*) devours by flame (*nsrt*) those who are in the islands (1.10). On the divine fire in the Bible see M. Weinfeld, *Deuteronomy and the Deuteronomic School*, 1972, p. 192, (Hereafter: Weinfeld, *Deuteronomy*). *nsrt* appears with the verb *wdi* and in this case means "sent forth fire" (see below, n. 43), which recalls the verse: "In Your great glory (גאון) You break Your opponents; You send forth Your blasting breath, it consumes them like straw" (Exod. 15:7). גאון is one of the expressions for the divine splendor, see M. Weinfeld, כבוד, *Theologisches Wörterbuch zum Alten Testament*, IV, 1982, 27-32, and compare Psalm 21:10, and n. 26 above.
29. Compare also in the story of the shipwrecked sailor: 'Then a star fell and because of it these went up in fire'; translation in W.K. Simpson (ed.), *The Literature of Ancient Egypt*, 1972, p. 54 (i. 130).

It is interesting to point out in this context that similar to the Song of Deborah, in whose beginning comes a hymn to God and a description of His going out to battle with His enemies, and only afterwards comes the concrete description of the battle itself,[30] so also in the Barkal Stela of Thutmose III comes first a eulogy for the king and only afterwards come the descriptions of the battles themselves.

It appears that in the adduced Egyptian parallel one may find an aid to the interpretation of ממסילותם 'from their courses' in Judg. 5:20.[31] Commentators are divided on the interpretation of this passage: whether the heavenly bodies waged war while arrayed in their courses, or whether their battle was waged while departing from the course (compare BT *Pesahim* 118b). From the Egyptian description it appears that the star came out of its course that is, a comet fell out of its fixed place, and it is reasonable to assume that so it is to be understood in the Bible too.

As in the Egyptian text, so also in the passage in Judges and in the description of the Egyptian defeat in Exodus 14:25, the horses and chariotry of the enemy are put out of commission as a result of the divine warfare. The same can be said of Psalm 76 in which God brings havoc upon the enemy, decimates their weaponry and incapacitates horse and chariot (vss. 4, 7). Moreover, there we find the expression 'they did not find their hands' (vs. 6), which is found also in the aforementioned Egyptian passage.

In the wars of ancient Greece we also find the star in the service of Zeus. Thus we read in the Iliad (IV, 75ff.) that Athene descended into the ranks of the fighters, just as a gleaming star is sent by Kronos as a sign into a great multitude of warriors.[32] Similarly, we read in the Homeric Hymn "To Apollo"[33] that Apollo leaped from the ship and

---

30. See H. Rabin, 'The Song of Deborah as a Cultural Document,' עיונים בספר שופטים, Jerusalem, 1966, pp. 108 ff. Rabin assumes that in vs. 19, "Then the kings of Canaan" the story begins; what comes before is a 'song of victory.'

31. It makes no difference to our case whether we read the verse according to the Massoretic punctuation: 'From heaven they fought, the stars from their courses fought against Sisera', or as many think it must be divided: 'from heaven the stars fought, from their courses they fought against Sisera.'

32. οἶον δ' ἀστέρα ἧκε...τέρας ἠὲ στρατῷ εὐρέϊ λαῶν, and see on this passage M.M. Willcock, *A Commentary of Homer's Iliad*, 1970. It should be pointed out that we have to do here not with a star which destroys the enemy, as in the previously mentioned cases, but rather a quick visit that will bring about the downfall of the Trojans. To be noticed, however, is the similarity of language between: 'the King like a star coming within a great multitude' in the Egyptian inscription and 'a star coming with a great multitude of warriors' in the Iliad.

33. Ll. 440 ff.

Moshe Weinfeld

the effulgence of his form was like a star at midday, from which many
sparks flew and whose brilliance reached unto the heavens, he ignited
the flame and revealed his arrows (κῆλα).

These descriptions of sparkling stars which venture forth to assail
the warriors' camp, might be understood against the background of
ancient Near Eastern mythology. As known, the god Resheph in the
Syro-Palestinian world[34] served as a warrior and also as the god of
plagues. In the Greek world, Apollo plays a similar role and is indeed
identical with Resheph.[35] In the Mesopotamian world the god Nergal
acts in this capacity and is explicitly equated with Resheph.[36] Resheph, Nergal and Apollo are connected with heavenly bodies, mainly
with falling stars (meteors)[37] which shoot like arrows – an action which

34. See recently D. Conrad, 'Der Gott Reschef.' *ZAW* 83 (1971), pp. 157ff., and also
A. Rofé, *The Belief in Angels in Israel*, 1969, pp. 120 ff. (Hebrew); S.E. Loewenstamm, רשף, *Enc. Miqr.*, VII, 1976, cols. 437 ff. In the Egyptian world we find the
name Resheph from the days of Amenhotep II and after. See recently W. Helck,
Die Beziehungen Ägyptens zu Vorderasien in 3. und 2. Jahrtausend v. Chr.², 1971,
pp. 450 ff. Compare now the inscription on a stone bowl from the days of Horem-
heb on which we read: "Resheph lord of heaven, Qodsha lady of the stars of
heaven;" see: D.B. Redford, *BASOR* 211 (1973), pp. 37 ff. In the Hittite milieu
Rešeph is represented by the god Yarri (the god of war and pestilence) who equals
Mesopotamian Erra-Nergal (see H.M. Kümmel, *Ersatzrituale für den hethitischen König, StBoT* 3, 1967, pp. 101ff.). Here we find that one dedicates to Yarri a
rhyton (in the form of a lion, cf. *KUB* XV S III:45–49, see L. Oppenheim, *Dreams
etc.*, p. 193) as we read in the treaty published by M. Otten, *Istanbuler Mitteil.* 17
(1967), p. 60, that the elders of Ura pledge to bring a rhyton to the god Yarri. An
identical practice is attested in Ugarit (*Ugaritica* VII, pp. 152–153) where an
inscription on a rhyton in the form of a lion reads: *pn arw dš'ly PN lršp gn* "the face
of a lion which PN offered to Resheph Gan." (This inscription has been discussed
by Y. Yadin in a lecture which is scheduled to appear soon.)
35. According to bilingual inscriptions from Cyprus, see *Répertoire d'Epigraphie
Sémitique* III, 1916, no. 1212, 1213; O. Masson, *Cultes indigènes, cultes grecs et
cultes orientaux à Chypre, Eléments orientaux dans la religion grecque ancienne*,
1960, p. 139 ff.
36. See in the list of the gods, *Ugaritica* V, pp. 45:26 and 57, in which Nergal=ršp. On
the identity of Nergal and Resheph see already W.F. Albright, in *Oriental Studies
Dedicated to Paul Haupt*, 1926, pp. 146ff.
37. σπινθήρ, mentioned in the text about Athene, quoted above, is explained as the
spark of a meteor, *LSJ* s.v., and in the hymn to Apollo, also mentioned above, the
word for sparks is σπινθαρίδες. Sparks or flames in connection with Resheph occur
in the verse: רשפיה רשפי אש שלהבתיה. "Its darts are darts of fire, a godly (mighty)
flame" (Song of Songs 8:6), and רשף is so rendered in the various versions to Job 5:7:
"and sparks (בני רשף) fly upwards", compare "arrow that flies" in Psalm 91:5 (see
below). The fire which issues from the planet of Mars, which appears in the role of
Nergal (see below), is called in Akkadian: *miqit išāti* – fall of fire; see E. von
Weiher, *Der Babylonische Gott Nergal* (*AOAT* 11) 1971, pp. 77, 84 (Hereafter:
von Weiher, *Nergal*), and see 1 Kings 18:38: "fire fell from the Lord", and also Job
1:16; "God's fire fell from heaven." The pestilence of Nergal and of the gods

128

characterizes a divinity of this type.[38] As we learned from the Homeric Hymn, Apollo leaps like a star, and similarly we find in Mesopotamia that Nergal acts in the role of a planet (*ṣalbatānu* = Mars), who dispatches plague,[39] especially among cattle.[40]

The last feature (pestilence among animals) is also characteristic of Apollo: First he sends his arrows against the mules and dogs and afterwards against men (Iliad I, 50ff.).

Nergal, Resheph and Apollo – each acts, therefore, in identical roles: 1. as a shooting star; 2. as a warrior; 3. as a bringer of plague and disease. Resheph together with Deber (plague), Qeteb (pestilence), indeed act in the Bible as deadly arrows sent forth (שלח) against the enemy, as in Deut. 32:23–24 (Resheph and Qeteb); Hos. 13:14 (Sheol, Death, and pestilence) (דבר, קטב); Ps. 78:48ff. (Deber, Resheph); Ps. 91:5ff. (Deber and Qeteb). In the Song of Songs 8:6–7 we find Reshaphim at the side of Death and Sheol (compare Hos. 13:14; and also Ps. 49:15).

identical with him also "falls", see von Weiher, *Nergal*, p. 33, n. 4, and compare Isa. 9:7: "The Lord let loose (see next note) *a pestilence* against Jacob and it fell upon Israel". Here the reading of the Septuagint *deber* must be followed, and not *dabar* ("word"). Compare Amos 4:10.

38. See *ršp ḥṣ* (*KAI* 32:4), and also *bʾl ḥz ršp* (*PRU* II, 1957, p. 3 (15.134), 1:3). For a possible interpretation of the entire line in the Ugaritic text see Rofé (above, n. 34), p. 124, n. 20. There is an interesting parallel between the above quoted passage from the Homeric hymn on the star of Apollo *at noon-time*, and Psalm 91:5–6: "*the arrow* that flies *by day*, or the pestilence that ravages *at noon*." In Mesopotamia Nergal is called "the lord of the bow and quiver", *bēl tillê u qašāte* (compare תליך וקשתך, "your quiver and bow" in Gen. 27:3); see von Weiher, *Nergal*, p. 71; or [*nāš*] *qasti uṣu u išpat* 'the one carrying bow, arrow and quiver', Böhl, *Bib Or* 6, 1949, p. 166:4). The Hittite god Yarri (see note 34) is also *bēl qašti*, see recently O.R. Gurney, *Some Aspects of Hittite Religion*, 1977, p. 16, note 3. Furthermore, Nergal's bow is considered delightful; cf. *qašat siḫat ana qātēšu ištakan* = '(Nin-lil) put into his (Nergal's) hands a delightful bow' (Ebeling, *AGH*, 1953, p. 118:21f). Apollo too carries a bow and quiver (Iliad I, 45ff), and is famous for his silver made bow (ἀργυρότοξος). His bow is beautiful (like that of Nergal) καλλίτοξος (Euripides, *Phoenissae*, 1162) and he is famous for his arrows (κῆλα, βέλεα). His arrows are released and dispatched (cf. e.g. Iliad I, 48 ἕηκε, from a ἵημι a phenomenon encountered in the Bible in connection with pestilence associated with Resheph [Deut. 32:23–24; compare Ezek. 5:16]. The verb used in this context שלח means releasing or sending forth, cf. Lev. 26:25; Ezek. 14:19; Amos 4:10; Is. 9:7 [LXX], Ps. 78:49–50). In Ps. 78:48 pestilence (read *ldbr* and not *lbrd*, see S.E. Loewenstamm, [above, n. 19], p. 3) stands next to שלח (v. 49) and is associated there with all sorts of deadly inflictions which are sent forth (שלח).

39. MUL *ṣalbatānu muštabarrû mûtanû* (von Weiher, *Nergal*, p. 79). *muštabarrâ* is derived from *šutabrû* which means "to make last" (see *CAD* B, p. 281a, s.v. *bitrû*).

40. MUL *ṣalbatānu innappaḫamma būla uḫallaq* – "the planet Mars (=Nergal) will flare up and destroy the cattle", see von Weiher, *Nergal*, p. 34; compare too "When the light of the planet Mars will be seen, there will be (lit. "fall" see n. 37) a pestilence in the land, there will be an epidemic against the cattle" (*ibid.*). In the

It must be admitted however that if the source of the motif of the smiting star and arrow is rooted in the mythology of Resheph, Nergal and Apollo, the stars of Judg. 5:20 and so Resheph, Deber, Qeteb etc. in other Biblical passages ceased to be independent divine forces. These are not considered divine entities, but rather heavenly bodies which serve as God's emissaries and servants. Thus we read in Hab. 3;4: 'Deber marches before Him and Resheph comes forth at his heels', comp. Ps. 97:3: 'Fire marches before Him, burning his foes on every side!'

Another scripture of ancient poetical character in which we find a star afflicting the enemy is found in Numbers 24:17: 'A star marches forth (דרך) from Jacob, a meteor (שבט) comes forth (וקם) from Israel.'

Rashi interprets *drk* from to draw the bow, 'that the star passes like an arrow.'[41] Ibn Ezra, who connects the verse with Judg. 5:20 explains *drk* as from path and course: "that he will be seen in his way as the stars from their courses." Actually, these two interpretations complement each other: the star, and especially the comet, shoot from their courses like an arrow, as we found in the inscriptions of Thutmose III. In this way the parallel stich (וקם שבט)[42] which refers to the position of the star in the stellar constellation (compare *mazal* = *manzaztu, manzaltu*, 'position' in Akkadian) is clarified. In Mesopotamian astrological accounts we find in connection with stars expressions like: 'taking course and path' (*ḫarranam ṣabātu*), in proximity to expressions of 'rising and standing' (*uzuzzu*).[43] These descriptions refer to planets standing up in their constellations.[44] In addition, Nergal, who shoots

Harper Letters: "Nergal will diminish the cattle," *Nergal būl uṣaḫḫir* (*ABL* 405:13). On this expression cf.: "He does not let their cattle decrease" (Ps. 107:38). In the pestilence of the plagues of Egypt it was the cattle which were afflicted (Exod. 9:3), and in the account of this plague in Ps. 78 we read: "He gave their beasts over pestilence (דבר), their cattle to Reshaphim" (vs. 48; see above, n. 38). It should be noted in this connection that Nergal, who is represented by a lion (cf. E. Porada-F. Basmachi, *Sumer* 7 [1951], pp. 66–68, and see above note 34 about rhytons in the form of a lion dedicated to Resheph and Yarri), usually has a star on its shoulder (see H. Kantor, *JNES* 6, [1947], pp. 250ff.)

41. See D. Kimchi, *Sepher haschoraschim*, (ed.) Biesenthal-Lebrecht, s.v. דרך p. 75: 'And because with the drawing of the bow the arrow is also drawn, therefore it is written "Let Him draw His arrows" דרכו חצם, (64:4) "they draw their arrows" חצו ידרך (Ps. 58:8).

42. On שבט meaning "comet" cf. TB *Berachoth* 48b.

43. See e.g.: *ina ḫarrāni šut Enlil izzaz* "it will arise in the courses of the planets of Enlil" (*ABL* 744, rev 10), cf. 1. 5; and cf. also R. Borger, *Die Inschriften Asarhaddons Königs von Assyrien* (*AfO* Beiheft 9), Graz, 1956, p. 18, Ep. 14b:6f.

44. See Th. Gaster, *Myth, Legend and Custom in the Old Testament*, 1969, p. 307.

with arrows-stars, is called "Nergal of the comet" (*Negal ša šibṭi*; *CT* 42, 41:68),[45] and to be sure, the verb *šabaṭu* is associated in Akkadian with a strike of plague (*AHw*, s.v.). In view of all this there is no place for the emendation of *darakh* to *zarakh* (shone), as proposed by modern commentators.

Even though the basic meaning of 'star' in this context is comet,[46] it is not inconceivable that Num. 24:7 contains a pun alluding to the meaning of king and kingdom implied by שבט (cf. Isa. 14:5; Gen. 49:10; Ps. 45:7), and perhaps also a double meaning is bound up in the verb *darakh*, which in Ugaritic connotes 'rule'.[47]

II. The Fire and the Cloud

Warfare from the heavens by means of fire and shining appearance (and not necessarily by means of a star) which causes the devastation of the enemy and the destruction of his chariotry, is found in Exod. 14:24ff. As in the inscription of Thutmose III we find here also fire confronting the enemy, panicky flight, and the destruction of the chariotry, at the time of the morning watch:

> At the morning watch, the Lord looked down upon the Egyptian army from a pillar of fire and cloud, and threw the Egyptian army into panic. He locked (ויסר)[48] the wheels of their chariots so that they moved forward with difficulty. And the Egyptians said, "Let us flee from the Israelites, for the Lord is fighting for them against Egypt."

The pillar of fire and cloud have various functions.[49] However, they are substantially the messengers of God who fulfill His mission – in this case the annihilation of the enemy. Emissaries of this type we find in Ps. 97:2–3: "Cloud and mist are around him . . . fire marches before him, burning his foes on every side", and similarly we read in Nahum

45. See von Weiher, *Nergal*, p. 86, n. 1, who accepts *šibṭu* as equivalent to Hebrew שבט.
46. Cf. Vulgate which translates שבט, *stella crinita*.
47. Cf. W.F. Albright, *JBL* 63 (1944), p. 219. On 'double meaning' in the Bible see D. Yellin, *Tarbiz* 5 (1933), pp. 1ff (Hebrew).
48. See n. 17 above.
49. They guide the people on their journeys (Exod. 13:21–22), serve as revelatory means and cover divine appearance (Exod. 33:9–11; Num. 11:25; 12:5; Deut. 31:15; Ps. 99:6–7; and see Weinfeld, *Deuteronomy* pp. 201 ff.), constitute signs for journeying or camping (Num. 9:15ff.), protect the people (Exod. 13:19 ff.;

131

1:23: "He (the Lord) rages against his foes ... He travels in whirlwind and storm and *clouds* are the dust on His feet".

Cloud and fire as divine messengers are to be found also in Ugaritic texts. *'nn 'ilm* which appear as messengers of Baal[50] are nothing other than the clouds which go before him[51] and serve as attendants similar to that of messengers called *ġlmm* (deputies(?) *CTA* 2, I:13ff), the attendants of Yam. In Exod. 14:19 the pillar of cloud is identified with the messenger of God.[52] On the other hand, in Ugarit we find also messengers of fire, and these are the messengers of Yam, depicted as two flames of fire ... as burnished swords,[53] which calls to mind the cherubim and the flaming sword which guards the Garden of Eden in Gen. 3:24, and the fire which proceeds before God and sets His adversaries aflame in Ps. 97:3.[53a]

It is reasonable to assume that the pillar of fire and the pillar of cloud as independent entities (as sort of angels), developed in fact out of "the fire and the cloud" which are the basic components in descriptions of the Deity, its effulgence and splendour. The fire and the cloud together describe the divine brightness which is set within the cloud, a phenomenon which is formulated in the priestly literature in the Pentateuch: "the glory (*kabod*) of the LORD appeared in the cloud" (Exod. 16:10; compare Num. 17:7; Exod. 40:34–35).[54] The cloud from which

Ps. 105:39), and throw the enemy into panic (Exod. 14:24; Ps. 97:2–3; cf. Hab. 3:5). On the pillar of divine fire cf. Euripides, *The Bacchae*, 1082–83, referring to Dionysus who sets up a pillar of fire between the heavens and earth. See the discussion of Cook, *Zeus*, II, p. 115. Apparently the functions of the pillar of fire and cloud are differently perceived in the different sources in the Bible.

50. *CTA* 3 IV:76, cf. 4 VIII:15 and see the discussion of J.C. de Moor, *The Seasonal Pattern in the Ugaritic Myth of Ba'lu*, 1971, pp. 129 ff.
51. F.M. Cross, *Canaanite Myth and Hebrew Epic*, 1973, pp. 165–166, n. 86; cf. also Th. Mann, *JBL* 90 (1971), pp. 19–24; G.E. Mendenhall, *The Tenth Generation*, 1973, pp. 54 ff., also compared Ugaritic *'nn* to the cloud in the Bible, but for some reason identifies the cloud with *melammu* (=halo, see above) and does not distinguish between the enveloping cloud and the *melammu*, which is the radiance set inside the cloud. As will be shown below, the *melammu* is embodied in the *pd* which Yam wants to take from Baal together with his clouds.
52. See below.
53. *'išt 'ištm ... ḥrb ltšt*, *CTA* 2 I:32, and see on this issue recently P.D. Miller, *The Divine Warrior*, 1973, 31ff.
53a. For divine messengers of fire and destruction in Mesopotamia compare the description of Esarhaddon in battle: 'before him goes the Zu-bird ... behind him the blazing flame (*nablu muštaḥmitu*), restless fire' (Borger [above, n. 43], p. 97, r. 14).
54. Apparently, the fire and radiance which are set within the cloud actually embody the lightning (see Exod. 9:23–24, etc.) and the fire which devours the enemies of the god is lightning, cf. 2 Sam. 22:15 (=Ps. 18:15).

light breaks forth actually appears in the theophanic descriptions of Job: 'scatters his light from the clouds' (37:11), 'makes appear the light of his cloud' (37:15).

In Ugarit also we find this image of cloud and light. *'nn 'ilm* who attend on Baal, as mentioned above, appear next to *pd* (=פד) which is the divine golden brilliance, and 'Yam' who seeks to deprive Baal of his superiority wants to take from him the *pd* with the clouds, similar to what we find in the Babylonian Creation Epic. There Ea removes from Apsu the *melammu* (=halo) and dresses himself with it (*En. Elish* I, 67–68).[55] "Golden cloud" in connection with the radiance which is over gods and warriors (=*melammu*) appears in a clear form in the Homeric Epic. Zeus wraps himself and Hera in a golden cloud, νε-φέλην . . . χρυσείην,[56] and in a similar way Athena crowns Achilles' head with a *golden cloud* from which a gleaming fire shines forth.[57] The brilliant appearance of Achilles caused a great panic among the enemy camp, as we shall see below.

As in Mesopotamia[58] and in Israel,[59] here also the deterring fire and the brightness are imparted from the god to those close to him. Thus, for example, it is related of Diomedes that Athena kindled an inexhaustible fire (see below, n. 68) in his helmet and shield, and also on his head and shoulders (Iliad V, 1–8). We have mentioned above the story of Athena who crowns Achilles with a golden cloud from which fire

---

55. Mendenhall (above, n. 51), pp. 54–55, perceived correctly the significance of *pd*, but wrongly determined that it is equivalent in its meaning to cloud. Likewise, there is no place for the understanding of פסים in כתנת פסים as related to פד, as Mendenhall endeavors to suggest.

56. Iliad XIV, 350–351 (cf. 343–344). In the continuation it is related that from the cloud issued droplets of sparkling dew. Perhaps this can be compared to the Ugaritic portrayal of *[t]l šmm . . . rbb [r]kb 'rpt...nskh kbkbm,* 'sky-dew . . . spray of the Rider of the Clouds . . . that is shed by the stars' (*CTA* 3 II:39–41) and to the description of the daughters of Baal: *pdry bt 'ar . . . tly [bt r]b* who are associated with light (*'ar*) and dew (*tl*) and who serve Baal 'the rider of the clouds' (*CTA* 3:23–24, 5 V:10–11). Compare also Isaiah 26:19: "For Your dew is like the dew of (sparkling) lights" and see U. Cassuto, *The Goddess Anat,* p. 113, (Hebrew). Compare similarly Job 36:28 ff.: "That trickle from the clouds, pour on men in showers . . . Lo, he spreads his light upon him." On the parallelism of "light" and "showers" in this passage see L.R. Fisher, *Ras Shamra parallels,* I, 1972, chap. II. 60, p. 21.

57. Iliad XVIII, 205ff. The fire is described there as smoke billowing up from flaming torches of a besieged city (11.214–297), and cf. the smoke of the fire of God who descends on Mt. Sinai: "the smoke rose like the smoke of a kiln" (Exod. 19:18).

58. See A.L. Oppenheim, *JAOS* 63 (1943), pp. 31ff., and recently E. Cassin, *La splendeur divine,* 1968, pp. 65ff.

59. See M. Weinfeld, כבוד, (above, n. 28), p. 32.

shines forth (Iliad XVIII, 250ff), to which must be added the radiance of Achilles which strikes terror in Hector who flees in panic from the battle (XXII, 136ff.). The Trojans depart from their city without fear because they do not see the gleaming visor of his helmet κόρυθος . . . μέτωπον . . . λαμπομένης (XVI, 69–71). What is unique in these accounts is that the brightness surrounds mainly the head of the warrior and his helmet, what is typical also of the Akkadian *melammu* and of *kabod* of the Bible.[60] But the most common element in the Greek Epic and the Bible is the fire enveloped by cloud,[61] which sheds light on the passage in Exod. 14:24 which we are discussing here.

Even though we found in Exod. 14:24 fire and cloud, there is no doubt that the destructive mission is given over to fire. That which caused panic among the Egyptians was the fire or the divine brightness which blinded the enemy and disabled them from advancing, similar to what we find among the men of Sodom (Gen. 19:11) and to the soldiery which surrounded Elisha (2 Kings 6:18). These were struck with blindness, that is, by the dazzling divine lightning,[62] and were thus halted in their tracks and were unable to carry on with their action. This blinding act is reflected in the inscription of Thutmose III which we quoted above: "The fire was before them, not one found his strength. Not one looked back. Their horses/chariotry were not."

The same phenomenon is reflected in the poetic section, where the diadem *3ḥt*, subjugates the enemy.[63]

A parallel phenomenon is found in the Epic of Gilgamesh. Humbaba prevents his enemies from penetrating the cedar forest by means of rays of *melammu* which were given to him by the gods.[64] Gilgamesh

60. See the studies of Oppenheim and Cassin (above, n. 58) and M. Weinfeld (above, n. 59). The gleaming helmet visor. κόρυθος...μέτωπον...λαμπομένης of Achilles is the tiara or diadem from which shines the brilliance which is the Akkadian *melammu* and the *3ḥt* in Egyptian. See note 27 above. Since the tiara or helmet visor embodies the divine brilliance, he who possesses the helmet or the tiara possesses also the divine glory. When Ea takes to himself the *melammu* of Apsu (see above) he loosens the strap of Apsu's crown, removes it from his head and places it on his own head.
61. On the *kabōd* of the Lord surrounded by cloud see Weinfeld, *Deuteronomy*, pp. 201 f.
62. In the view of Speiser, the source of סנורים is Akkadian *šunûrum* (Shaphel conjugation of *nwr*), which means to illumine with a strong light (*JCS* 6 [1952], p. 89), and see his commentary to *Genesis* (*Anchor Bible*), 1964, p. 139.
63. See above n. 27.
64. So for example, in the dream of Gilgamesh in connection to Humbaba: "The brilliance increased," *šalummatu udannin* (*KUB* IV 12 rev. 15; cf. R.C. Thompson, *The Epic of Gilgamish*, 1930, p. 43, and see recently on the whole matter E. Cassin

and Enkidu, who desire to enter the forest, must know how to get rid of these rays of *melammu*.

The most instructive parallel to Exod. 14:24–25 is found in the Homeric Epic whose literary formulae[65] are most ancient and many of them are rooted in the East. Thus we read in the Iliad XVIII, 220ff., that after Athena crowned the head of Achilles with the cloud from which fire gleamed forth, a great panic gripped the Trojans:

> Amid the Trojans he roused confusion (κυδοι-μός)[66] . . . the hearts of all were moved[67] and the fair-maned horses turned their cars backward . . . and the charioters were stricken with terror when they beheld the inexhausible (ἀκάματος)[68] fire blaze in fearsome wise above the head of the great-souled son of Peleus; for the goddess, flashing-eyed Athene, made it blaze.

As in Exod. 14, so also in Homer we hear of a panic which fell upon the camp when the warriors saw the divine fire, and of the chariots which turn to flee from such. In other places we hear of Zeus himself dispatching fire (lightning) against the horses of the fighters in order to dazzle them. So we read in the Iliad VIII, 133ff., that Zeus thundered and sent[69] gleaming lightning at the feet of the horses and chariotry of Diomedes, and that fire broke out and the horses cringed in fear. In yet another place: 'he thundered aloud from Ida, and sent a

(above, n. 58), pp. 53ff. On this same topic in the Sumerian Epic see recently J. Klein, *S.N. Kramer Anniversary Volume* (*AOAT* 25), 1976, pp. 209–291.

65. See especially M. Parry, *The Making of Homeric Verse*, 1971.

66. Like מהומה in the Bible (see below) so also κυδοιμός appears in a context of battle. In the Homeric Epic we find also a personification of this concept, see Iliad V, 593; XVIII, 535. In these passages κυδοιμός appears as a demon who causes panic and astonishment at the side of "Ενυω, who embodies Ares, the god of war, and "Εριζ, the goddess of contention (apparently these couples reflect the pairs of destroying angels, like Pestilence and Resheph, who accompany the god on his going out to battles [Hab. 3:5]). The "uproar" is bound up in general with "(smite) one another by the sword", see Iliad XVIII, 534, and also XI, 337; Cf. 1 Sam. 14:20: "every man's sword turned against his fellow", and also Zech. 14:13.

67. πᾶσιν ὀρίνθη θυμός (1.223). The basic meaning of ὄρνυμι is "to move", and if so, we have here an idiom which is found also in the Bible, Isa. 7:2: 'their hearts moved (וינע) as trees of the forest'.

68. Compare the account of the burning bush, Exod. 3:2–3: 'and there was a bush all aflame, yet the bush was not being burnt up'.ἀκαματος in Homer always refers to fire.

69. ἀφίημι and also ἵημι, which mean "to set loose" (an arrow), etc. Compare also Iliad I, 48; VIII, 76; and see above, n. 38.

blazing flash[70] amid the host of Acheans and at sight thereof they were seized with wonder and pale fear got hold of all.'[71] On the matter of putting the horses and chariots out of commission which is prominent in Exod. 14:25 and also in Judg. 5:22,[72] the portions which speak of lightning sent forth against the horses and chariots of Hera and Athena are most interesting; there Zeus says[73] that he will disable the horses (will make them stumble $\gamma\upsilon\iota\delta\omega$) and will break the chariots, similar to what we find in Exod. 14:25; Judg. 5:22; Ps. 76:7 (see below).

Moreover, the "looking down from the (pillar) of fire" which we find in Exod. 14:24 also finds its clarification in the Greek mythological descriptions. So, for example, "the blazing eyes" $\delta\sigma\sigma\varepsilon\ \varphi\alpha\varepsilon\iota\nu\dot{\omega}$ of Zeus are none other than the lightning which he dispatches,[74] and to be sure, Hesychius explains "the eyes of Zeus" as the spark of lightning.[75] In this context we find also the "looking down" ($\kappa\alpha\theta\rho\rho\dot{\alpha}\omega$). In the Iliad XI, 337 Zeus looks down from Ida and thus the warriors kill each other (see above, n. 66).

The dazzling glance of the god, which brings about defeat of the enemy, is found also in Mesopotamia, and this feature is especially prominent (as expected, see above) with the god Nergal. Thus we read in the Hymn to Nergal: "Nergal, the warrior of the gods, . . . whose countenance radiates in the heavens (ša ina šamê bunnanûšu ittanabitu), who rides a horse . . . whose glory/radiance is high in the heaven . . . who in battle flashes evilly (ša ina annat lemniš iṣṣanarrara) . . . to whom in battle and war there is no competitor . . . who destroys the enemies . . . and defeats the hostile country."[76]

III. The Annihilating Divine Forces

a. Arrows, lightning, hail and brimstone, which are showered upon the enemy by the thundering God, who resides in a cloud-enveloped splendor, are found in 2 Sam. 22:12ff. (=Ps. 18:11ff.). All these factors

70. σέλας, in contrast to κεραυνός in the previously cited passage, is not necessarily lightning, but rather any fire or flame. But it must be admitted that in connection with thunder, this fire signifies lightning, like fire in the Bible (cf. Ps. 148:8).
71. Iliad VIII, 75ff.
72. See n. 17 above.
73. Iliad VIII, 402ff; 416ff.
74. See Cook, Zeus II, pp. 502ff.
75. See the references and discussion in Cook, loc. cit.
76. See E. Ebeling, AGH, p.116.

cause מהומה, "panic"[77] in the midst of the enemy, an expression which is found also in Exod. 14:24 and in other passages which treat of God's war against his enemies, e.g. Josh. 10:10; Judg. 4:15; 1 Sam. 7:10; Pss. 144:6, 18:15; (cf. also Exod. 23:27; Deut. 2:15; 7:23; Zech. 13:13; Isa. 22:5). It is interesting that in this ancient psalm we find also, as in God's warfare with Egypt, the drying up of the sea:

> *The ocean beds* (אפיקי ים) *were exposed*, the foundations of the world were laid bare (ויגלו) by Your mighty roaring, O Lord, *at the blast of* the breath of Your nostrils[78] (2 Sam. 22:16 = Ps. 18:16).

A similar phenomenon is found in the Song of the Sea: *At the blast of Your nostrils* [78] . . . *the deeps froze in the heart of the sea* (קפאו תהמת בלב ים) (Exod. 15:8).

The revealing of the depths of the sea[79] by means of the breath of God's nostrils, is linked in both passages to the divine war.[80] Indeed this is a general topos in the ancient epic. Thus we find in the Homeric Epic that when Poseidon ventures forth in his chariot to the aid of the Acheans, the earth quakes before him and even the sea parts before him (Iliad XVIII, 17ff.), a description to which one may compare Hab. 3:8–10[81] and also Ps. 77:19–20 (see below).

b. A picture similar to that in 2 Sam. 22 (=Ps. 18) is found in Habakkuk 3. Here also God acts from within splendor and light (see above) while riding in his chariot,[82] shaking the mountains, sending forth a torrent of water and letting loose his arrows in order to trample the nations.

77. On this concept מהומה and its parallel in the Greek Epic (κυδοιμός) and in Mesopotamian literature see above, n. 66.
78. Cf. above, n. 26.
79. Ocean beds and deeps (אפיקי ים, תהמות) which we find in these passages, belong to the ancient epic idiom. Compare El, who dwells "at the sources of rivers in the midst of the ocean beds" (*'m 'il mbk nhrm qrb 'apq thmtm*) (*CTA* 4 IV:21–22), and El who dwells "in the heart of the seas" according to Ezek.28:2. It is interesting that after *qrb 'apq thmtm* in the Ugaritic text we read: *tgly dd 'il* which can be interpreted: She revealed the "torent" of El (cf. זה in the Siloam inscription) that is, Anat arrives unto the source of the seas and the rivers.
80. Other passages speak of roaring גער, (which is bound up with the blowing of wind) at the sea and its drying up, See Is. 50:2; Nahum 1:2; Ps. 104:7; 106:9. S.E. Loewenstamm argued (above, n. 19), p.103ff., that the parting of the Red Sea is based on a theophanic description widespread in the ancient Near East of the god who drives back the waters of sea and river (see e.g. Pss. 66:5–6; 77:17; 114:3f.). Only later was this motif integrated in the national epic of Exodus.
81. See Weinfeld, (above, n. 2) p. 422, n. 7.
82. *Ibid.*

Moshe Weinfeld

c. Ps. 46 – Here God comes to the aid of his people in battle by daybreak (vs.6) with thunder which shakes the earth,[83] breaking the bow and snapping the spear,[84] and consigning of wagons[85] to the flames.[86]

d. Ps. 97 – In this psalm are depicted the dense clouds which surround God and the fire which is his vanguard,[87] burning his foes, together with convulsions of nature (4–5). His righteousness (צדק) and his glory (כבוד) which are revealed to the nations (v. 6), are comparable to the Akkadian *melammu*, the Egyptian *3ḫt*[88] and the Hittite *handan datar* which will be discussed below.

To these needs be added:

Ps. 21:11: "The Lord in anger destroys them; fire consumes them." Ps. 144:6: "Make lightning flash and scatter them; shoot Your arrows and rout them." Isa. 30:30:33 ". . . In raging wrath, in a devouring blaze of fire . . . and with the breath of the Lord burning in it like a stream of sulfure;" and also Ezek. 18:21 and other places where the devouring fire does not appear in a context of Theophany: Gen. 19:24; Num. 11:1, 3; 2 Kings 1:10, 12, 14; Isa. 66:15; Jer. 15:14; 17:4; Joel 3:3; Amos 7:4;[89] Ps. 11:6 and others.

83. "At the sound of His thunder the earth shakes (read תמוט, see BH) " cf. Ps. 68:34: "To Him who rides the ancient highest heavens, who thunders forth with His mighty voice". נתן בקול is more intensive than נתן קול (cf. Gesenius-Kautzsch §119q).

84. Cf. Ps. 76:4: "There He broke the fiery sparks of the bow, and shield and the sword of war." It is, to be sure, tempting to see in "fiery sparks (רשפי)" the subject of the verse, as does Dahood in his commentary, *Psalms, II (Anchor Bible)*, 1968, p. 218; and perhaps it should be read שבר רשפו קשת. But on the other hand, it must be admitted that רשף also means arrow. The breaking of bow and arrows we find also in a curse in the Aramaic treaty from Sefire: ואיך זי תשבר קשתא וחציא אלן (I a 38), and see J.A. Fitzmyer, *The Aramaic Inscriptions of Sefire*, 1967, p. 14.

85. Wagon, עגלה in contrast to chariot, generally serves for transport, however, from the parallels which we bring here it seems that wagon connotes also vehicle in general, cf. Ps. 76:7: "At Your blast, O God of Jacob, horse and chariot (רכב) lay stunned" (נרדם). The original meaning of רדם is the dulling of the senses, cf. Dan. 8:18; 10:9. The Septuagint translates תרדמה by ἔκστασις (Gen. 2:21; 15:12), and most instructive is the fact that תמהון in connection with horse in Zech. 12:4 ("I will strike every horse with dumbfoundedness") is also translated by ἔκστασις.

86. For אש as lightning see e.g. Ps. 148:8; σέλας/φλόξ in Greek indicate fire, flame and lightning at once, and cf. above, n. 70.

87. On pillar of cloud and fire as two messengers of God see above, and cf. Joel 2:2–3: "A day of darkness and gloom, a day of densest cloud . . . In front of him a consuming fire, behind him a devouring flame."

88. See above, n. 27.

89. See P. D. Miller, *CBQ*, 26 (1964), pp. 22 ff. Cf. also "send fire" in the refrain of Amos 1–2.

138

On this topic of the devouring fire we find instructive parallels from the ancient Near Eastern world. In the Gebel Barkal inscription of Thutmose III we read of the fire which destroys the enemy.[90] But a more detailed parallel is to be found in the annals of the Hittite king Muršili. There we read:[91]

> As I marched and arrived at the Lawasa Mountains, the mighty stormgod,[92] my lord, showed his 'divine power'[93] and shot a 'thunderbolt'.[94] My army saw the 'thunderbolt' and the land of Arzawa saw it and the 'thunderbolt' went and struck the land of Arzawa . . .[95]

Friedrich[96] made a comparison between the phenomenon described in the inscription of Gebel Barkal of Thutmose III mentioned above and the Hittite description. We, however, distinguish between the star (meteorite) in the Egyptian account and the *'thunderbolt'* in the Hittite account.[97]

In Assyria also the god wages warfare by means of fire rained down from the heavens upon the foe. Thus we read, for example, in the epic

90. See above, p. 125.
91. A Goetze, *Die Annalen des Mursilis* (*MVAG*, 38), 1933, p. 46:15ff. (KBo III 4 II:15ff).
92. ᵈU NIR GAL (*muwatalliš* in Hittite, meaning "the strong warrior"), see H. Güterbock, *Symbolae Hrozny*, III, 1950, p. 216f.
93. An expression particular to supernatural phenomena of salvation by the gods. See A. Goetze, *Kleinasien*², 1957, pp. 146,148. In my opinion the expression is identical to the Biblical (כבוד) which is comparable to the Akkadian *melammu*, For *kabod* = *melammu* see *Tarbiz* 37 (1968), 116ff; *handandatar* is equivalent to NÍG.SI.SÁ which is Akkadian *mīšarum* (=צדק "righteousness"). In the Bible צדק is parallel to כבוד (see e.g. Ps. 97:6) and is *revealed*, as is כבוד. Cf. e.g. Ps. 98:2: "He has revealed His צדקה in the sight of the Nations" and also Isa. 56:1: "and my righteousness (וצדקתי) shall be revealed". See on this matter Weinfeld, *JAOS* 92 (1972), p. 468.
94. ᵍⁱˢ*kalmišanaš* means splinter of wood for starting a fire and also thunderbolt, see A. Goetze (above n. 91), pp. 212ff., and cf. now 'ṣ *brq* in a description of Baal who sends forth lightning (*Ugaritica* V, ch. III no. 3:4), and see the discussion of M. Pope and J. Tigay, *UF* 3 (1971), p. 124. Cf. on this matter Baal who holds in his right hand "*arz*" (*CTA* 4 VII:41), which is none other than a kind of "lightning-wood". See recently J.C. de Moor, *The Seasonal Pattern in the Ugaritic Myth of Baʿlu*, 1971, p. 167. (On the various figurative images of lightning in the hands of the storm god, and in particular in the hands of Zeus, see Cook, *Zeus*, II, 722ff., and his attempts to explain and sketch lines of historical development). "Lightning-wood" (apparently cedar) can be seen in a most clear form in the hands of Baal on a stone stela from Ugarit (*ANEP*, n. 490).
95. Compare the comprehensive annals, Goetze (above, n. 91); (*KUB* XIV 15 II:2f).
96. J. Friedrich, *OLZ* 39 (1936), pp. 135ff.
97. As demonstrated above, the star which strikes the enemy is a different motif.

Moshe Weinfeld

of Tukulti Ninurta: "The god (Ashur) ignited against the foes the deterring fire ... the god Enlil set the flame in the midst of the foe ..."[98] In the inscription of Ashurbanipal we read of the fire (^{d}GIŠ. BAR)[99] which fell from the heavens[100] and burned the enemy,[101] and of Ishtar, enclothed in fire (^{d}GIŠ. BAR) and charged with splendor (*melammu*), who rains down flames.[102] In the Hymn to Ishtar we read: "Like a light enkindled in the heavens, I am the burning fire showered upon the land of the foe."[103]

The fire which destroys the enemy is reflected in its most prominent form in mythological wars. Thus it is related of Zeus who battles with Typhon that he leaped from Olympus, struck the monster Typhon with his fire, and burned all its heads.[104] In depictions of the struggle with a monster in the ancient Near East, we indeed find the god burning the dragon and its heads.[105]

IV. Stones from the Heavens

In the war of Joshua with the Amorite kings in Joshua 10 we read that the Lord threw the Amorites into panic before the Israelites (vs. 10) and hurled huge stones on them from the sky (vs. 11). In the continuation we learn that these stones were "hailstones." "Hailstone" alongside "flame of devouring fire" which are dispatched by God are mentioned also in Isa. 30:30.

We find a similar account with regard to hail in the Plague stories: ... "the Lord sent thunder and hail, and fire streamed down to the ground, as the Lord rained down hail upon the land of Egypt. The hail was very heavy – fire flashing in the midst of the hail ..." (Exod.

98. E. Ebeling, *Mitteilungen der altorientalische Gesellschaft*, 12 (1938), p. 7:25–26.
99. A divine personification of fire, and so also ^{d}GIBIL.
100. ^{d}GIŠ BAR ultu šamē imqutma.
101. Cf. Job. 1:16: "*Fire of God fell from heaven* and burned the sheep and the boys and consumed them." The divine fire here is of the type of fire of Nergal who destroys the cattle at the outset of battle. See above, p. 136.
102. R.C. Thompson, *Annals of Archaeology and Anthropology* 20 (1933), p. 150, and cf. *CAD* I/J, p. 228, s.v. išātu.
103. See G.A. Reisner, *Sumerisch-babylonishe Hymnen*, 1896, p. 104: 27f and cf. *CAD* I/J, p. 229.
104. Hesiod, *Theogony*, 839ff., and cf. Iliad II, 780ff.
105. *ANEP*, no. 691, and see, nos. 670, 671. Perhaps a reference to the burning or a dragon is to be found in the Ugaritic text dealing with the submission of the serpent by Anat (C.H. Gordon, *Ugaritic Textbook*, no. 1003) where we find tongues (or fire?) licking the heavens and afterwards read: ttrp ym (on the interchange of š and t in Ugaritic cf. ḫtbn, ibid., Glossary, 179, with ḫšbn, ibid., 908).

140

9:23–24). In Job 38:22 it is said of the "hoards of hail" that they are reserved by God "for troublous times, for the day of attack and war." Ezekiel also describes God's war with Gog with "hailstones" (38:22; cf. 13:11, 13), and apparently Ben Sira as well makes use of this concept in his description of Joshua's above-mentioned battle (46:6).[106] We find similar phenomena in the Assyrian account of warfare. In the Hymn to Ishkur (=Hadad/Adad/Baal)[107] we read that Enlil commanded his son Ishkur to take *small and large stones* (cf. Josh. 10:11) and to hurl them down upon the despised rebellious earth. In the inscription of the third campaign of Sargon, king of Assyria, we read that Adad the warrior let forth his voice against the enemy, "with *torrentuous* cloud and *stones of the heavens* he destroyed the survivors."[108] In other places we hear of Adad who showers fire (*aban išāti*)[109] and burning stones (*anqullu/aqqullu*) against the foes.[110] In Greece also, Zeus hurls stones.[111]

In this context must be mentioned as well the raining down of burning coals by God in Psalms 11:6,[112] and in a curse found in the treaty of Asarhaddon with the vassals.[113]

V. The Thunder

Thunder is considered the voice of God in Israel (1 Sam. 2:10; 2 Sam. 22:14 = Ps. 18:14; 29:3; 77:19; 104:7; Job. 37:4–5; 40:9), as well as in Mesopotamia and in Greece.[114] At times thunder itself, without the accompaniment of lightning, rain and hail, constitutes a bad omen for the enemy, as in 1 Sam. 7:10: ". . . the Lord thundered mightily against

---

106. In the text: ויענהו אל עליון באבני ...
107. See S.N. Kramer, *ANET*³, pp. 577ff.
108. *ina urpat riḫṣi u aban šamê uqatti rēḫa*, F. Thureau-Dangin, *Une relation de la huitième campagne de Sargon (TCL* 3), 1912, p. 24:147.
109. For *išātu* see above, nn. 102–103. Contrariwise, אבני אש in Ezek. 28:14 are precious stones, and in my opinion are equivalent in meaning to *'abn ṣrp* in Ugaritic and Aramaic, which are stones (metal) purged in fire. On *'abn ṣrp* see J. Greenfield, *JCS* 21 (1967), pp. 91–92.
110. See *CAD* s.v. *anqullu, aqqulu.*
111. Cook, *Zeus*, vol. III, pp. 482ff.
112. פחים here is an alternate form of פחם; cf. כנים as against כנם and see regarding this orthography A.B. Ehrlich, *Die Psalmen*, 1905, and the Midrash to Psalms (ed. Buber) on this verse: וימטר וגו' גומרין דאשא כמה דאת אמר: פחם לגחלים ועצים לאש' (מש' כו, כא) and subsequently are quoted other places in which the Lord wreaks judgement by fire.
113. D.J. Wiseman, *The Vassal Treaties of Esarhaddon*, (=*Iraq* 20[1958]), p. 69:533.
114. See above. On ancient Greece see Cook, *Zeus*, II, 827ff.

Moshe Weinfeld

the Philistines that day. He threw them into confusion, and they were routed by Israel." In the Homeric Epic we find Zeus's thunder as an omen of distress (Iliad VIII, 170–171; Odyssey XXI, 413).

Most instructive for the understanding of thunder in the Bible is the passage from Psalm 77:19: "Your thunder rumbled like wheels (קול רעמך בגלגל), lightning lit up the world; the earth quaked and trembled." The wheels are the wheels of the divine chariot, as can be learned from Ezekiel. There the גלגל mentioned in the description of the chariot in chapter 10 (vss. 2, 6, 13) is parallel to the אופן in the description of the chariot in chapters 1–3, and the prophet even explicitly states: "It was these אופנים that I had heard called the גלגל " (10:13).[115] We hear of the wheels, גלגלין, of the throne of glory in Daniel 7:9, and as demonstrated elsewhere,[116] in Israel, as among the peoples of the ancient Near East, the concept that the god rides in a chariot was prevalent (see for example Hab. 3:8, and compare 1 Chron. 28:18 "model of the chariot"), a concept which lies at the base of the description of the chariot in Ezekiel and of "Ma'aseh Merkabah" in the later literature.[117]

Accordingly, " thunder rumbling like wheels" is none other than the sound of God's chariot, and Ezekiel also speaks of the "sound of the wheels" and "a great roaring sound" in his describing the movement of the chariot (3:13). The simile of thunder as the sound of the wheel of the god's chariot, which shakes heaven and earth, is found in a description of the chariot of the god Ninurta, considered also to be the god of thunder and rain.[118] In the literary work called Angim-dimma we read of the god Ninurta: "When you step into your chariot, whose creaking is a pleasant sound, the heaven and earth tremble."[119]

115. For our purposes it is unimportant whether the description in Ezek. 10 is later than the description in chapter 1, see recently on this matter D.J. Halperin, *VT* 26 (1977), pp. 129ff.
116. M. Weinfeld, (above, n. 2).
117. The origin of the mysteries of *Ma'aseh Merkabah* is most ancient and is found already in Sumerian Hymns from the 20th century BCE. Cf. Weinfeld, *B.Z. Luria Anniversary Volume*, 1980, p. 241 (Hebrew).
118. Th. Jacobsen, *Toward the Image of Tammuz*, 1970, p. 32.
119. giš gigir-za gù du₁₀ ur₅ša₄ -bi gìr gub-ba-zu an ki tuk₄-e-bi, in the Akkadian version: *narkabtaka ana rigim ramīmiša ina alakika šamû u erṣetim inuššu* (J.C. Cooper,*The Return of Ninurta to Nippur* [*Analecta Orientalia* 52], 1978, pp. 70–71 (lines 83–34). On the roar of the chariot cf. the Hymn of Išme-Dagan to the chariot of Enlil (M. Civil, *JAOS* 88 [1968], p. 5): giš gigir nim-gim gír-gír-re [gù-de]-ur₅-sa₄-bi dug-ga-am, "the chariot shines like lightning, the sound of its roar is a pleasure" (1.70); see also bilingual dedicatory inscription of Nebuchadnezar I: *tabū rigim ramīmišu*, 'Adad's pleasant roaring noise' (F.M.T. Böhl, *Bib Or* 7 [1950], p. 43:10), and also in connection with Baal in Ugarit (Aqhat I 44–46): *bl ṭl bl rbb . . . bl ṭbn ql b'l* "No dew, no rain . . . no pleasantness of Baal's voice" and see

142

A. Ehrlich[120] understood Ps. 77:19 as presenting the lightning illumining and announcing the coming of the thunder of the chariot and is thus a sort of advance-deputy before the chariot who proclaims the coming of the Lord. An image such as this, to be sure, lies behind the descriptions of the storm god in ancient Mesopotamia. Thus we read in the hymn to Ishkur cited above: "Let lightning, your vizier, go before you." On thunder as the noise of the chariot of the god we hear in ancient Greece. Cook[121] already commented on the fact that even though we do not find this image explicitly in the epic, it appears frequently in other examples of Greek literature and art and was permeated with worship practices and myths during a long period of time.

VI. The Hiding Cloud

In Exod. 14 we read of the cloud which comes between the Egyptians and the Israelites and thus saves Israel: "The angel of God, who had been going ahead of the Israelite army, now moved and followed behind them; and the *pillar of cloud* shifted from in front of them and took up a place behind them, and it came between the army of the Egyptians and the Army of Israel. Thus there was the cloud with the darkness, ויאר את הלילה, *it lit up* (?) the night, so that the one could not come near the other all through the night" (Exod. 14:19–20).

This passage is complex and is not sufficiently clear. In the opinion of many, two sources have been integrated in verse 19: One source (J) according to which the pillar of cloud functioned as a barrier between the Israelites and the Egyptians, and a second source (E) according to which the messenger of God fulfills this function.[122] However, as demonstrated above,[123] the cloud is considered to be God's deputy or messenger, and it is thus possible that the redactor of this section intentionally identified the cloud with the messenger.

on this last sentence M. Held, *JANES* 6 (1974) p. 108, n. 8. Cf. also Enuma Elish VII: 119–120: *Addu . . . tāba rigmašu* ("Adad . . . his pleasant voice"). The pleasant sound of the wheels of the chariot became the song of the wheels in Jewish Merkabah literature, see I. Gruenwald, *Tarbiz* 35 (1967), p. 274 (Hebrew).

120. A.B. Ehrlich, *Die Psalmen,* 1905, *ad loc.*
121. Cook, *Zeus,* II, pp. 830ff.
122. According to the Classic critical analysis the verses dealing with a messenger of God who accompanies the Israelites on their way to the land of Israel belong to the source E, cf. Exod. 23:20; Num. 20:16.
123. p. 131f.

Greater difficulties exist in verse 20 in the interpretation of the words: "Thus there was the cloud with the darkness, and it lit up the night." The Aramaic Targums and Rabbinic Midrashim (see *Mechilta de Rabbi Yishamel* on this verse) interpret that there was cloud and darkness for the Egyptians, and light for the Israelites. But this is not the plain meaning of the passage. Apparently ויאר את הלילה is an explanatory note which is brought here under the influence of 13:21: "... and a pillar of fire by night, to give them light."[124] The main intent of the verse is to say that the cloud and the darkness[125] prevented the Egyptians from attacking the Israelites during the whole night, an intent which is confirmed by Josh. 24:7: "He put darkness between you and the Egyptians."

On this matter we find an instructive Hittite parallel. In the Annals of Muršili[126] we read: "The mighty Storm-god (^{d}U.NIR.GAL)[127] [my lord, helped me] (*piran ḫuwaiš*) and it continually rained all night, [so that the enemy] did not see the fire of the camp. But when it became light ... the mighty Storm-god ... and in the morning suddenly a cloud (IMBARU)[128] [arose; ...] 'put' cloud(s), and as long as [...] the cloud [went] before my troops".[129]

The text is not continuous but its meaning is clear: The cloud hid the army from the enemy, similar to what is related of the Israelite camp. In another military context Muršili relates: "the storm-god called out

---

124. See S.E. Loewenstamm (above, n. 19), p. 119. The Septuagint translates ויאר את הלילה καὶ διῆλθεν ἡ νύξ "and the night passed" which was accepted by Ehrlich in *Randglossen*. E. Speiser (*JAOS* 80 [1960], pp. 198–200) takes ויאר as Hiphil conjugation of אור, as if the angel of God adjured the night to increase its darkness, an explanation which seems far-fetched. Nevertheless, there is something to this interpretation, especially in view of Judg. 5:23, where the angel of God curses the inhabitants of Meroz.

125. ויהי הענן והחשך can be interpreted "and the cloud and the darkness endured/rose up". The verb היה means also to stand and rise up. Cf. 33:9: "For He spoke, and it was (ויהי), He commanded, and it endured (ויעמד)" and also the interchangings of "there was none (לא היה כמוהו) like him among all the kings of Judah after him" (2 Kings 18:5, Hezekiah) with "nor did any like him arise (לא קם כמוהו) after him" (2 Kings 23:25, Josiah). On קום, "arise" in the meaning of היה, "be" in Samaritan Aramaic see Z. Ben-Haim, *Samaritan Hebrew and Aramaic*, III, Book 2, 1967, p. 143 (Hebrew), and there are given additional references for the interchange of היה/עמד in the Bible.

126. A. Goetze (above, n. 91), p. 194:11ff. (*KUB* XIV 20). I wish to express my thanks to Professor H.G. Güterbock for his kind assistance in connection with this parallel.

127. See note 92.

128. For *imbaru* = cloud fog, see *CAD* I/J, pp. 107ff, cf. e.g. *naspiḫi kīma imbari, tebī kīma nalši,* "scatter like a cloud, arise (=vanish) like dew," *JRAS* 1927, 537:12, and cf. to this expression: "your goodness is like morning cloud כענן בקר like dew so early gone" (Hosea 6:4, and also 13:3).

129. Geotze reconstructs here "und machte sie (the army) unsichtbar."

for Hašammeliš and he held me hidden".[130] The god Hašammeliš appears in two Hittite lists of gods at the side of Star (MUL) and Night (*ispanza*-GE$_6$-*anza*)[131] which is appropriate to the context.[132]

Similar phenomena are to be found in the Homeric Epic, except that there it is spoken of the concealment of solitary warriors since the waging of battle was individual. Thus, for example, Priam, the king of Troy, was concealed in a *thick cloud* [133] by Aphrodite when he was in mortal danger (Iliad III, 381); Idaeus was enfolded in the darkness of night (V, 23); Apollo conceals Hector in thick cloud (XX, 444–445) and likewise conceals Agenor (XXI 549, 597). Similarly we find in Virgil's Aeneid that Venus shrouded Aeneas in a *thick mantle of cloud* (I, 411ff.).

In the course of the discussion of this topic it must be indicated that as in the Bible, also in the Greek Epic the cloud is a sort of camouflage for the divinity himself. Zeus is called κελαινεφής, "the one (cloaked) in a black cloud" (Iliad II, 412; VI, 267; XV, 46; XXI, 520 – cf. XV, 192 – etc.), similar to the God of Israel who "dwells in concealment" (Ps. 91:1) "abides in a mist" (שכן בערפל), (1 Kings 8:12).[134] Just as the God of Israel's dwelling is covered in cloud (Exd. 40:34; cf. 1 Kings 8:11) so also Zeus and Hera spread thick cloud upon their riding animals (Iliad V, 776;[135] VIII, 50); and just as the God of Israel is seen in the *cloud of incense* (ענן הקטרת) [136] over the ark-cover (Lev. 16:2, 13), it is related of Zeus that he is enveloped in a cloud of incense (Iliad XV, 153).

130. A Goetze, (above, n. 91), p. 126 (*KBO* IV, 4 Rs. iii:33–35), see P.H.J. Houwink Ten Cate, *JNES* 25(1966), pp. 172, 180, (Fragment VIII).
131. *KBo* IV 13+VI 32f; *KBo* XIX 128, vi:18ff., both of these are lists of fifteen gods. On these lists see H. Otten, *Ein hethitisches Festritual* (*KBo* XIX 128) (*STBoT* 13), 1971, p. 46.
132. A. Goetze (*Kleinasien* ², 1957, p. 134, n. 11) brings up the assumption that the role of Hašammeliš was to close and to open the gates of heaven.
133. ἠέρι πολλῇ, an epic formula (cf. Iliad XX, 444; XXI 549, 597) whose parallel in Hebrew is possible to find in עב הענן "thick cloud" in Exod. 19:9; cf. also ענן כבד "heavy cloud" in vs. 16 (for the latter compare *imbaru kabtu* = IM DUGUD, *CT* 17, 19, 1:27).
134. Cf. Ps. 18:12: "He made darkness His screen; dark thunderheads, dense clouds of the sky, were His pavilion around about Him"; 97:2 "Dense clouds are around Him"; Job. 22:14: "Clouds hide him, he cannot see."
135. Hera arrives with her horses to a place where two rivers join their streams (V, 773f) which is to compare to El who dwells 'at the sources of the rivers', see note 79.
136. The *imbaru* (see n. 128) is also used with *qatāru* "to smoke". See *CAD* I/J, p. 108.

VII. "Stand still, O sun, at Gibeon, O moon, in the Valley of Aijalon!" (Josh. 10:12)

To the phenomenon reflected in this verse different explanations have been given. Several scholars have tried to understand the event against the background of eclipses of the heavenly bodies which occured in Joshua's time.[137] Others understood the words of Joshua as a request or demand for the creation of a special heavenly constellation which would bring an auspicious omen.[138] B. Margulis[139] finds here a reordering of nature which accompanies the appearance of God in battle. However, it seems that in all these explanations there is some attempt to read into one text what is not there. The phrase "until a nation had taken vengeance" (vs. 13) is organically connected with the poetic section under discussion in verse 12. The organic connection of the sentence עד יקם גוי אויביו in vs. 13 with the poetic section in vs. 12[140] explains the phenomenon. The sun needs stop from its course in order to lengthen, as it were, the day and thus enable the fighting nation to take vengeance on its foes. And so the prose narrator explains: "Thus the sun halted in midheaven, and did not haste to set for almost a whole day" (vs. 13). God, who does battle here for Israel (vs. 14; cf. Exod. 14:14), performs an extraordinary act in order that the warriors will be able to complete their victory while it is still day. A parallel phenomenon is found in the battle of Saul with the Philistines (1 Sam. 14), except that there the extraordinary act is on the part of the people following the swearing in of the leader: "For Saul had laid an oath upon the troops: 'Cursed be the man who eats any food before night falls and I take revenge on my enemies' " (v. 24). In both instances comes a declaration on the part of the fighting leader whose goal is "vengeance

---

137. See recently J.F.A. Sawyer, *PEQ* 1972, pp. 139–146.
138. This is the assumption of W.L. Holladay (*JBL* 87 [1968], pp. 155–178), who claims that Joshua adjures the sun and the moon to stand in equilibrium one against the other, which signifies "a good omen" according to Babylonian belief.
139. B.Margulis, "The Ancient Israelite Epic and the Origin of Biblical Astrology," חקר ועיון במדעי היהדות, Haifa, 1976, pp. 166ff. According to his assumption, דם is to be understood here as from *da'amu* in Akkadian, meaning "the darkness", and in the original tradition it was related to the darkening of the heavenly light bearers in the war of God against the Cannanites, a motif which belongs to the theophanic accounts of the day of the Lord. In order to uphold this assumption Margulis is forced to say that the narrator who placed the command in the mouth of Joshua and explained the event as the halting of the sun from its course, acted out of his non-understanding the original motif (p.169). This accompanying assumption is in my opinion the weak point of his thesis.
140. On the place of this poetic section in its present context see B. Margulis, *ibid.*, p. 165.

on the enemy",[141] except that Joshua turns to God requesting that He lengthen the day, whereas Saul turns to the people requesting that they prolong their fighting by abstaining from eating. These two phenomena, which are essential for the successful outcome of the battle: prolonging the day (by God) on the one hand, and prolonging the battle (by the people) on the other, are also found in ancient Greek literature. In the Homeric Epic we hear Agamemnon declaring in battle:

> Zeus, most glorious, most great, the one of the dark
> clouds, that dwellest in the heaven, grant that the sun
> set not, neither darkness come upon us, until I have
> cast down in headlong ruin the hall of Priam . . .
> burned with consuming fire.[142] (Iliad II, 412–415)

Comparable to this declaration we find in ancient Greece an oath of warriors not to return home before vanquishing the enemy (Strabo 279c; Polybius XII, 6b), which calls to mind the oath of Saul in 1 Sam. 14 and also the obligation of the tribes in the war over the concubine at Gibeah (Judg. 20:8).

Apparently, also in the account of the divine warfare in Habakkuk 3 we find a phenomenon identical to that in Joshua 10: "Sun (and) moon stand in his high abode,[143] as Your arrows fly in brightness, Your flashing spear in brilliance. You tread the earth in rage, You trample nations in fury" (Hab. 3:11–12).

---

141. עד יקם גוי אויביו is not grammatically difficult, and thus it is unnecessary to emendate to יקם מגוי, as assumes F.Delitsch, *Die Lese-und Schreibfehler im Alten Testament,*1920, p.6. Cf. e.g. לא תקם ולא תטר את בני עמך (Lev. 19:18). Only the Niph'al of נקם necessitates מ, as in 1 Sam. 14:24, and also Judg. 16:28; Jer. 46:10; Esther 8:13.

142. Cf. Ps. 140:11: "May He drop fire down upon them באש יפילם and they be cast into pits, never to rise again." See also Ps. 73:18–19: "make them fall through blandishments, (הפלתם למשואות). How suddenly are they ruined . . .".

143. Read זבלה, see Tur-Sinai, פשוטו של מקרא, 1967, III, pp. 522–523.

THE AMMONITE OPPRESSION OF THE TRIBES OF GAD AND REUBEN: MISSING VERSES FROM 1 SAMUEL 11 FOUND IN 4QSAMUELª

FRANK MOORE CROSS

Harvard University

1. The manuscript 4QSamª is one of three important manuscripts of Samuel found in Cave 4, Qumrân. It came to light in excavations of Cave 4 carried out under the direction of the late Roland de Vaux in September, 1952. Some twenty-seven fragments of the second and third columns were recovered in the excavation, and in the summer of 1953 were cleaned and assembled by the writer and given immediate, preliminary publication.[1] Subsequently thousands of fragments of the same manuscript 4QSamª, were found in a lot of materials purchased from the Taʿâmireh tribesmen. It is the most fully preserved of the biblical scrolls from Cave 4 and will in published form consist of more than twenty-five plates.

   The manuscript is inscribed in an elegant Late Hasmonaean bookhand of *circa* 50 B.C.E.[2] Its text is non-Massoretic, standing much closer to the *Vorlage* of the Old Greek translation – the "Septuagint" – than to our received text, and has notable affinities with the so-called Proto-Lucianic text.[3] Among its other striking

1. F.M. Cross, "A New Qumran Biblical Fragment Related to the Original Hebrew Underlying the Septuagint," *BASOR* 132 (1953), pp. 15–26; for corrigenda, see F.M. Cross, "The Oldest Manuscripts from Qumran," *JBL* 74 (1955), p. 165, n. 40. The latter is reprinted in F.M. Cross and S. Talmon (eds.), *Qumran and the History of the Biblical Text*, Cambridge, Mass., 1975, p. 109, n. 40.
2. On the date of this manuscript, see F.M. Cross, "The Development of the Jewish Scripts," G. Ernest Wright (ed.), *The Bible and the Ancient Near East*, New York, 1961, pp. 133–202.
3. The Lucianic witnesses in Samuel include the minuscules bboc₂e₂; less trustworthy but useful are minuscules gi and the quotations of Theodoret and Chrysostom. The early stratum of the Lucianic text, untouched by the "Lucianic" activity of the fourth century with its heavy Hexaplaric content, has its witnesses in the Old Latin and in the Greek text of Samuel used by Josephus.

features are numerous agreements between the text of 4QSam[a] and the Chronicler's text; examination of these agreements has shown that the Chronicler in composing his work used a form of the Deuteronomistic History which was by no means identical with the later *textus receptus*, but which was ancestral to the 4QSamuel manuscript.[4] There are intimate relations also between the text of 4QSam[a] and the biblical text used by Josephus. These have recently been investigated in an important study by Eugene Ulrich.[5] There can now be little doubt that Josephus' Greek text of Samuel was also allied with 4QSam[a], over against the Massoretic Text.

4QSam[a] in column 10, lines 6–9 [see plate], contains a long addition, introducing chapter 11 or 1 Samuel, replacing the familiar *crux* ויהי כמחריש at the end of chapter 10 (1 Sam. 10:27b).

5. [זה וי]בזוהו ולא הביאו לו מנחה   [   ] *vacat*

6. [ונ]חֹש מלך בני עֹמון הוא לחץ את בני גד ואת בני ראובן בחזקה ונקר להם כֹ[ול]

7. [עין ימין ונתן אי]מה ופחד] על [י]שראל ולוא נשאר איש בבני ישראל אשר בעֹ[בר]

8. [הירדן אש]רֹ לֹ[וא נ]קֹרֹ לו נח]ש מלך] בני עֹמֹון כל עין ימין רֹק שבעת אלפים איש

     ויהי כמו חדש ויעל נחש העמוני ויחן על יביש [גלעד]

9. [נסו מפני] בֹני עמון ויבאו אל [י]בֹש גלעד ויאמרו כל אנשי יבש אל נחש

     [*vac*]at

10. [העמוני כרת] לֹ[נו ברית ונעבדך ויאמר א]לֹ[יה]ֹם נחש [העמוני בזאת] אכֹרת לכם]

6. [And Na]hash, king of the Ammonites, sorely oppressed the children of Gad and the children of Reuben, and he gouged out a[ll] their

7. right eyes and struck ter[ror and dread] in Israel. There was not left one among the children of Israel bey[ond]

8. [Jordan who]se right eye was no[t go]uged out by Naha[sh king] of the children of [A]mmon; except seven thousand men

9. [fled from] the children of Ammon and entered [J]abesh-Gilead. / About a month later, Nahash the Ammonite went up and besieged Jabesh-[Gilead]/ and all the men of Jabesh said to Nahash

10. [the Ammonite, "Make] with [us a covenant and we shall become

4. See F.M. Cross, "The History of the Biblical Text in the Light of Discoveries in the Judaean Desert," *HTR* 57 (1964), pp. 281–299, especially 292–297 (reprinted in Cross-Talmon (above, n. 1), pp. 177–195); and W. Lemke, "The Synoptic Problem in the Chronicler's History," *HTR* 58 (1965), pp. 349–363.

5. *The Qumran Text of Samuel and Josephus* (*HSM* 19), Missoula, 1978.

Frank M. Cross

your subjects."] Nahash [the Ammonite said t]o [th]em, ["After
this fashion will] I make [a covenant with you] . . .

In copying the text the scribe committed a haplography owing to
homoioteleuton in line 9, his eye skipping from יבש גלעד to יביש גלעד; the
scribe himself corrected the error by copying in above the point of the
omission: ויהי כמו חדש ויעל נחש העמוני ויחן על יביש [גלעד]. There is no doubt
that the supra linear correction is *prima manu*. It is clear also that the
scribe corrected his omission before he completed the line. There is a
blank at the end of line 9 separating נחש and העמוני (beginning of line
10) which is otherwise inexplicable. Moreover, the last words of the
correction curved down into this blank (יביש [גלעד]).

Most of the restorations I have made impose themselves and require
no comment. Several are problematical. In line 7 we are inclined to
read: תפל עליהם אימה [מה ופחד] אין ונתן comparing Exod. 15:16
על ישראל ויהוה נתן את־פחדו על־כל־הגוים and such expressions as ופחד (1 Chr. 14: 17),
and פחדכם ומוראכם יתן יהוה אלהיכם על־פני כל־הארץ (Deut. 11:25).[6] In line 9
we have restored [נסו מפני] בני עמון comparing such passages as 1 Kings
20:30; 2 Sam. 10:18; 23:11; etc.[7] On the restoration בע[בר הירדן אש]ר,
see below. Finally in line 10 we must restore [העמוני] at the beginning of
the line. Considerations of space require a word of this length; the
restoration follows the reading of the Old Greek (τὸν ’Αμμανείτην) in
accord with the general tendency of 4QSam[a].

We have read the sequence of verbs in lines 6 and 7; לחץ . . . ונקֹר . . .
ונתֹן , the perfect followed by infinitives absolute. This usage is well
known and is especially frequent in the seventh–sixth centuries B.C.E.
in the Bible and in Hebrew inscriptions. For example, in Jer. 32:44 we
read: שדות בכסף יקנו וכתוב בספר וחתום והעד עדים. Again we read in the
Yabneh-yam inscription in line 5 *way-yákol wě-’asōm* "and he took
measure and stored," and again in line 6/7 *kāl ‘abdak . . . wě-’asōm*
"thy servant measured . . . and stored."[8]

6. This restoration is not my initial reading, but was pressed on me by several scholars
   in slightly variant forms, among them Kyle McCarter, Alexander Rofé, and Moshe
   Greenberg, each independently. After some reluctance I have accepted it. It can be
   squeezed into the lacuna, but it makes a tight fit.
7. One might restore as an alternative [נצלו מיד]. Compare ואציל . . . מיד . . . הלחצים
   (1 Sam 10:18).
8. Cf. F.M. Cross, "Epigraphic Notes on Hebrew Documents of the Eighth-Sixth
   Centuries B.C.: II The Murabba‘ât Papyrus and the Letter Found Near Yabneh-
   yam," *BASOR* 165 (1962), pp. 42–45, especially p. 44, no. 43. Dennis Pardee,
   "The Judicial Plea from Mesad Hashavyahu (Yavneh-Yam)," *Maarav* 1 (1978),
   pp. 42f. has recently argued that *w'sm* is actually the (anomalous) perfect with *waw*
   consecutive (see below, n. 9), rejecting an "unmarked infinitive absolute." Pardee

150

Of course, it is possible to read a sequence of perfects with *waw* conjunctive. This usage is abnormal, not to say anomalous, in early Hebrew, but not rare in the received biblical text.[9] In 2 Kings 18:4, for example, we read:

הוא הסיר את־הבמות ושבר את־המצבות יכרת את־האשרה וכתת ...

However, many such sequences are probably mispointed in the Massoretic Text. In view of the frequency of the use of the infinitive absolute in sequences following imperfect or perfect verbs in Hebrew inscriptions of Pre-Exilic date, I am inclined to read in Kings:

הוא הסיר את־הבמות ושבר את־המצבות וכרת את־האשרה וכתת ...

That is to say, the sequences of perfects with conjunctive *waw* in the Deuteronomistic history are suspect and may be the result of unconscious "modernizing." This is especially the case when early orthographies (ō of the infinitive absolute unmarked by a *mater lectionis*) survived into the period when infinitives absolutes were ordinarily written *plene*, and the "anomalous" perfects with *waw*-conjunctive had ceased to be anomalous. In any case I prefer to read infinitive absolutes in the 4QSam[a] text.

2. There can be no doubt that Josephus had the missing account before him in his Bible. We note the following indirect quotations.[10]

ויהי כמו חדש] *Μηνὶ δ' ὕστερον Antiquities* 6.5,1 (§68) ("However, a month later") Cf. *Καὶ ἐγενήθη ὡς μετὰ μῆνα* in G[BO+].

נחש מלך בני עמון] *Ναάσην . . . τὸν τῶν Ἀμμανιτῶν βασιλέα Antiq.* 6.5,1 (§68) ("Naas, king of the Ammanites")

הוא לחץ את בני גד ואת בני ראובן בחזקה] *οὗτος γὰρ πολλὰ κακὰ τοὺς πέραν τοῦ Ἰορδάνου ποταμοῦ κατῳκημένους τῶν Ἰουδαίων διατίθησι Antiq.* 6.5,1 (§68) ("For this one dealt very harshly with the Jews who had settled beyond the river Jordan")

here, however, goes against the whole weight of the orthographic practice in pre-Exilic Hebrew. Internal *matres lectionis* are excessively rare, and *waw* as a marker for ō<ā makes its first appearance in the third century B.C.E. Indeed, it is still not regularly used in 4QSam[b]. See D.N. Freedman, "The Massoretic Text and the Qumran Scrolls: A Study in Orthography," in Cross-Talmon (above, n. 1), pp. 206f.

9. See A. Rubinstein, "The Anomalous Perfect with Waw-Conjunctive in Biblical Hebrew," *Biblica* 44 (1963), pp. 62–69 who reviews the discussions of Driver, Mayer Lambert, and Stade.

10. Quotations follow the *LCL* edition: H. St. J. Thackeray and Ralph Marcus (eds.) *Josephus*, V, Cambridge, Mass., 1934.

Frank M. Cross

Josephus' πέραν τοῦ Ἰορδάνου confirms the restoration [בע]בר הירדן in lines 7/8. The expression πολλὰ κακὰ . . . διατίθησι reflecting הוא בחזקה . . . לחץ may be compared usefully with Josephus' paraphrase of Judg. 4:3 בחזקה . . . הוא לחץ with ἐκάκωσε δεινῶς *Antiq.* 5.5,1 (§199).[11] [ונקר להם כול עין ימין] τοὺς δεξιοὺς ὀφθαλμοὺς ἐξέκοπτεν *Antiq.* 6.5,1 (§69) ("he cut out the right eyes . . ."). [ולוא נשאר איש בבני ישראל אשר בעבר הירדן] καὶ ὁ μὲν τῶν Ἀμμανιτῶν βασιλεὺς ταῦτ' ἐργασάμενος τοὺς πέραν τοῦ Ἰορδάνου *Antiq.* 6.5,1 (§71) ("Having then so dealt with the people beyond Jordan, the king of the Ammanites . . .")

This is, of course, not close to the Hebrew text save for the reference to "those beyond Jordan," i.e., the Gadites and Reubenites whose eyes have been mutilated. However, it notes the accomplishment of his campaign against the south, and provides the transition to the attack in the north against the Gileadites of Jabesh.

[ויעל נחש העמוני ויחן על יביש גלעד] ἐπὶ τοὺς Γαλαδηνοὺς λεγομένους ἐπεστράτευσε καὶ στρατοπεδευσάμενος πρὸς . . . Ἰαβίς *Antiq.* 6.5,1 (§71) ("against those called Galadenians he [then] mounted an expedition and pitched his camp at . . . Iabis.")

Josephus' account in *Antiquities* thus follows the overall sequence and content of the text of 4QSam[a]. He begins with a reference to Nahash the king of the Ammonites, the title used in the initial reference in 4QSam[a] but missing in the account in the Massoretic Text. He then describes the harsh oppression of the "Jews of Beyond Jordan." He specifies the treatment of the defeated Israelites: the putting out of the right eye. Finally he records that when this program of war and maiming was completed, the Ammonite king then took up arms against the Gileadites and pitched his camp at Jabesh-Gilead.

There are also some odd changes and omissions in Josephus' rendering of the account. While he mentions that all who surrendered were maimed and rendered incapable of revolt, he omits reference to the escape of the seven thousand men of Israel and their flight north to Jabesh. This would appear to be an important element for the historian, motivating Nahash's campaign to the far north, beyond the borders traditionally claimed by Ammon.[12] The most surprising feature of Josephus' account is his placement of the expression "However, a

---

11. I owe this observation to Professor Emanuel Tov.
12. Judges 11:13 records the Ammonite claim to all lands north to the river Jabbok, some twenty-five km. south of Jabesh. Cf. Josh. 12:2–5; Deut. 3:12–17; Josh. 13:8–28. Compare the expression "land of Gad and Gilead" in 1 Sam. 13:7.

month later" (*Μηνὶ δ' ὕστερον*) in his lead sentence rather than at the transition where it is found in 4QSam[a]. It may be an arbitrary reshaping of the narrative. More likely, I believe, the Hebrew *Vorlage* of Josephus' text had suffered corruption, a so-called vertical dittography, the phrase ויהי כמו חדש being anticipated and incorrectly inserted at the beginning of the paragraph. In this case both the first and second paragraphs of the chapter would have begun with ויהי כמו חדש. The loss of a paragraph in a text of this kind would have resulted from a simple haplography owing to homoioteleuton, the commonest of all scribal errors.

At the same time it must be said that the omission of the passage by parablepsis, the scribe's eye jumping from one paragraph break to another (both with Nahash as subject) is an entirely adequate explanation of the loss of the paragraph. There is no reason to suppose that the passage was suppressed in the course of transmission; most losses in textual transmission arise from unconscious scribal lapses.

3.   The expression נחש מלך בני עמון in line 6 warrants further comment. In the received text the king of the Ammonites is introduced in his first appearance in Samuel simply as "Nahash the Ammonite" (נחש העמוני). This is most extraordinary. In the books of Samuel and Kings there is otherwise an invariable pattern: when a reigning king of a foreign nation is introduced for the first time, his full or official title is given, "So-and-so, king of So-and-so." Some twenty examples are found:

אכיש מלך גת (1 Sam. 3:3); תלמי מלך גשור (1 Sam. 15:8); אגג מלך עמלק (1 Sam. 21:11); חירם מלך צור (2 Sam. 5:11); הדדעזר בן־רחוב מלך צובה (2 Sam. 8:3); תעי מלך חמת (2 Sam. 8:9); שישק מלך מצרים (1 Kings 14:25); בן־הדד מלך ארם (1 Kings 15:18); בן־הדד בן־טברמן בן־חזיון מלך ארם (Ben-Hadad II, 2 Kings 6:24); אתבעל מלך צדנים (1 Kings 16:31); מישע מלך מואב (2 Kings 3:4); חזאל מלך ארם (2 Kings 8:28); תגלת פלאסר מלך אשור (2 Kings 15:29); רצין מלך ארם (2 Kings 15:37); שלמנאסר מלך אשור (2 Kings 17:3); מרדך בלאדן בן בלאדן מלך בבל (2 Kings 18:13); סנחריב מלך אשור (2 Kings 18:13); פרעה נכה מלך מצרים (2 Kings 23:29); נבכדנאצר מלך בבל (2 Kings 24:1); אויל מרדך מלך בבל (2 Kings 25:27).[13]

---

13.   See also 1 Kings 11:14 הדד האדמי מזרע המלך of a pretender to the crown. Ben Hadad III is named first in association with his father Hazael "king of Aram" (2 Kings 13:3), his accession in 2 Kings 13:24. In 2 Sam. 10:1 we read: "the king of the children of Ammon (1 Chr. 19:1 Nahash king of the children of Ammon) died and Hanun his son ruled in his stead."

Thus the Massoretic omission of Nahash's full title is the sole exception to the practice. Indeed, the pattern obtains for the whole of the Deuteronomistic History, violated in the Massoretic Text only here.[14] However, if the paragraph from 4QSam[a] is original, Nahash is introduced first as "king of the children of Ammon," his full title, precisely in accord with the historian unvarying practice. This is a very strong argument for the originality of the passage in Samuel and its subsequent loss by simple scribal error.

We should add that the Ammonite king's official title was in fact מלך בני עמון. We know it from the royal Ammonite inscription from Tell Sirān;[15] and, of course, in a later passage in 1 Sam. 12:12 the Deuteronomistic editor himself used the full title נחש מלך בני עמון.[16]

The paragraph is introduced by a *casus pendens*, elegant and frequent in biblical Hebrew and in early West Semitic inscriptions. In line 6 the words הוא לחץ את בני גד ואת בני ראובן בחזקה constitute a Deuteronomistic cliché. Compare, e.g., והוא לחץ את בני ישראל בחזקה in Judg. 4:3, and וחזאל מלך ארם לחץ את ישראל in 2 Kings 3:22. One can argue that such usage points to the authenticity of the paragraph's style; on the other hand such clichés are easily imitated.

In line 8 "seven thousand" are said to have escaped. This number is a round number, not unlike the "seven thousand" who were left who had not "bowed the knee to Ba'al" (1 Kings 19:18; cf. 2 Kings 24:15), and is appropriate to the style of such a narrative. Even in a monumental inscription – that of Mesha' – we find round numbers: "the seven

---

14. In Deuteronomy, Joshua, and Judges, among the many kings introduced, the only variations found are references to nameless kings who are designated only "king of Edom," "king of Moab," and "king of Ai" (Judg. 8:14, 29) in the Conquest, "king of children of Ammon" in the Jephthah story (Judg. 11:12, 14, 28), and the pair of kings זבח וצלמנע מלכי מדין (Judg. 8:5, 12). None of these instances really violate the Deuteronomist's style. The one genuinely problematic case is that of אדני בזק בבזק (Judg. 1:5; cf. 1:6, 7). Who is this man with the strange name/title who has mutilated seventy kings, and in turn is brought to Jerusalem, and dies there? His name, of course, has been explained as a corruption of אדני־צדק who is introduced in standard fashion in Josh 10:1, 3 as "king of Jerusalem." The association with Jerusalem, the suspicious sequence בזק בבזק, and, indeed the violation of the pattern – unless he be the king of Jerusalem earlier mentioned – tend to support this view. Moreover, the tradition of his mutilating seventy kings can hardly be fitted to a lesser figure than the king of a major city-state claiming these many vassals.

15. Professor Jeffrey Tigay reminded me of this reading – to my considerable embarrassment for having overlooked it. Cf. F.M. Cross, "Notes on the Ammonite Inscription from Tell Sīrān," *BASOR* 212 (1973), especially p. 15 where the title on the Tell Sīrān Bottle and the 'Amman Theatre Inscription is discussed.

16. Cf. Jer. 40:14 (בעליס מלך בני עמון).

thousand" put under the ban by Mesha', and the "forty years" Israel controlled Madeba.[17]

The episode recorded in lines 6–9 also presumes the traditional conflict between Ammon and the Israelite inhabitants of Transjordan who lived between the rivers Arnon and Jabbok, territory claimed by both. Yet in Judg. 10:6–11, 40, the account is very different and there are few verbal contacts. Nor is there any direct dependence on the narrative of Judg. 21:1–25 in which the origin of the close ties between Jabesh-Gilead and Benjamin are graphically described. Yet both passages in Judges provide a backdrop and lend plausibility to the 4QSam^a account of the Ammonite conquest of the south, the flight of survivors to Jabesh-Gilead, and Saul's readiness to succour the besieged city and its refugees. In other words, the full narrative fits into the presuppositions of the Deuteronomistic history, and echoes its language, while going beyond any information that can be culled directly from parallel passages in Judges.

The phrase ויהי כמו חדש is clearly an archaic expression. In early Hebrew orthography כמו חדש would have been written simple כמחדש.[18] The Massoretic reading כמחריש, always an awkward and troublesome reading, is a corruption of כמו חדש, surviving as a remnant of the lost paragraph. In the older orthography the corruption is merely כמחדש read כמחרש; involving the perennial confusion of *dalet* and *reš*. Indeed, since the first important studies of the text of Samuel, כמחריש has been recognized as a corruption (Thenius, Wellhausen, S.R. Driver). A like archaism is found in Gen. 38:24: ויהי כמשלש חדשים (Samaritan ויהי כמשלשת חדשים), "and it came to pass after about three months." Here too we should read *kamō-* (*šĕlōšet ḥodāšīm*) preserved in an older orthography, later misunderstood.

ויהי כמו חדש as a temporal phrase, providing the transition between the escape of the seven thousand men of Gad and Reuben and the expedition of Nahash north against the city which provided them sanctuary, makes perfect sense. It fits exquisitely in the text preserved in 4QSam^a. On the contrary we do not expect a temporal connection of short duration between the events of king-making at Mizpah recorded in chapter 10 and the battle of Jabesh. The victory of Saul in the

---

17. Mesha' Inscription lines 16 and 8. Professor Moshe Weinfeld called my attention to the Mesha' parallel.
18. *km* is often written with its following noun without the word divider in Ugaritic, and no doubt also was so written in Hebrew.

Ammonite wars indeed motivates the establishment of the kingship in Gilgal, an independent narrative.[19] In any case the reading ויהי כמו חדש found in 4QSam[a], and in Greek translation in Josephus and the Septuagint is the superior reading: an unexpected and transparently archaic expression which at the same time makes sense in the context.

4. The initial reaction of some textual critics to the extra paragraph will be to propose that it is a late addition, a haggadic expansion of post-biblical times – despite the evidence accumulated above. I must say that I can detect no evidence of the extra paragraph originating in a haggadic addition. The text gives rather flat historical facts. There is no edifying element, no theological bias, no "theory" developed, no hortatory or parenetic motif, in short no "haggadic" element that I perceive. Moreover, while the loss of a full three lines of text in the textual family ancestral to the Massoretic Text is remarkable, it is by no means unparalleled. The traditional text of Samuel has long been recognized as uniquely defective and haplographic, and the Qumrân manuscripts of Samuel have confirmed this judgment. In the immediate environment of this passage are two well known extended haplographies in the Massoretic Text: at 1 Sam. 10: 1 and at 1 Sam. 14: 24.[20] Nor can the agreement of 4QSam[a] and the Greek Bible used by Josephus[21] be treated lightly or given an *ad hoc* explanation. The evidence collected by Ulrich demonstrates that the Greek text used by Josephus has a systematic relationship to 4QSam[a]. There are other demonstrable haplographies in the Massoretic Text where 4QSam[a] and Josephus share the original (full) reading in passages controlled by G or the Chronicler, or where the original reading survives only in 4QSam[a] and Josephus.[22]

One may argue too that the episode without the paragraph omitted in the *textus receptus* is incomplete on its own. Why the harsh, even vengeful punishment – eye gouging – insisted upon by Nahash when asked for surrender terms by the men of Jabesh? It is not enough that they give the city over to him and become his subjects or slaves? Why

19. Here we touch upon problems of the sources of Saul's rise to kingship, problems too complex to discuss in detail here. See most recently, P.K. McCarter, *1 Samuel* (Anchor Bible), New York, 1980, pp. 205–207 and references.
20. See J. Wellhausen, *Der Text der Bücher Samuelis*, Göttingen, 1871, pp. 72f., 90f.
21. On the Greek Bible of Josephus, see Ulrich (above, n. 5) pp. 223–255 ("Josephus' *Vorlage*").
22. An example of two lines' length is found at 2 Sam 24:16+. (See Ulrich [above, n. 5] pp. 156f.). On agreements between Josephus and 4QSam[a] against all other witnesses, see Ulrich, pp. 165–173.

must Nahash heap an ignominy? Mutilation is the standard treatment meted out to rebels, or to arch-enemies of long standing, or to violators of treaty.[23] It is not the treatment due a newly conquered city lying outside the conqueror's domain. The commentators have had no satisfactory explanation.[24]

The prior episode found now in 4QSam[a] gives a wholly unexpected but sensible answer. Jabesh-Gilead was, in fact, giving shelter to ancient adversaries from Nahash's own domain (as Ammon viewed it), to ancestral enemies from Reuben and Gad who occupied Ammonite soil as the kings of Ammon had always claimed. In this light the requirement of mutilation as a treaty term is understandable and (so to speak) appropriate in the light of ancient practice.

All in all, the text as preserved in 4QSam[a] makes excellent narrative and historical sense,[25] as part of the Deuteronomistic work. Nahash, leading a resurgent Ammonite nation, reconquered land, long claimed and fought over with the tribes of Reuben and Gad, punishing his old enemies with a systematic policy of mutilation. The Deuteronomistic sources may exaggerate its extent – from a modern historian's point of view – but the account is not different from other traditional accounts used by the editor in writing his history. Those Israelite warriors who survived defeat at the hands of Nahash's forces, some seven thousand in number, fled and found haven to the north of the traditional border (at the river Jabbok) in the Gileadite city of Jabesh, a city allied to

---

23. Examples of blinding rebels or arch foes include the putting out of the eyes of Samson by the Philistines (Judg. 16:21), and of Zedekiah by the Babylonians (2 Kings 25:7; Jer. 39:7 = 52:11). Moshe Weinfeld has called my attention to Num. 16:14 where there may be a similar reference, and to Zech. 11:17 where the right eye of the "foolish shepherd" is threatened. Blinding as a punishment for rebels is also documented in the Assyrian annals. Hayim Tadmor has cited to me the extraordinary list of techniques of maiming, mutilating, dismembering, including putting out of eyes, found in the records of Aššur-nāsir-apli II [see for example, D.D. Luckenbill, *Ancient Records of Assyria and Babylonia*, Chicago, 1926, I, p. 445–480]. Mutilation or dismemberment for violation of treaty is also well documented in biblical and extra-biblical sources. See F.M. Cross, *Canaanite Myth and Hebrew Epic*, Cambridge and London, 1976, p. 266 and references.
24. Commentators have resorted to the explanation that the proposed mutilation is a mark of the sheer barbarity of Nahash, this "wild man of the desert." Such an *ad hoc* explanation is less than satisfactory, however, in view of what we know of Ammon's high level of development at this period; and it ill accords with the later report of David's cordial relationship with this same Nahash (2 Sam. 10:1f.).
25. This is not to say that all the details in the narrative are in fact historical. Rather I mean to say that the material conforms to the Deuteronomistic historiographic technique: its style, language, and treatment of sources.

Benjamin and Saul. A month or so after their escape, Nahash determined to subjugate Jabesh for sheltering his escaped "subjects." This is the motivation – or pretext – for striking far north of his claimed boundaries, and so he marched to the city and besieged it. When asked for terms for a treaty by the men of Jabesh, he insisted on the same harsh punishment that he had inflicted on Gad and Reuben, the gouging out of the right eye of all able-bodied men. But he thereby overreached and sealed his own fate. Saul of Benjamin, enraged by news of the affair, and seized by the Spirit, rallied elements of the Western tribes, and leading the Israelite militia, crossed Jordan and "slaughtered the Ammonites until the heat of the day." His great victory brought, or extended, the recognition of his kingship throughout Israel, and was celebrated with feasting at Gilgal.[26]

26. A first draft of this paper was read to a seminar of the Fellows of the Institute of Advanced Studies, the Hebrew University of Jerusalem in 1979. I learned much in the discussion with my colleagues, and the present form of my paper owes much to their suggestions and corrections. Some detailed acknowledgements are found in the notes above. But my debt is greater than these specific credits can indicate. I am particularly grateful to Professor Emanuel Tov for several long discussions of the problems of this text.

EZEKIEL'S VISION:
LITERARY AND ICONOGRAPHIC ASPECTS

MOSHE GREENBERG

The Hebrew University of Jerusalem

The following attempt at comprehending the vision of Ezekiel 1 is based on the working assumption that all the components of the celestial vehicle enumerated in the MT and all versions belong to its original conception, and that the description, though occasionally obscure and defective, follows an organic and intelligible pattern. Recent commentators do not make this assumption; on the contrary, thoroughly typical of their approach is Wevers' affirmation: "One thing is certain: the original text was much shorter – and much clearer!"[1] As a result, they simplify the vision in various ways – most notable being the elimination of the wheels.[2] But simplicity is nowhere a feature of Ezekiel's thought, symbolism, or expression; it is a highly dubious principle of exegesis of his book. All the elements of the vision of the divine vehicle have a foundation in ancient Israelite and West-Asian imagery; it remained for Ezekiel to combine them in his characteristically baroque manner.

Reduced to its essentials, this is the narrative of the vision of the divine majesty: While the prophet stood beside the River Chebar one summer day, a tempestuous north wind (not unusual for the season) bore toward him an incandescent cloud, encircled by a radiance. As the cloud neared, four glowing creatures became visible in its lower part, like humans in their erect posture, their leg(s) and hands, but having four faces and four wings. The creatures, disposed perhaps in a

---

1. W. Wevers, *Ezekiel (The Century Bible: New Series)*, London, 1969, p. 40.
2. W. Zimmerli, *Ezekiel (Biblischer Kommentar-Altes Testament* 18. 1–2), Neukirchen-Vluyn, 1955–1969; W. Eichrodt, *Ezekiel (Old Testament Library)*, Philadelphia, 1969, [Trans. by C. Quin from the German *Der Prophet Hesekiel (Das Alte Testament Deutsch* 22. 1–2), Göttingen, 1965–1966.].

square, were joined at their wing tips to one another. They gave the impression of a unity as they moved, and, facing in every direction, always went in the direction they faced, without needing to turn. Amidst them was a flashing, torch-like apparition. The prophet noted that below each creature, and alongside it, was a high, complex wheel, rimmed with eyes.

The prophet's gaze moved from the creatures upward, to take in a dazzling, ice-like expanse borne above their heads and outspread wings. As they neared, he grew aware of the terrific noise made by their wings in motion.

Then the wings slackened and the apparition came to a halt; the prophet heard a sound from above the expanse that drew his gaze further upward. He saw a sapphire throne standing upon the expanse, upon which an effulgent human figure sat, all brilliant and fiery, and encased by a rainbow-like radiance. Only then did the prophet realize that what he beheld was the majesty of God; at that, he fell awestruck to the ground.

The order of the narrative represents the order of the prophet's perception: first sights, then (as the apparition drew near) sounds; first the lower part of the vision (that nearer the earth), then the upper; first the motion of the apparition, then its halting. Verses 4 and 27f. form an envelope for the entire narration: the undifferentiated, uncomprehended pyrotechnics in the cloud of vs. 4 are by stages put in their proper place and finally deciphered in vss. 27f. There is an evident aim to reconstitute for the reader the movement of the prophet's senses and the course of his understanding of the experience. However, at places, the good order of the narrative breaks down (e.g., vss. 8b–12); this is most likely due to the accumulation of doublets in our text from which G is freer. Moreover, the depiction of the various motions of the apparition – the ability of the creatures to change direction without turning, the unity of wheels and creatures in ascending and traveling – seems to be based on observation of more complex motions than the mere approach of the apparition involved in this vision; it would seem therefore that at least here later information gotten otherwise from elsewhere has been incorporated in chap. 1 (cf. 3:12f.; 10:15, 19; 11:22).

Recent commentators (e.g., Fohrer, Zimmerli[3]), go far in reducing the narrative to a hypothetical original terseness, but their criteria for

---

3. G. Fohrer-K. Galling, *Ezekiel (Handbuch zum Alten Testament)*, Tübingen, 1955; Zimmerli (above, n. 2).

originality are arbitrary (e.g., the assumption of a system in the present vacillation of gender in reference to the creatures) and the resultant creativity ascribed to copyists or the (assumed) circle of the prophet's disciples is excessive. There is little reason to suppose that the original conformed exactly and consistently to any single norm.

The frequent use of comparison in the description is an aspect of the desire to be faithful and exact. The most frequent expression of comparison is $k^emar'e$, lit. "like the appearance of"; this does not signify a reservation with respect to looks but with respect to substantial identity. When Manoah's wife describes the man of God who appeared to her as one "whose appearance was like the appearance of an angel, very dreadful" (Judg. 13:6), she intends the comparison to convey exactly the looks of the man, though in substance he was no angel. Similarly here, "something with (lit. like) the appearance of torches" (vs. 13), "of sapphire-stone" (vs. 26), "of a human being" (vs. 26), signifies that what was seen looked just like that with which it is compared; however, the use of (and of k^ecen and d^emut also) signifies unwillingness to commit oneself to the substantial identity of the seen with the compared: it looked like torches, sapphire, a human being, but that is not to say that torches, sapphire, and a human being were actually there. The use of these buffer terms indicates that the prophet wished to prevent his reader from assuming the substantial identity of the seen with the compared, although there is no ground for supposing he had any reservations respecting the precision and adequacy of these comparisons.[4]

To such a vision, as the first element in the account of a prophet's call, few analogies exist. Moses was prepared for his commissioning by a miniature theophany in a burning bush (Exod. 3). Isaiah 6 describes a vision of the celestial court that has points in common with Ezekiel – winged attendants on God, who is seated on his throne – and that is generally taken to be an account of Isaiah's call. (A similar scene in Micaiah's vision, 1 Kings 22:19ff., is not part of a prophet's call.) But in these, God is neither seen nor said to have come to the prophet from heaven, or from afar; he is statically there throughout the vision. On the other hand, God is commonly pictured as riding in heaven

---

4. For exact parallels, note the dream report of a Hittite queen: "In a dream something like my father has risen again, alive" (A. L. Oppenheim, *The Interpretation of Dreams in the Ancient Near East*, Philadelphia, 1956, p. 204a) and of the Egyptian king Merneptah: "Then his majesty saw in a dream as if it were the image of Ptah standing in the presence of the Pharaoh" (*ibid.*, p. 251a).

(Ps. 68:5, 34; 104:3) and coming as judge or king to save his faithful or punish the wicked (Deut. 33:26; Isa. 19:1).

The characteristics of the divine manifestation in Ezekiel – the storm, the cloud, lightning, fire and radiance – are regularly associated with awesome public theophanies; cf. Exod. 19; Deut. 33:2f.; Judg. 5:4f.; Isa. 63:19; Nahum 1:3ff.; Hab. 3:8–15. The closest analogue to Ezekiel's private vision occurs in Ps. 18 (2 Sam. 22), vss. 8–14: in answer to the psalmist's cry for help,

> The earth quaked and trembled . . .
> [God] tilted the sky and came down
> Thick clouds were under his feet
> He rode on a cherub and flew
> He appeared (var. soared) on wings of wind
> He put darkness about him as his pavilion . . .
> In the radiance before him fiery coals burned
> YHWH thundered from heaven
> The Most High gave forth his voice

The image of God as a rider in the sky with the clouds his chariot is common to the Bible, Ugaritic texts (who describe Baal thus), and Mesopotamia (see below); in itself it is not remarkable.

The closest approach to an ancient illustration of the divine figure seen by Ezekiel is *ANEP* 536, a colored ceramic from Ashur depicting the god Ashur floating amidst rain clouds accompanying his army and shooting with a bow. "The flying god . . . is . . . unusually beautiful . . . The head and uppermost part of the body seem to have been white, and the wing feathers yellow and blue . . . a double yellow ring [is] in his flaming nimbus. Great flaming streamers fly back from him . . . "[5]

The appearance of the majesty of YHWH in cloud and fire (but without visible shape) is a feature of the wilderness narratives of the Pentateuch. The majesty appears in order to support the leader(s) of Israel when they are set upon by the people in the episodes of the manna (Exod. 16:10), the spies (Num. 14:10), and Korah's rebellion (Num. 16:19). On Mount Sinai (Exod. 24:17), on the tabernacle on the day of its inauguration (40:34f.), at the inauguration of the priests (Lev. 9:23), as later at the inauguration of Solomon's temple (I Kings 8:11), the majesty appeared to signify God's proximity to and presence

---

5. W. Andrae, *Colored Ceramics from Assur*, London, 1925, p. 27.

amidst his people. Moses' plea to see God's majesty (Exod. 33:18) indicates that its revelation to an individual is the highest token of divine favor. The combination of features in the divine appearance to Ezekiel thus expressed powerfully and in concentrated form God's support of and intimate presence with the prophet.

The search for analogues to the structure of the apparition and particularly to its creatures gives the same result: individual elements are found in the tradition, but the ensemble is unique. God is said to ride "on the wings of the wind" (Ps. 18:11) – of which the "cherub" (*ibid.*) is a personification; elsewhere God is said to be "the one enthroned on the cherubs" (1 Sam. 4:4; 2 Sam. 6:2; Ps. 99:1). The shape of the cherubs is not indicted by the sources; they were winged – and their two wings covered the ark in the holy of holies (1 Kings 6:27); between the outspread wings of the cherubs on the desert ark God "met" Moses to speak to him. Combining this data, it seems that the cherubs were celestial winged bearers of God, upon which he was imagined as sitting enthroned; the sanctuary images were but representations of them. Modern scholars have compared the winged sphinxes and other composite quadrupeds that are pictured as supporting (or constituting) the thrones of ancient near eastern kings (e.g., Ahiram, *ANEP* 458, cf. 332) or serving as pedestals for gods (*ANEP* 534). On the other hand, the cherub of Ezek. 28:14ff. – a denizen of God's garden, Eden – appears to be human in form; moreover, the "creatures" of ch. 1 are, in Ezek. 10, named cherubs – and they are here said to have a human shape. That Ezekiel did not immediately identify the creatures as cherubs indicates that some difference marked them off from the sanctuary images, but it was not so great as to exclude his later identifying them as such. What the difference was eludes us.

Like the seraphs seen by Isaiah, Ezekiel's creatures had several sets of wings; the seraphs had one set more, in order to cover their faces, since they hovered above the divine throne and might otherwise gaze upon God, while Ezekiel's creatures were positioned below and looked straight ahead.

The composite nature of Ezekiel's creatures accords entirely with Mesopotamian and Syrian iconography. Composite deities and mythical beings are common in Egypt and Mesopotamia; an Egyptologist explains the symbolism as follows: " . . . whenever possible they combined [the zoo- and anthropomorphic] ideas in a composite whole. Thus the anthropomorphized gods were given a human body, but only seldom a human head, this being mostly replaced by that of the animal in whose form the god originally used to appear." "Also for the purposes of art . . . some material personification of deities was indispensable, and if the human bodies of gods kept the heads of various animals, this was certainly largely because it was a convenient means of distinguishing their various personalities. That the head of the animal should in some way recall the qualities attributed to the god is only natural."[6] In Mesopotamia, it is the lesser divinities (e.g. guardian genii and demons) that are portrayed in composite form, including winged quadrupeds with human faces (*ANEP* 644–666); here too we are to understand the combination to express attributes conjoined in these imaginary creatures.

Multiplication of faces in the manner of Ezekiel's creatures is, however, extremely rare. Two tiny bronzes from Old Babylonian times show a god and a goddess each with four identical human faces; the impression is of all-observing potency.[7] Janus (=two)-faced gods are more common (not usually great gods; e.g. an attendant upon Ea, *ANEP* 685, 693), a variation of which is the following late description of the Phoenician El (=Kronos) in Sanchuniathon: "[The god Taautos] . . . devised for Kronos, as insignia of royalty, four eyes, before and behind [of which two were awake] and two quietly closed; and on his shoulders four wings, of which two were as flying and two as folded. The symbolic meaning was: Kronos could see when he was sleeping, and being awake he slept; similarly for the wings – that being at rest he flew and when flying he rested."[8] However, the symbolism of four distinct faces must be different, and for that we have no analogues.[9] To get at its meaning we must note the figurative use of each of the animals whose faces are found on the head of Ezekiel's creatures.

6. J. Cerný, *Ancient Egyptian Religion*, London, 1952, pp. 29, 40.
7. A. Parrot, *Sumer*, London, 1960, p. 285, Figs. 351–352.
8. Eusebius, *Praeparatio Evangelica* I, 10. 36–37; (eds.) J. Sirinelli and E. des Places (*Sources Chrétiennes* 206) I, Paris, 1974, pp. 200–201.
9. The evidence collected by S. Landersdorfer (*Der BAAΛ ΤΕΤΡΑΜΟΡΦΟΣ und die Kerube des Ezechiel* [*Studien zur Geschichte und Kulture des Altertums* 9/3], Paderborn, 1918), contrary to his intent, all bears on four-faced deities whose faces are the same; cf. the rationale given by Basil of Caesarea (4th c.) for the four-faced idol allegedly made by Manasseh (J. Migne, *Patrologia graeca*, CXXI, p. 228; cited by Landersdorfer, p. 7), "so that one might pray to the images from whatever side one approached" (=*Deut. Rabba* 2.20) – a rationale based necessarily on the idol's showing the same aspect every way. Compare also *Pesikta de-Rab Kahana's* depiction of God's revelation at Sinai as like "a statue with faces on every side so that though a thousand persons looked at it, it would be looking back at each one" (Piska 12.25).

The lion is proverbially the fiercest of beasts (Num. 23:24; 24:9; Judg. 14:18; 2 Sam. 1:23; 17:10, etc.); the eagle, the most imposing (swift, high-flying) of birds (Deut. 28:49; 2 Sam. 1:23; Jer. 48:40; Job 39:27; Lam. 4:19); the bull, the most valued of domestic animals (for plowing, breeding: Prov. 14:4; Job 21:10; cf. Exod. 21:37). Man, of course, rules them all (Gen. 1:28; Ps. 8:7). In ancient near eastern art, these animals, or combinations of them, served as bearers or pedestals of images of gods (*ANEP* 472–474, 486, 830 [lion]; 500, 501, 531, 835 [bull]; 534 [winged lion with bull's head]; 537 [number of gods mounted on different animals]). An eagle-headed human figure, with two sets of wings supports overhead a symbol of a god (*ANEP* 855). Horned bull-men hold a stool on which the divine symbol rests (*ANEP* 653; cf. 645). In Ezekiel's vision, the traditional bearers of God are portrayed as combining the attributes of the "lords" of animate creation in their countenances, the dominant shape of their bodies being human. A midrash to Exod. 15:1 gives as fine an interpretation of the creatures as can be found: "Four kinds of proud beings were created in the world: the proudest of all – man; of birds – the eagle; of domestic animals – the bull; of wild animals – the lion; and all of them are stationed beneath the chariot of the Holy One . . . " (*Exod. Rabba* 23.13). That is to say, the most lordly of creatures are merely the bearers of the Lord of lords.

Two concepts appear to be fused in the apparition, taken as a whole: that of a deity borne by mythical beings and that of a throne-chariot. For the two-level image of a deity enthroned and riding on an animal or a mythical being (cf. YHWH's epithet "the one enthroned on the cherubs") good Mesopotamian and west-Asiatic representations exist, to help us envision the general aspect of this apparition. A goddess enthroned and borne by a lion is a commonplace.[10] Particularly suited for comparison owing to its complexity is the depiction in the Maltai procession scene (*ANEP* 537). The second divine figure from the left is a goddess seated on a throne resting on a high pedestal whose side shows a griffin, a scorpion man with upraised wings, and a (worshiping?) human figure. Between the pedestal and the seat of the throne appear three views of a king, between which are two composite creatures (upper half human, lower, animal) whose upraised hands support

---

10. M. Jastrow, *Bildermappe zur Religion Babyloniens und Assyriens* (plates), Giessen, 1912, No. 204; C.L. Woolley, *Charchemish*, II, London, 1914–52, Pl. B 19a; E. Strommenger, *5000 Years of the Art of Mesopotamia*, London, 1964, Pl. 179, 2nd row, right.

the seat of the throne. The whole rides on the back of a walking lion. Related to this image is *ANEP* 653, in which "bull men" support a legged "table" on which the symbol of a god rests; or *ANEP* 855 in which a four-winged "eagle-man" with upraised arms supports a divine symbol over his head.

This straightforward concept is complicated by the wheels in Ezekiel's apparition. Four wheels belong to a cart (cf. the bases of the temple lavers, 1 Kings 7:27–37, with four wheels and decorated by figures of cherubs, lions, and cattle!) or a primitive type of chariot (*ANEP* 303). Comparable is the early disk-wheeled divine chariot with a god standing in it shown in *ANEP* 689 (the chariot is drawn by a winged lion, on whose back a goddess rides). Now, YHWH is said to ride in a chariot too (Hab. 3:8; Isa. 66:15), and it appears that Ezekiel's vision combined the two modes of locomotion. In the vision of divine judgment in Dan. 7:9 God's throne is also equipped with wheels. What facilitated the combination was the actuality of throne-chariots in near eastern antiquity. A scene from an 8th c. Assyrian palace relief depicts servants carrying an empty wheeled throne: the visible wheel is quite large, and, interestingly, though spoked, has a thick rim made up of three concentric bands (cf. our "wheel within a wheel"); above and alongside the wheel, beside and below the seat of the throne, is the figure of a harnessed, striding horse. This vehicle has a yoke shaft for draft animals.[11] In the vision of the divine judgment of Daniel 7, God's throne is again equipped with wheels (vs. 9). Perhaps even more apt is the high-backed, wheeled sedan chair of Assurnasirpal II depicted on the as yet unpublished bronze gates found at Balawat;[12] a device normally borne by bearers may thus be furnished with wheels.

The dominance of four in the apparition must be connected with the division of the world into four parts (Isa. 11:12, "the four corners [*kanfot*] of the earth") or the circle of the horizon into four directions ("seaward [west] and forward [east] and north and south", Gen. 13:14; 28:14). It symbolizes the divine capacity to control the whole world – to see all, to be everywhere effortlessly. These traditional Israelite notions can only have been enforced by contact with the Babylonians whose literature was full of "the four regions of the world" (*kibrāt arba'i* or *erbetti*) and "the four winds" (*šār*

11. G. Parrot and C. Chipiez, *Histoire de l'art dans l'antiquité*, II, *Chaldée et Assyrie*, Paris, 1884, fig. 23, p. 100.
12. E. Sollberger, *Iraq* 36 (1974), p. 232. I owe this reference to Dr. Irene Winter.

erbetti) – a notion that occurs in the Bible from the Babylonian period onward (Jer. 49:36; Ezek. 37:9, etc.).

The eyes with which the rims of the wheels were inlaid may be supposed to signify the constant divine watchfulness. Compare what was adduced above concerning the many eyes of Kronos, and the many "eyestones" (Akk.*abanīnu*) that adorned the tiaras of the Assyrian gods' statues.[13]

If a basis in some earthly reality exists for the fiery appearance moving about among the creatures, it escapes us. As a sign of divine fierceness – the fire will figure in the punishment of Jerusalem in 10:2 – it recalls the poetic allusions to fire "going" or "consuming" before God (Ps. 50:3; 97:3), and to the "coals of fire" that "burned out of the radiance that was in front of him" (Ps. 18:13f.). Here the position of the fire has changed in accord with the disposition of the entire apparition vertically (throne beneath which are the ministers-bearers) instead of horizontally (chariot ahead of which are draft-animals and outrunners).

Virtually every component of Ezekiel's vision can thus be derived from Israelite tradition supplemented by neighboring iconography – none of the above cited elements of which need have been outside the range of a learned and curious Israelite. Indeed the divine imagery of the Bible resembles closely that of the surrounding (especially west-Asiatic) cultures; it was not in imagery but in divine attributes and manner of worship that Israel's religion differed. The specific combinations (such as the four distinct faces) and the ensemble remain unexampled for us – and for the prophet. There is no ground for asserting that he saw an exact earthly equivalent anywhere, or for supposing he followed a Babylonian prototype.

As a captive domiciled away from the great centers of culture, Ezekiel had little opportunity to study the art-work of Babylonian temples or witness the grand processions of the gods. Even in the event that he had, he was so concerned over the purity of Israel's worship (see esp. chaps. 8–11) that he would hardly have imported into it images drawn directly from the pagan sphere.[14] The whole tenor of the description bespeaks wonder at the unfamiliar. Here was a new revelation of the suite of Israel's God, displaying, indeed, enough of the

13. S. Parpola, *Letters from Assyrian Scholars to the Kings Esarhaddon and Assurbanipal* (*AOAT* 5/I), Pt. 1, Neukirchen-Vluyn, 1970, no. 276, obv. 11: "26 'eyestones' for the tiara of the god Nabu"; cf. E. Vogt, *Biblica* 59 (1978), pp. 93–96.
14. H. Schmidt, "Kerubenthron und Lade", in *Eucharisterion* (H. Gunkel Festschrift I, *FRLANT* 19), Göttingen, 1923, p. 124, n. 2.

known to be in the end identifiable (vs. 28), yet so unfamiliar as to exclude for the prophet the possibility that he was merely drawing out of the stock of memory a sight that his heart craved.[15]

15. After submitting this article, I was apprized, by courtesy of Professor Moshe Weinfeld, of O. Keel's *Jahwe-Visionen und Siegelkunst*, Stuttgart, 1977, in which an extensive iconographic study is made of (among others) the visions of Ezek. 1 and 10. Keel's textual basis is essentially the commentary of Zimmerli (see nn. 1 and 2, pp. 125, 126), which entails several departures from the composition of the vision as given in the received text. The most important of these is the treatment of the wheels as a secondary accretion to the supposed original text. Keel's work is a rich collection of pictorial material well worth earnest consideration. My conclusions often enough coincide with his, but perhaps as often diverge, owing in part to my reluctance to disregard elements presently found in the vision.

AN EARLY TECHNIQUE OF AGGADIC EXEGESIS

Jeffrey H. Tigay

University of Pennsylvania

Nothing has been more characteristic of Jewish intellectual endeavor than the explication of Scripture. The typical expression of new ideas is not the systematic philosophical treatise but the Biblical commentary, showing that these ideas had been deposited, if not necessarily revealed, in the Biblical text long ago. Not only the midrashim and medieval Bible commentaries, but even Philo's treatises, Maimonides' *Guide*, and the Kabbalists' *Zohar* took the form of Biblical exegesis. The reason for this was expressed concisely by Fritz A. Rothschild:

> . . . the view that the Bible contains God's message to man has led to ever new interpretations, since it constantly forced believing readers to reconcile the words of the sacred text with whatever they held to be true on the basis of their own experience, the canons of logic, contemporary science, and their moral insights.[1]

Judaism became a text-centered religion during the Biblical period with the canonization of Deuteronomy under Josiah and of the entire Torah under Ezra, but prophecy still co-existed with scripture as a source of divine revelation. However, with the cessation of prophecy in the Second Temple period, the Bible took on a double burden. Not only was it the repository of past revelation; as interpreted by its scholars it now took the place of prophecy as the source of guidance for the

---

1. F. Rothschild "Truth and Metaphor in the Bible," *Conservative Judaism* 25 (1971), p. 4; cf. Solomon Schechter, *Studies in Judaism: A Selection,* New York, 1960 pp. 11–12.

Jeffrey H. Tigay

present and near future.[2] Now more than ever[3] it was necessary for scholars to develop a system of Biblical interpretation which would make clear the contemporary message of the ancient text. In the development of this system ancient Biblical scholars drew upon techniques which had been developed in various disciplines.[4] A

2. See S. Spiegel, "On Medieval Hebrew Poetry," in L. Finkelstein (ed.) *The Jews: Their History, Culture, and Religion,* 1961, I, pp. 854–856.
3. Several studies trace the beginnings of both halakhic and aggadic exegesis back to the Biblical period, in some cases to pre-exilic times. See I.L. Seeligmann, "Voraussetzungen der Midraschexegese", *VTS* 1 (1953), pp. 150–181; H.L. Ginsberg, *Studies in Daniel,* New York, 1948, p. 78, n. 21b; *idem,* "Daniel", *EncMiqr,* II, cols. 692–693, 949–952; idem, "The Oldest Interpretation of the Suffering Servant," *VT* 3 (1953), pp. 400–404; Y. Kaufmann, *History of Israelite Religion,* Tel Aviv, 1956, IV, pp. 291–293, 327–329, 331–338 (Hebrew. Hereafter: Kaufmann, *HIR*); idem, *Mikivshonah shel HaYesirah HaMiqrait,* 1966, pp. 161–168; M.H. Segal, *Parshanut HaMiqra,* Jerusalem, 1971, pp. 5–7; N.M. Sarna, "Psalm 89: A Study in Inner Biblical Exegesis", in A. Altmann (ed.) *Biblical and Other Studies* 1963, pp. 29–46; D.R. Hillers, *Lamentations (Anchor Bible),* Garden City, 1972, p. 25 (on Lam. 1:10); M. Fishbane, "Torah and Tradition", in D.A. Knight (ed.) *Tradition and Theology in the Old Testament,* Philadelphia, 1977, pp. 275–300; E.Z. Melammed, *Bible Commentators,* Jerusalem, 1975, I, pp. 10–12 (Hebrew). Some studies use a loose definition of exegesis, including under it such phenomena as literary allusion, revision, re-use or adaptation, variant tradition, related topic, imitation, and reflexes of exegesis, rather than limiting the inquiry to exegesis proper. Some of the cases discussed may actually reflect interpretations of older passages, but in most studies the difference between these phenomena and exegesis is not considered. These phenomena are what Seeligmann termed *"Voraussetzungen der Midraschexegese,"* not Midraschexegese itself (note his definition of the term, pp. 150–152); cf. E.Bickerman, *Four Strange Books of the Bible,* N.Y., 1967, pp. 112–113. See also below, n. 14.
4. See S. Lieberman, *Hellenism in Jewish Palestine,* N.Y., 1950, pp. 28–37, 47–82 (Hereafter: Lieberman, *Hellenism*). Although rabbinic exegesis is a product of the Hellenistic-Roman world, many exegetical techniques developed earlier in the ancient Near East, where texts were studied intensively in scribal academies. Note the reference to understanding proverbs in Prov. 1:2b, 6. An Egyptian letter refers to a scribe "who can explain the difficulties of the annals like him who composed them" (*ANET,* p. 475b), while another tells a schoolboy that "Another fine occasion is when you penetrate the sense of a papyrus-book" (R.J. Williams, "Scribal Training in Ancient Egypt," *JAOS* 92 [1972], p. 218). For Egyptian commentaries, see J.W.B. Barns, "A Note on the Egyptian Background of the 'Demotic Chronicle'," *apud* C. Rabin, "Notes on the Habakkuk Scroll . . .," *VT* 5 (1955), pp. 151–152, and M. Fishbane, "The Qumran Pesher and Traits of Ancient Hermeneutics", *Proceedings of the Sixth World Congress of Jewish Studies* (1973), Jerusalem, 1977, p. 101, n. 21. Mesopotamian texts refer to "discussing" or "interpreting" *(šutabūlu)* omen series (M. Streck, *VAB* 7/2, p. 254:15 [*CAD* A/I, p. 28a] and "explaining" *(kullumu)* an omen text (*ABL* 688, rev. 10, as understood in *CAD* K, p.523c) and the creation epic (*ANET,* p. 72c; cf. A.L. Oppenheim, "Mesopotamian Mythology I," *Orientalia* 16 [1947], p. 237; cf. Wilcke, "Die Anfänge der akkadischen Epen", *ZA* 67 [1977], pp. 171–174). See also A. W Sjöberg, "Examenstext A," *ZA* 64 (1975), pp. 140: 13–14, 152–156. There are Akkadian commentaries on texts of various genres (astrological, grammatical

number of these techniques have been found to resemble mantic techniques, that is, techniques employed in certain types of divination. That the exegesis of Scripture at times resembles the exegesis of dreams was recognized in Midrash Haggadol:

> Behold it says: "A dream carries much implication" (Eccl. 5: 2). Now by using the method of *qal vahomer* we reason: if the contents of dreams, which have no effect, may yield a multitude of interpretations, how much more, then, should the important contents of the Torah imply many interpretations in every verse.[5]

This tolerance for a multiplicity of interpretations became a major asset of Biblical exegesis. It permitted a text-centered religion to avoid fundamentalism and dogmatism, stimulating the growth of a rich body of legal and homiletic exegesis in response to ever changing conditions and ideas, while at the same time permitting scientific exegetes to state their view of the plain-sense even when that contradicted the *halakha*.[6] These achievements are little diminished despite their degeneration, in the late Middle Ages, into extravagant pilpulistic attempts to find

medical, mythical, wisdom, etc.). The native terminology recognizes four classes of commentary: *sâtu*, "excerpt;" *šūt pî*, "according to" (often, but debatably, taken as based on oral tradition); *mukallimtu*, "explanation;" and *maš'altu*, "questioning, inquiry" (cf. *miḏrāš*?). The precise signification of these terms is not really clear (cf. M. Civil, "Medical Commentaries from Nippur," *JNES* 33 [1974], p. 329). The classification may depend more on format and source of information than exegetical techniques, and commentaries are sometimes described in their colophons as combining several types. On the whole, they are simply glossaries and elementary explanations, although difficult words sometimes call forth fanciful explanations, guesswork, or confessions of ignorance (some typical commentaries may be seen in W.G. Lambert, *Babylonian Wisdom Literature*, Oxford, 1960, pp. 32–56, 70–88; E. Leichty, *The Omen Series Šumma Izbu* [*TCS* 4], Locust Valley, 1970, pp. 22–23, 211–233). The greatest ingenuity is devoted to interpreting gods' names by such techniques as *notariqon* (see below, n. 31). Some passages speak of texts' "secrets" (see Sjöberg, *ZA* 64 [1975], p. 152). Modern scholars have described some commentaries as "esoteric" (e.g., R.D. Biggs, "An Esoteric Babylonian Commentary," *RA* 62 [1968], pp. 51–58), but this characterization may only reflect our difficulty in understanding those commentaries. For an impression of the nature of cuneiform commentaries, see B. Landsberger, "Die babylonische Theodizee, *ZA* 43 (1936), pp. 37–38; W.G. Lambert, "An Address of Marduk to the Demons", *AfO* 17 (1954–56), pp. 311, 318, 320; E. Leichty, "Two Late Commentaries, "*AfO* 24 (1973), pp. 78–86.

5. *Midrash Haggadol*, Genesis (ed. Margulies), p. 39, quoted and translated by S. Lieberman in *Hellenism* p. 70; cf. *Gen. Rabba* 17:5 (ed. Theodor–Albeck), p. 157: גובלת נבואה חלום, "a dream is an inferior variety of prophecy," and TB *Berachot* 57b: חלום אחד מששים לנבואה, "A dream is one-sixtieth of prophecy."
6. Cf. M. Greenberg in *Judaism* 12 (1963), p. 232, citing Rashbam's introduction to Exod. 21–24.

hundreds of clever interpretations of a single passage.[7] Whatever we can learn about the origins of this flexibility may contribute to understanding something of the vitality of Judaism itself.

It has often been thought that such exegetical flexibility was first sought in order to permit conforming the Bible to the intellectual and moral standards of later times. As far as mantic techniques are concerned, however, we shall see that the earliest sources in which such techniques are regularly applied to the Bible were motivated primarily by the need to conform the Bible to new geographic and political conditions. It may well be that these conditions gave the major impetus to the use of mantic techniques in Biblical exegesis, and that after their ability to meet these conditions was proven, the use of these techniques was then extended to meet new moral and intellectual needs.

I

Recognition of similarities between interpretation of the Bible and the interpretation of dreams and other kinds of oracles is rooted in the Bible itself, where it is indicated that God reveals himself to prophets other than Moses in visions, dreams, and riddles (Num. 12:6–8). Scripture is but a written counterpart of such modes of revelation, and it was therefore a natural inference that the Bible could be interpreted by techniques similar to those employed in wresting meaning from visions, dreams, and riddles.[8] The Bible itself reports a precedent for a written revelation being interpreted by such techniques, namely the writing on the wall in Daniel 5: the Aramaic names of three weights or coins – mina, shekel, and half-mina *(měnē, těqēl,* and *pěrēs)* – being interpreted paronomastically as the homonymous verbs meaning "numbered, weighed, and divided," with *pěrēs* simultaneously taken to refer to Persia *(pārās).*[9]

At the heart of the common exegetical techniques lay the assumption that the *texts* treated in these ways were valid far beyond the time

7. W. Bacher, "Bible Exegesis – Jewish," *The Jewish Encyclopedia*, 1901–1905, III, p. 172.
8. Cf. E.E. Halevy, "Biblical Midrash and Homeric Exegesis,", *Tarbiz* 31 (1961–62), p. 159 (Hebrew); M.P. Miller, "Midrash," *IDB Supplement*, p. 595b; A.S. van der Ploeg, *Bib Or* 16 (1959), p. 163, citing A.S. van der Woude, *Bijbelcommentaren en bijbelse verhalen*, 1958; L.H. Silberman, "Unriddling the Riddle," *RQ* 3 (1961–62), pp. 330–331.
9. Cf. H.L. Ginsberg, (above, n. 3), pp. 24–26; J. Barr, *Comparative Philology and the Text of the Old Testament*, Oxford, 1968, p. 49; Kaufmann, *HIR*, IV, pp. 425–426, n. 14.

of their composition. This is what necessitated their preservation, their accurate transmission, their distinction from extraneous material,[10] and their interpretation in the light of changing conditions. This assumption was at home in omen literature, where the compendia consulted by diviners introduced each omen with the Akkadian conditional particle *šumma*, "if, whenever," or the Hebrew *ha-* functioning as the relative particle, "whoever" (TB *Berachot* 56b-57a). Such introductions mean, "whenever the following phenomenon is observed / whoever sees the following phenomen in a dream, it portends such and such." This wording implies that the applicability of the portent is, in theory, endlessly repeatable. What was new in the application of diviners' techniques in Biblical exegesis was in treating Biblical prophecies and even non-prophetic passages as if they, too, addressed distant generations and spoke in veiled language. In the case of apocalyptic exegesis the prophecies were not thought to be applicable repeatedly, but to apply to the final age, in which the interpreter thought he lived. The innovation was aptly summed up by Bickerman, with reference to Daniel's interpretation of Jeremiah's prophecy of seventy years' destruction:

> The method of *pesher* was not new, but the Daniel of chapter 9 applied it to the already realized prophecy. Here he was a revolutionary innovator.[11] It had occurred to no one that the oracle to Croesus (that he would destroy a great kingdom by crossing the river Halys, his frontier with Persia), already realized in

10. The correspondence between the treatment of Biblical and oracular or mantic literature expressed itself not only in exegetical techniques, but in the very distinction between canonical and uncanonical texts. It is precisely in the case of vital mantic and related ritual texts that we find ancient Mesopotamian scribes distinguishing between passages which are "good," "near" (i.e. belong), "(part) of the series" *(damqu, qurbu, sä iškari),* on the one hand, and "extraneous," "not part of the series" *(aḫû, la ša iškari),* on the other. See references in *CAD* D, p. 73d sub 9; *CAD* A/I, p. 212 a–b; W.G. Lambert, "A Late Assyrian Catalogue," in B.L. Eichler (ed.), *S.N. Kramer Anniversary Volume,* 1976, p. 314:11, 14; brief discussion by Oppenheim, "Divination and Celestial Observation in the Last Assyrian Empire," *Centaurus* 14 (1969), pp. 123 and 134 n. 54. Note in the passages cited that even "external" omens were sometimes collected and consulted, implying that some significance was attributed to them.
11. But contrast Kaufmann, *HIR*, III, 46–47, on the earlier re-use of old prophecies. Cf. also E. Tov, "Some Aspects of the Textual and Literary History of the Book of Jeremiah", in P.–M. Bogaert (ed.), *Le Livre de Jérémie (Bibliotheca Ephemeridum Theologicarum Lovaniensium* 54), 1981, p. 153 § c.

Jeffrey H. Tigay

his defeat, could have a second meaning realizable generations later. The new insight immediately found favor with clerks of Jerusalem. A new and limitless field opened to their ingenuity. For the author of Daniel 11 (33ff.) the Suffering Servant of Isaiah (52) is the figure of the steadfast "enlighteners" (*maskilim*) of Epiphanes' persecution. For the author of First Maccabees (7:17) pious Jews slaughtered by a Seleucid general in 161 died "according to the word of the Psalmist" (79:2). The commentator of Habakkuk whose work has been found among the Dead Sea Scrolls was positive that God told the prophets to write down the things that were to come upon the later age . . . The ancient oracles became perennially valid just as astrological predictions were true indefinitely.[12]

This contemporizing, predictive or oracular use of the Bible[13] constitutes one of the earliest significant types of Biblical exegesis. Evidence for this use begins to appear in the second century B.C.E.[14] In Dan. 9–12 such prophecies as Num. 24:24; Jer. 25:11–12; Isa.

12. Bickerman (above n. 3), pp. 111–112. The adverb "perennially" in the final sentence is not quite precise; unlike astrological predictions, which could indeed recur repeatedly, the applicability of ancient Biblical prophecies was transferred only to the exegete's own time.
13. What J. Goldin calls "prophetic interpretation"; see his *The Song at the Sea*, New Haven, 1971, pp. 14, 22–23. M.P. Miller (above n. 8), speaks of "mantic characteristics" in Midrash. Cf. R.P.C. Hanson, "Biblical Exegesis in the Early Church", in P.R. Ackroyd and C.F. Evans (eds.), *Cambridge History of the Bible,* I, 1970, pp. 419ff. on the "oracular" view of the Bible in early Christianity (further references in index, p. 620, s.v. "oracles").
14. This is not to deny that the Bible was interpreted by other techniques earlier (cf. n. 3), nor that ancient motifs were applied typologically or as precedents to later events. Allusions in Exod. 15 to the ancient myth of the Lord's suppression of the primordial sea make the crossing of the sea seem like a recurrence of the primordial event (cf. Isa. 51:9–10; see U. Cassuto, *A Commentary on the Book of Exodus*, Jerusalem, 1942, pp. 122–125 [Hebrew]); in Isa. 27:1 Leviathan stands for the forces of evil in Isaiah's time (Cassuto, *The Goddess Anath* [Hebrew], pp. 39–40; on Rahab as a designation for Egypt see Sarna, רהב, *EncMiqr,* VII, col. 329). Isaiah 43:16–19 describe the coming redemption as a new crossing of the sea. Cf. also the explicit analogies in Isa. 54:9 and Ps. 83:10–13. However, these passages do not necessarily have specific Biblical verses in mind, nor do they imply that the new event was *intended* by an earlier passage. See Seeligmann (above, n. 3), pp. 169–70, where he distinguishes between historicizing adaptation as such and exegesis.

52:13–53:12 and others are applied to Seleucid times.[15] 1 Macc. 3:48 states that on the eve of the Battle of Emmaus Judah's army "opened the Book of the Law[16] for what the gentiles would have inquired/ searched from the images of their idols" (*exepetasan to biblion tou nomou peri hōn exēreunōn ta ethnē ta homoiōmata tōn eidōlōn autōn*). According to the most plausible interpretation of this passage,[17] the scroll was opened for the purpose of seeking divine guidance, although the method followed is not indicated.[18] Considering the kind of advice normally sought by divination before a battle, the comparison to divination[19] suggests that Judah sought such advice as whether, when,

15. See Ginsberg (above, n. 3); Bickerman (above, n.3), pp. 110–113; Tigay, שבוע, *EncMiqr*, VII, col. 477. On Num. 24:24 see below, §III, text accompanying n. 40.
16. Not necessarily the Torah: see W.F. Arndt–F.W. Gingrich, *A Greek-English Lexicon of the New Testament*, Chicago, 1957, p. 545 sub 4b.
17. See J. Wellhausen, "Über den geschichtlichen Wert des zweiten Makkäbaerbuchs," in *Nachrichten von der Königl. Gesellschaft der Wissenshaften zu Göttingen. Philologisch-historische Klasse* (1905), pp. 161–162; F.–M. Abel, *Les Livres des Maccabées*, Paris, 1949, pp. 68–70, where previous views are summarized and discussed; this interpretation is followed in *La Sainte Bible/The Jerusalem Bible* and *The New English Bible*. The practice of the Syrians was to destroy Torah scrolls, which they regarded as subversive (I Macc. 1:56–57, cf. 49 and see J. Goldstein, *I Maccabees [Anchor Bible]*, Garden City, 1976, pp. 255f.); this (along with linguistic objections) argues against interpretations of the verse to the effect that the Syrians had drawn pictures of their gods on the scrolls or had sought to find support for their own religion and myths in the Torah.
18. According to the account of the same event in 2 Macc. 8:23, Judah had the scroll read by Elazar and afterwards announced the watchword *(synthēma)*, "God's help" *(theou boetheias)*. In the light of this passage Wellhausen concluded that Judah found the watchword in the scroll. However, the text does not state that the watchword came from the scroll, and later, in 2 Macc. 13:15 Judah announces another watchword ("God's victory," *theou nikēn*) without resort to a holy book. The use of such watchwords was conventional (cf. Y.Yadin, *The Scroll of the War of the Sons of Light against the Sons of Darkness*, Jerusalem, 1957, p. 53, n. 66 [Hebrew]) and they were not normally chosen by divination; those in 2 Macc. are similar to those in 1QM 4:6–14 and others cited from classical sources by Abel (above, n. 17), p. 392, and virtually identical to some of them. While that in 2 Macc. 3:48 is reminiscent of certain Biblical passages (e.g., Ps. 61:8 [MT 62:8] LXX: *ho theos tes boetheias mou)*, J. Moffatt takes it as a play on the name of Elazar who had just read the scroll (see Moffatt in Charles, *APOT*, I, p. 143) and, indeed, the watchword is no less reminiscent of the explanation of that name in Exod. 18:4 (LXX: *ho gar theos tou patros mou boēthos mou*); note how the watchwords on the standards of the military divisions in 1QM 4:1–5, play on the names of the divisions, e.g., *'lp-'p-'l, m'h-m't;* see P.R. Weis, "The Date of the Habakkuk Scroll," *JQR* 41 (1950–1951), p. 149, n. 149; W.H. Brownlee, "Biblical Interpretation among the Sectaries of the Dead Sea Scrolls," *BAr* 14 (1951), p. 70; Yadin, pp. 53–54, n. 67, 279; T.H. Gaster, *The Dead Sea Scriptures*, Garden City, 1976, pp. 404, 453, nn. 26–28.
19. For divination by idols, to which the verse compares Judah's action, cf. Ezek. 21:26; Hab. 2:18–19; Zech. 10:22; and see the passage from Pausanias and

Jeffrey H. Tigay

or where to fight, or an indication of the battle's outcome (cf. Judg. 20:28; 1 Sam. 23:2–12; 28:4 24; 1 Kings 22:1–28; Ezek. 20:21). Seeking answers to such questions by opening a sacred scroll suggests bibliomancy, a practice widely known in the classical, Jewish, Christian, and Muslim worlds.[20] One might imagine that the scroll was opened at random, with the passage discovered being regarded as the answer. The predictive implication of many verses discovered this way was naturally not always transparent, and the hermeneutic techniques already established for other forms of divination would be just what was needed to make a recalcitrant text yield its secrets.

Whatever the method may have been, the predictive use of Scripture became widespread. This was especially true among groups which cultivated apocalyptic, as vividly illustrated in the *pĕšārîm* from Qumran. Josephus hinted at this use of Scripture among the Essenes, the group which also produced the dream interpreter Simon the Essene:[21]

> There are some among them who profess to tell the future, being versed from their early years in holy books, various forms of purification and apothegms of prophets; and seldom, if ever, do they err in their ‚predictions (*War* 2.8,12 [§159]).

Note the association of predictive ability with knowledge of Scripture.

II

The similarity of some of the hermeneutic rules of the *aggadah* to techniques used for interpreting dreams and oracles was discussed by

Mesopotamian analogues cited by A.L. Oppenheim, "Sumerian: inim. gar, Akkadian: *egirru* = Greek: *kledon*," *AfO* 17 (1954–1956), p. 54. For diviners accompanying an army see *ARM* 2, 22 (*ANET*, 482c). For pre-battle divination cf. *ARM* 10, 4 (*ANET*, pp. 629–630 and W.L. Moran, "New Evidence from Mari on the History of Prophecy", *Biblica* 50 [1969], pp. 47–50).

20. In the various articles on divination and related topics in J. Hastings (ed.), *Encyclopedia of Religion and Ethics*, N.Y., 1913–1922 note the following: vol. II, p. 611b; IV, pp. 776b, 789a, 790–791a, 813a, 818, 822a, 826d. See also TB Hulin 95b; Kimchi at 2 Kings 22:11; M. Grunwald and K. Kohler, "Bibliomancy," *Jewish Encyclopedia*, III, pp. 202–205; J. Trachtenberg, *Jewish Magic and Superstition*, Philadelphia, 1961, pp. 216, 307 n. 16; J. Mann, *The Jews in Egypt and Palestine under the Fātimid Caliphs*, New York, 1970, II, 307; J. Blau, *Teshubot HaRambam* , II, Jerusalem, 1960, pp. 321–322 (Hebrew); J. Morier, *The Adventures of Hajji Baba of Ispahan*, New York, 1954, p. 74.

21. Josephus, *Jewish War* 2.7, 3 (§112–113). For prediction among the Essenes see also Thackeray's note at *Jewish War* 2.8, 12 (§159): *Josephus, [LCL]* II, p. 384.

Saul Lieberman in 1950.[22] This similarity is underscored by the use of the term *pešer* for the interpretation of scriptural verses in the Dead Sea Scrolls, for in its exegetical sense this term is used in Biblical and ancient Near Eastern literature primarily for the interpretation of dreams and omens.[23] Reflexes of oneirocritical techniques in the Qumran commentaries have since been pointed out in a number of studies.[24] Although Lieberman's study focused on oneirocritical[25] techniques in Hellenistic and rabbinic sources, he noted that these methods "were invented neither by the Jews nor by the Greeks. They go back to hoary antiquity".[26] Their antecedents in the Near East were recently surveyed by M. Fishbane.[27]

For purposes of illustration, Lieberman studied five of the techniques listed in the thirty-two hermeneutic rules of the Aggadah: (1) *mashal*: "parable or allegory or symbol"; (2) *remez*: "paronomasia, amphiboly, playing with homonymous roots"; (3) *gematria*: "computation of the numerical value of letters"; (4) "substitution of letters, the so-called *Athbash* alphabet"; and (5) *notariqon*, interpreting the letters or syllables of a word as abbreviations for other words, or as anagrams. Several of these techniques can be found in mantic literature in the ancient Near East and in the Bible as well as Hellenistic and rabbinic dream interpretation.[28]

22. Lieberman, *Hellenism*, pp. 68ff.; I. Heinemann, *Altjüdische Allegoristik (Bericht des Jud.-Theol. Seminars)*, Breslau, 1935.
23. Cf. J. van der Ploeg, *Bib Or* 8 (1951), p.2. In Dan. 5 the term is used for the explanation of the handwriting on the wall, and in Eccl. 8:1 for the meaning of an adage; see van der Ploeg, *loc. cit.*; K. Elliger, *Studien zum Habakuk–Kommentar*, Tübingen, 1953, p. 123; H.L. Ginsberg, *Koheleth*, 1961, p. 105 (Hebrew). In Akkadian *pašāru* and *pišru* are normally used for dreams and omens (sporadically speech), *kullumu* for interpreting texts. For *pšr* and *ptr* in rabbinic sources see H. Yalon, *Studies in the Dead Sea Scrolls* (Hebrew), p. 65; L. Gertner, "Terms of Scriptural Interpretation: A Study in Hebrew Semantics," *BSOAS* 25 (1962), pp. 17–18; W. Bacher, *Erkhei Midrash*, II, pp. 270, 272–274; Silberman (above, n. 8), pp. 326–330; Heinemann (above, n. 22), p. 19. On Arabic *tafsir* and *fassara* see C. Rabin, *Qumran Studies*, New York, 1957, p. 117.
24. Silberman (above, n. 8), pp. 330–334; A. Finkel, "The Pesher of Dreams and Scriptures," *RQ* 4 (1963–1964), pp. 357–370; Fishbane (above, n. 4), pp. 97–114.
25. Cf. Lieberman, *Hellenism*, p. 78, n. 249.
26. *Ibid.*, p.75.
27. See n. 24; Fishbane notes the antiquity of such techniques in Israel as well (above, n. 4), pp.105–112.
28. In order to retain the proper perspective on Biblical interpretation and the interpretation of mantic phenomena, it should be kept in mind that the techniques mentioned here are only a small percentage of those used in the Aggadah, and they are likewise only a few of those used in mantic literature. The hermeneutic principles followed in interpreting most omens are not all understood; see Leichty (above,

(1) Parable, allegory, and symbol are well-known in Biblical exegesis, as in the rabbis' frequent reading of water as referring to the Torah (TB *Baba Kama* 82a; *Taanit* 7a), the interpretation of "well" (Num. 21:18) as the Torah at Qumran (C[airo] D[amascus] C[ovenant] 6:4), Philo's interpretation of the serpent in Eden as the symbol of passion (*Questions and Answers on Genesis*, No. 31), and the messianic interpretation of "star" (Num. 24:17) among the Qumran sect and in rabbinic Judaism (CDC 4:18–20; Targum Onkelos Num. 24:17; TP *Taanit* 4:8, 68d). In mantic contexts symbols are found in Biblical dreams, such as Pharaoh's seven cows and seven ears of grain each indicating seven years (Gen. 41:1–31), the Midianite soldier's tumbling barley loaf which represented the sword of Gideon (Judg. 7:13–14), and Daniel's four animals representing four kingdoms (Dan. 7). In Mesopotamian omen literature, if something in the configuration of the liver of a sacrificial animal resembles a ring it indicates that "the land will close ranks and unanimity will prevail" (*YOS* 10, No. 11, II, 7–9); if the liver looks like a corpse and is perforated, it means that "a man's wife will commit adultery (apparently suggested by perforation, i.e. penetration), he will catch her at it and kill her" (*YOS* 10, No. 14:6); "if a ewe gives birth to a lion with matted or unkempt hair (*malî*) it means that there will be a reign of mourning (*malî*, literally unkempt hair, a mourning rite)" (Leichty, *TCS* 4, p. 77: V, 39).

(2) Paronomasia is another standard exegetical technique, as in Ben Azzai's interpretation of *pĕrî 'ēṣ hādār* as the *'eṭrôg* because it is the fruit which "dwells" (*haddār*) on the tree year-round (Rashi at Lev. 23:40, citing *Sifra 'Emor* 16, 16:3 [ed. Weiss p. 102d]; TB *Sukkah* 35a). In the Qumran commentary on Habakkuk *lō' tûkāl*, "you cannot" (Hab. 1:13) is interpreted as *lō' yĕkaleh*, "he will not destroy" (1QpHab 5:3). In the Bible paronomasia is used mantically in prophetic visions, such as the interpretation of *qayiṣ*[29] as *qēṣ* in Amos 8: 1–2 (cf. *šāqēd* in Jer. 1:11–12). Daniel's interpretation of the writing

---

n. 4), pp. 6–7; I. Starr, "In Search of Principles of Prognostication in Extispicy," *HUCA* 45 (1974), pp. 17–23. Many of the omen apodoses in cuneiform omen texts are not based on hermeneutic principles but upon observed correlations between ominous phenomena and actual events; see W.W. Hallo, "New Perspectives on Cuneiform Literature," *IEJ* 12 (1962), pp. 17–18; Oppenheim, *Ancient Mesopotamia*, Chicago, 1964, pp. 210–211.

29. In northern Israel, where Amos preached, this word may have been pronounced *qēṣ*, owing to the contraction of diphthongs in north-Israelite Hebrew; see E.Y. Kutscher, *The Language and Linguistic Background of the Isaiah Scroll*, Jerusalem, 1959, p. 47 n. 10 (Hebrew) [Eng. trans., Leiden 1974, p. 64, n. 4.]

on the wall is also paronomastic (Dan. 5:25–28) as is his interpretation of Jeremiah's "seventy" *(šib'îm)* years as "seventy weeks" *(šib'îm šābû'îm)* of years. In Mesopotamian omen literature a mark called an *erištum* indicates a request or desire, also called *erištum* (*YOS* 10, No. 11, V, 14–21; *RA* 44, 41:26). In a dream a raven *(arbu)* portends income *(irbu)*.[29a]

(3) *Gematria* is known from such interpretations as that of the 318 men who accompanied Abraham (Gen. 14:14) as referring to his servant Eliezer, the letters of whose name have the numerical value of 318 (TB *Nedarim* 32a). The use of letters of the alphabet as numeral signs was a relatively late practice among Semites, borrowed from the Greeks.[30] However, cryptographic writing of personal names with numbers is attested in Mesopotamia as early as the seventh century B.C.E., where it is based on the equation of divine names and other cuneiform signs with numbers.[31] It is not so far known to have been used in the interpretation of oracular texts. In Greek dream interpretation, to see a weasel *(galē)* portends a lawsuit or penalty *(dikē)*, since the two Greek words have the same numerical equivalent.[32] The use of numerological interpretation of oracular texts among Christians is required by such passages as Rev. 13:18 where the beast is identified by his number, 666, the reference being to Nero (*nrwn qsr*=666; a variant reading 616 reflects the Latin form *nrw qsr*).[33]

(4) Letter substitution has not yet been found as a technique in mantic interpretation, but cryptographic writing was known.[34]

(5) *Notariqon* is well-illustrated as an exegetical technique. The salutation with which Joseph was greeted, *'abrēk* (Gen. 41:43), was

29a. A.L. Oppenheim, *The Interpretation of Dreams in the Ancient Near East (Transactions of the American Philosophical Society,* N.S. 46.3), Philadelphia, 1956, p. 241.
30. Lieberman, *Hellenism*, p. 73 n. 211. At the time of Lieberman's writing the earliest examples known in Semitic languages were from coins of the First Jewish Revolt (66–70 C.E.; see Ginsberg, *Studies in Koheleth*, N.Y., 1950, pp. 31–33). Earlier examples were subsequently found on Hasmonean coins (J. Naveh, "Dated Coins of Alexander Jannaeus," *IEJ* 18 [1968], pp. 20–25). Prof. F. M. Cross has kindly informed me that an example is now attested on a Phoenician ostracon from Cyprus which he dates to the fourth century B.C.E., which he will shortly publish.
31. E. Leichty, "The Colophon", *Studies Presented to A. Leo Oppenheim,* Chicago, 1964, pp. 152–153.
32. See Lieberman, *Hellenism*, p. 72, citing Artemidorus.
33. See Bruce M. Metzger, *A Textual Commentary on the Greek New Testament,* United Bible Societies, 1971, p. 752; cf. Sibylline Oracles I, 144–145 and 326–330 (cited by Y. Kaufmann, "Apokalyptik," *Encyclopaedia Judaica,* Berlin, 1928–1934, II, 1149) and V, 1–42, in Charles, *APOT,* II, pp. 397–398.
34. Lieberman, *Hellenism*, p. 73; Leichty (above, n. 31), p. 152 n. 18.

Jeffrey H. Tigay

taken by some rabbis as composed of two words, either '*āḇ* and *raḵ*, yielding "father (in wisdom) though tender (in years)," or '*aḇ* and Latin *rex*, yielding "father to the king," as Joseph is actually called in Gen. 45:8 (*Sifre Deut.* 2, 1, [ed. Finkelstein, p. 8]; *Gen. Rabba* 90, 3 [Gen. 41:43; ed. Theodor-Albeck, p. 1102]; Targum Onkelos *ad loc.;* cf. Pesh). The interpretation based on Latin *rex* recalls another notariqon employing a foreign language, R. Akiba's explanation that the head *tĕfillîn* consists of four compartments because *ṭoṭāpôṭ* consists of two words for "two", one from Coptic (? or Egyptian) and the other from "African" (TB *Menachot* 34b). In Qumran exegesis '*ml* "iniquity" (Hab 1:3) is taken as an anagram for *m'l*, "treachery," and *wysphw* (the reading in Hab 1:15), "gathered it," is taken for two words, one written defectively and the other abbreviated, equivalent to *wywsypw* (*'t) hwnm*, "they increase their wealth" (1QpHab VI, 1). Analysis of a word as if it consisted of several smaller words or abbreviations is known in non-mantic uses in Israel and Mesopotamia[35] and is found in Greek and Jewish dream interpretations. Lieberman cites from Artemidorus the case of a military commander who saw the letters *iota, kappa,* and *theta* on his sword in a dream; the commander died in the Jewish war in Cyrene, and it turned out that the letters had stood for *Ioudaiois, Kurēnaiois,* and *thanatos,* Jews, Cyrenians, death.[36] In rabbinic dream interpretation, seeing barley (*śʿwrym*) portends forgiveness of sins, since *śʿwrym* can be dissolved into *sār 'āwon*, "sin has departed" (TB *Berachot* 57a).

In addition to specific techniques shared by Biblical exegesis and the interpretation of mantic phenomena, we find other shared features as well. The multiple interpretations tolerated by the same omen or dream (*šaniš*, etc.) are paralleled by the same multiplicity of interpretations which may be proposed for a single Biblical passage simultaneously (*dābār 'aḥēr*). In Dan 5:28 *pĕrēs* is interpreted as both the verb "divided" *(pĕrîsaṭ)* and the noun "Persia" (*pārās*) while the "seventy weeks" of years in Dan. 9:24 construes the "seventy" (*šiḇʿîm*) of

35. This is quite common in the exegesis of names, as in Abraham = '*aḇ hămôn*..., Gen. 17:4–5; cf. Lambert (above, n. 4), p.320; see especially the fifty names of Marduk in Enuma Eliš (*ANET*, pp. 69–72) and the discussions of F.M. Th. Böhl, *AfO* 11 (1937), pp. 191–218 = *Opera Minora*, Groningen–Djakarta, 1953, pp. 282–312, 504–508; J. Bottéro, "Les noms de Marduk, l'écriture et la logique en Mésopotamie ancienne," in Maria de Jong Ellis (ed.), *Essays on the Ancient Near East in Memory of Jacob Joel Finkelstein* (Connecticut Academy of Arts and Sciences, Memoirs 19), Hamden, Conn.,1977, pp. 5–28.
36. Lieberman, *Hellenism*, p. 74

Jer. 25:11–12; 29:10 as both "seventy" (*šib'îm*) and "weeks" (*šā-bû'îm*).[37] In the realm of terminology we find not only the shared use of *pišru/pešer*, but also similar formulae. For example, the standard rabbinic lexicographical formula *'ên* X *'elā'* Y, "the word X means nothing else than Y" has a Biblical forerunner in the Midianite's interpretation of his companion's dream: *'ên zōt biltî 'im hereb gid'ôn*... "this is nothing else than the sword of Gideon..." (Judg. 7:14).

III

Most of these similarities between Biblical exegesis and techniques used for interpreting oracular texts have been pointed out by others. To date the question has not been raised as to when, how, and for what reason such techniques first came to be applied to the aggadic interpretation of the Bible. Before offering a suggestion on this subject, we turn to another important technique whose mantic counterpart has rarely been noticed[38] and which can help us focus on a possible explanation for the application of these techniques to Scripture.

In applying Scripture to contemporary events, it was necessary for exegetes to find in it hints of their own times. This was often accomplished by identifying nations mentioned in the Biblical text as other nations of the interpreter's time. This type of symbolism was crucial for preventing an ancient text from becoming outdated with the rise and fall of nations.[39] An early example of this technique employed in finding contemporary meaning in ancient prophecy is reflected in the Bible itself, in Dan. 11:30, where Balaam's prophecy about the Kittim, Asshur and Eber of Num. 24:24 are taken as the Romans, Seleucid Syrians, and Hebrews (these interpretations are partly reflected in the versions as well).[40] The Habakkuk commentary from Qumran

---

37. Tigay, שבע, *EncMiqr*, VII, col. 477.
38. I have found this noted only by Bickerman (above, n. 3), p. 81.
39. For the homiletic use of *pšr* in the sense of matching the words of Scripture to contemporary personalities and events see Yalon, *Qiryat Sefer* 27 (1951), pp. 172–173 = *Studies*, p. 65; cf. Seeligmann, *Qiryat Sefer* 30 (1954–1955), pp. 41–42. Ph. Bloch pointed out that this "petirah" technique is present in many midrashim even when the verb *ptr* is not used (Ph. Bloch, "Studien zur Aggadah," *MGWJ* 34 [1885], pp. 268–269).
40. See Ginsberg (above, n. 3), p. 78 n. 21; J.C. Greenfield, "Kittim," *IDB* III, p.41; cf. J. Goldstein, *I Maccabees (Anchor Bible)*, Garden City, 1976, pp. 191–192. On the contemporarizing interpretation of Kittim in Num. 24:24 see the Vulgate and the

(IQpHab 2:10–12) identifies the Chaldeans of Hab. 1:6 etc. as "the Kittim" (itself an archaism), and various later sources took Esau/ Edom and Amalek as Rome and Byzantium.[41] Such interpretations presuppose that the ethnic and geographic names used in ancient texts refer to something other than what they mean literally. In principle this supposition seems simply to recognize two commonplace linguistic phenomena: on the one hand, old places acquire new names; on the other hand, words develop new and non-literal meanings, including archaic ethnic and geographic terms which outlasted their original referents and came to be used for people and places other than those to which they originally and literally referred. Even the plain-sense interpretation of ancient texts often has to deal with such developments.[41a] The Biblical text itself sometimes glosses antiquated place names with their subsequent replacements, for example *'ēmeq haśśiddîm hû' yam hammelaḥ* (Gen. 14:3, with many more examples throughout the chapter),[42] and translations frequently render the old names with those in contemporary use (see, e.g., the renderings of "Ararat" [Gen. 8:4] in the Targums, Vulgate, and Peshitta). The Near East has witnessed many shifts in the meaning of geographic and ethnic terms. Certain ethnic terms lost all ethnic meaning and came to refer to professions or social types. Thus "Canaanite" developed into a common noun for "merchant,"[43] "Chaldean" for "magician/soothsayer," and the like,[44] and, in Sumerian, "Subarian" for "slave."[45] Hittite scribes borrowed the name of a Mesopotamian nomadic tribe, the

Targums; on Eber there see LXX and the Vulgate; on Kittim in Dan. 11 see LXX and Vulgate.

41. See J. Heinemann, *Darke HaAggadah*, p. 209, n. 71 (Hebrew); M.D. Herr, "Edom, In the Aggadah" and "Esau, In the Aggadah," *EJ*, VI, pp. 379, 858–859; K. Kohler, "Amalek, Amalekites–In Rabbinical Literature," *Jewish Encyclopedia*, I, p. 483; Seeligmann (above, n. 3), pp. 168–171.

41a. Cf. the interpretation of Gen. 15:19 in Gen. Rabba 44, 23 and parallels cited in ed. Theodor-Albeck, pp. 445–446.

42. Note that antiquarian glosses and contemporizing exegetical glosses are often phrased in the same way: "A *hû'/hî'* (etc.) B" or "A B *hû'* (etc.)" (Gen. 14:13; I Kgs. 6:1, etc.; IQpHab 12: 3–4; CDC 7:15–20). This is a standard form for any sort of explanatory note (e.g., Exod. 16:36; Isa. 9:14; Esther 2:7; 3:7 twice; A.E. Cowley, *Aramaic Papyri of the Fifth Century B.C.*, Oxford, 1923, p.10, No. 5:1, etc.; E. Reiner, *Šurpu*, Graz, 1958, p.50 [Akkadian *šû*, etc.]).

43. See J. Liver, כנען במקרא, *EncMiqr*, IV, col. 204.

44. L. Koehler and W. Baumgartner (eds.), *Hebräisches und Aramäisches Lexikon zum Alten Testament*³, Leiden, 1967, pp. 477–478.

45. For šubur, "Subarian," as "slave" in Sumerian see *CAD* A/II, p. 243d, lexical section, and the variants šubur and ìr, "slave," in *Gilgamesh and Agga*, line 42, cited by C. Wilcke, *Das Lugalbandaepos*, p. 44:116. Hallo compares the derivation

"Sutaeans" (*Sutu*), and applied it to the barbarian tribes (the Gaš-gaeans) of Anatolia.[46] In other cases ancient tribal names are simply transferred to newly-encountered ethnic groups. A Babylonian text of the Hellenistic period "foretelling" the succession of empires ruling Mesopotamia in a manner reminiscent of the book of Daniel,[47] refers to "the army of the Hanaeans" ($^{lú}umm\bar{a}ni^{meš\ kur}\underset{.}{H}a\text{-}ni\text{-}i$). According to A. K. Grayson,

> The context as well as internal clues strongly indicate that [this passage describes] the invasion of Asia by Alexander the Great. The term Ḥanû, which was originally the name of an Amorite tribe in the Old Babylonian period, is known from other late cuneiform contexts to refer to inhabitants of Thrace. Its use here, rather than Makkadunû, with reference to the conquerors who had come by way of Thrace, reflects an archaizing tendency.[48]

The geographic term "Palestine," originally *hē Syria hē Palaistinē*, "Philistine Syria," was based on the Philistines and later extended to cover the entire country long after the Philistines had disappeared as a distinctive group.[49] An earlier name for the Syro-Palestinian region, $^{kur}\underset{.}{H}atti$, "Hatti-land," developed similarly from the Neo-Hittite kingdoms of Syria.[50] The terms "Magan" and "Meluḥḥa,' which refer in first millennium cuneiform literary texts to Egypt and Ethiopia, are

of "slave" from "Slav" (W.W. Hallo and W.K. Simpson, *The Ancient Near East – A History*, N.Y., 1971, p. 24 n. 47; cf. *Oxford English Dictionary* s.v. "slave"); cf. also "vandal" and "gypsy".

46. H.G. Güterbock, "The Deeds of Suppiluliuma as Told by His Son, Mursili II," *JCS* 10 (1956), pp. 62ᶜ, 126.

47. The literature on Akkadian prophetic or apocalyptic literature continues to grow. For the most recent survey (with previous bibliography) see Hallo, "The Expansion of Cuneiform Literature,"*Proceedings of the American Academy of Jewish Research* 46–47 (1979–80), pp. 307–322.

48. A.K.Grayson, *Babylonian Historical-Literary Texts*, Toronto, 1975, pp. 26, 34–35.

49. See M. Noth, "Zur Geschichte des Namens Palästina," *ZDPV* 62 (1939), pp. 125–144; idem, *The Old Testament World*, Philadelphia, 1966, pp. 7–9; B. Mazar, ארץ ישראל, *EncMiqr*, I, col. 615; M. Stern, *Greek and Latin Authors on Jews and Judaism*, I, Jerusalem, 1974, pp. 3, 6. On the extension of originally narrow geographic terms cf. Hallo (above, n. 45), p. 23, n. 45, and I.J. Gelb, "Makkan and Maluḥḥa in Early Mesopotamian Sources, " *RA* 64 (1970), pp. 6–7; O. Weber, in J.A. Knudtzon, *Die El-Amarna-Tafeln*, II, p. 1173; W.F. Albright in *BASOR* 70 (1938), p.22.

50. See J. D. Hawkins, "Hatti," *RLA*, III, pp. 152–159.

Jeffrey H. Tigay

thought by many scholars to have referred in third and second millennium texts to eastern Arabia and India.[51] "Gutium" was still used as a geographic term long after the Gutians had ceased to exist in an ethnic and political sense; Sargon even undertook a campaign against Muṣaṣir in Urartu (south of Lake Van) partly on the strength of an omen portending "the defeat of Gutium" (*šulput* $^{kur}Guti^{ki}$).[52]

Such shifts in the meaning of geographic and ethnic names are a natural consequence of the rise and fall of nations, and they are variously facilitated by (1) the location of contemporary nations in or near the territory occupied by ancient nations; (2) a sense of analogy and recognition of typological similarity between the role, actions, or characteristics of contemporary people and nations and ancient nations; and, perhaps, (3) coincidental similarity of names between unrelated nations. Usages such as those described in the previous paragraphs established the precedent that a name appearing in a text may mean something other than what it seems to mean. This is precisely what is supposed by the ancient interpreters of mantic texts. Omens often specify that they refer to a specific land or group, sometimes ancient ones such as Akkad or Amurru. By the first millennium B.C.E. at least some of these referents had become ambiguous. "The land of Akkad" was no longer an independent political entity, and its name had come to be used sometimes for other places, such as Babylon.[53] The Amorite states of Syria had long since lost their independence.[54] Still, the ancient omens had spoken of Akkad and Amurru, and they were presumed to be still valid. When astral phenomena indicated a recurrence of these omens in Neo-Assyrian times, it was vital to know what *contemporary* city or state was the object of the portent. When royal astrologers reported their observations to the king and quoted the omen which covered what they had observed, they added notes identifying the contemporary equivalents of the ancient nations. One report to the

51. Oppenheim (above, n. 28), p. 398; Gelb (above, n. 49), p. 108; contrast S.N. Kramer, *The Sumerians*, Chicago, 1963, pp. 276–281.
52. Luckenbill, *ARAB*, II, §170; cf. Hallo, "Gutium," *RLA*, III, pp. 717–719.
53. Cf. H. Weiss, "Kish, Akkad and Agade," *JAOS* 95 (1975), pp. 446–447; B. Landsberger, *Brief des Bischofs von Esagila an König Asarhaddon*, (*MKNAW*, N.R. 28 no. 6), Amsterdam, 1965, pp. 46–49.
54. Cf. Honigmann, "Amurru," *RLA*, I, p. 100. The meaning of the ancient geographic term Subartu, though still used as a name for Assyria, had to be explained even to an Assyrian in R.C. Thompson, *The Reports of the Magicians and Astrologers of Nineveh and Babylon*, London, 1900, II, no. 62 obv. 4 (also cited in *CAD* A/II, p. 123a).

king of Assyria reports on omens that portend an attack of the Umman-manda and well-being for Akkad. In the course of the report the writer pauses to identify the mysterious Umman-manda as the Cimmerians of the Caucasus (ERIM- *manda* ˡⁱ*Gimirajē*) and to indicate that the land of Assyria is what is meant by Akkad (ᵏᵘʳ*Aššur*ᵏⁱ ᵏᵘʳ*Akkadim-ma*; *ABL* 1391: obv. 16, rev. 22).⁵⁵ Another report tells of an eclipse which portends evil for the Land of Amurru, which the writer explains as follows: "The Amurru-land is the Hatti-land (i.e. Syria) or, alternatively, the Land of Chaldea" (ᵏᵘʳ*Amurru* ᵏᵘʳ*Hattu šaniš* ᵏᵘʳ*Kaldu*; *ABL* 337: rev. 14'-15'; Parpola 278). A third report does the latter one better. With reference to an eclipse which portends evil for the land of Amurru the author writes:

> The king of the Amurru-land will die, his land will diminish, or, alternatively, it will be lost. Perhaps the scholars can tell the king my lord something about the Amurru-land: the Amurru-land means the Hatti-land (i.e., Syria) and the Sutu (i.e., desert nomads)-land or, alternatively, the land of Chaldea. Someone or other of the kings of the land of Hatti or the land of Chaldea or of Arabia must bear this portent ... Either the king of Cush or the King of [Tyre ?] or Mugallu (ruler of Tabal in Asia Minor) must [meet] the ap[pointed] death... (*ABL* 629: obv. 17- rev. 2)⁵⁶

This technique of finding a contemporary meaning for the geographic objects of ancient omens enabled the omens to retain significance in later generations. Biblical exegetes, as we have seen, helped to perpetuate the significance of the Bible in the same way. It is another

---

55. S. Parpola, *Letters from Assyrian Scholars to Kings Esarhaddon and Assurbanipal*, Pt. I (*AOAT* 5/1) Neukirchen–Vluyn, 1970, no. 110. The text is discussed at length by L. Hartman, "The Date of the Cimmerian Threat against Ashurbanipal according to *ABL* 1391," *JNES* 21 (1962), pp. 25–37.
56. Parpola (above, n. 55), no 279; *ANET* ³, p. 626. It is interesting to note how these identifications are rooted in historical reality but move away from it. To identify Amurru as the land of Hatti (Syria–Palestine) is historically reasonable, for "Hatti" was the contemporary name of the region which once included the homeland of the Amorites and where the Amorite states had existed. But to interpret Amurru as Chaldea is stretching things. It can rest at most on the fact that a thousand years earlier southern Mesopotamia had come under the domination of Amorite dynasties, or upon similarities in the way of life of the Chaldeans and the old Amorites. cf. A. Schott, *ZA* 47 (1958), p. 111.

example of techniques shared by Biblical exegesis and the interpretation of dreams, omens, and oracles.

IV

In the remaining discussion it will be helpful to view the phenomena we are discussing from two perspectives: that of the author of a text, who uses such phenomena as symbols, paronomasia, archaic geographic terms, or cryptographs, etc., as literary *devices*; and that of the interpreter whose explanation of the text or oracular manifestation as if it contains such devices constitutes an interpretive *technique*.

The techniques we have been discussing were never *specifically* mantic techniques, because the corresponding literary devices were not limited to oracular manifestations. The techniques were always used in plain-sense exegesis because the corresponding literary devices were more or less commonly used by authors. Such devices as parables, allegories, and symbols are often part of a writer's intention, as indeed are paronomastic allusions such as the double entendre (e.g. Isa. 54:9 *ky-my* "for the waters/like the days"; Jonah 4:6 *lhṣyl* "to save/ shade"). Even devices such as *gematria, notariqon* abbreviations, and cryptographs are sometimes employed intentionally by writers and scribes.[57] The updating of a text's geographic references is often a reasonable act of clarification necessitated by changed nomenclature or social and political conditions (cf. Gen. 14). Akkadian writers did sometimes use the names of ancient lands and peoples to refer to contemporary ones, and at least some of the identifications of Amurru in the Assyrian astrologers' reports are accurate in a geographical though not a political sense. The normal use of these devices by authors indicates that techniques which treat a text as if it contained such devices do not of themselves point to an affinity with mantic literature. Indeed these techniques must have been employed in a reasonable way in interpreting some passages as soon as they were composed. What demands explanation is the forced use of these techniques in an aggadic manner to produce far-fetched interpretations in passages where these devices were never intended. It is in these extremes, which

---

57. See Lieberman, *Hellenism*, pp. 73 top, 75 top; Leichty (above, n. 31), pp. 152–153; Fishbane (above, n. 4), p. 111 and idem, "Abbreviations," *IDB Supplement*, pp. 3–4 with bibliography.

eventually became common, that Biblical exegesis seems indebted to mantic interpretation.

V

We may now pose the question of why Biblical exegesis began to use these techniques in an aggadic manner. Num. 12:6–8 implies a theoretical readiness to interpret Scripture as oracular in early times. How did this readiness first come to be applied in practice? Studies of allegorical interpretation often account for this development in terms such as the following:

> Whenever the literature of a people has become an inseparable part of its intellectual possession, and the ancient and venerated letter of this literature is in the course of time no longer in consonance with more modern views, to enable the people to preserve their allegiance to the tradition it becomes necessary to make that tradition carry and contain the newer thought as well.[58]
>
> The allegorical interpretation marks a stage in the history of any civilized people whose literature is 'primitive.' They dispose of what conflicts with their present moral and intellectual standards by reading their past as an allegory.[59]

Both of these quotations indicate that allegorical interpretation arises out of the need to depart from the plain-sense of Scripture. But the earliest examples of the regular use of these techniques in an aggadic way in Biblical exegesis were prompted not by a conflict with "more modern views" or contemporary "moral and intellectual standards" to which Scripture had to be conformed, but primarily by new geopolitical conditions.[60] In Daniel, at Qumran, and generally in apocalyptic and in messianic speculation these were the conditions that had to be faced, and under these conditions the assumption that Biblical prophecies were still applicable necessitated maximum flexibility and avoidance of literalism. To meet this need Biblical exegetes began to apply

58. L. Ginzberg, *On Jewish Law and Lore,* Philadelphia, 1962, p. 127.
59. B. Smalley, *The Study of the Bible in the Middle Ages,* Notre Dame, 1970, p. 2.
60. Similarly what Kaufmann calls the earliest halakhic midrash (Ezra 9; cf. Neh. 13:1–3) was prompted by new ethnic conditions in Ezra's time; see Kaufmann, *HIR,* IV, pp. 291–293.

Jeffrey H. Tigay

exegetical techniques in a way which had long met similar needs in mantic practice. They were preceded in this by the Egyptian author of the "Demotic Chronicle" (ca. 300 B.C.E.), who applied ancient oracles to the geopolitical situation of his own time by means of symbolic and paronomastic interpretations.[61]

The earliest Jewish source attesting to this kind of scriptural exegesis is Daniel 9–12. It is probably no accident that the Book of Daniel describes its hero not only as understanding the true meaning of ancient Biblical prophecies, but also as a master interpreter of dreams, visions, and oracular inscriptions, just as the Essenes, who responded to a similar historical challenge with the same kind of Biblical exegesis, were also known for their dream interpreters and prognosticators (see above, p. 176). Chapters 9–12 of Daniel were composed in a time of political and religious crisis, the days of Antiochus IV Epiphanes. Among the questions confronted in these chapters was the apparent delay in the end of the seventy years' punishment prophecied by Jeremiah (Jer. 25:11–12; cf. 29:10). To earlier writers (Zech. 1:12; 7:5; 2 Chr. 36:21) it seemed that the prophecy had been fulfilled during the Return to Zion; but to the author of Dan. 9, writing in the days of the Antiochian decrees, it seemed that the redemption had not come and therefore Jeremiah's prophecy limiting the punishment to seventy years had not been confirmed. The problem was solved by a paronomastic double interpretation of "seventy" (*šibʿîm*) as "seventy weeks," i.e. heptads (*šibʿîm šābûʿîm*) of years namely 490 years, whose culmination was approaching. In Dan. 11 allusions to other ancient prophecies imply that the current crisis and its eventual outcome were foretold. This is accomplished in part by understanding the personalities and nations mentioned in those prophecies as those involved in the current events; for example the Kittim, Assyria, and Eber of Num. 24:24 are understood as the Romans, Seleucid Syria, and Israel, as noted above.

This "new exegesis" enabled Biblical exegetes – Daniel, the "Teacher of Righteousness," and their successors – to find in the text a preconceived meaning, namely hints of a historical situation or event. In this the predictive use of Scripture shares the aim of much of rabbinic legal and aggadic exegesis, which seek to find in Scripture indications of, respectively, a predetermined law or spiritual or moral

61. See the passage quoted by Rabin (above, n. 4), p. 149, where earlier bibliography is cited.

188

teaching. Typical of rabbinic exegesis was the sermon which, often following similar techniques, identified concisely expressed spiritual and moral teachings in the Hagiographa and proceeded by means of the hermeneutic rules of the *aggadah* to find these teachings expressed in the Torah as well.[62] This form of exegesis retained its popularity long after centuries of frustration had deprived the oracular use of Scripture of its early predominance.[63] In the long run these techniques made their most extensive contribution to Biblical exegesis through the moral and spiritual interpretation of the Bible, but they owe their original place in the interpreter's repertoire to the contemporizing, predictive or oracular use of Scripture which was so visible from the second century B.C.E. onward and which has not been entirely abandoned even in modern times.

62. For an example of moralizing exegesis at Qumran see CDC 4:14–18.
63. For prediction on the basis of the Torah in early Islamic times see Rabin (above, n. 23), p. 116.

LIST OF ABBREVIATIONS

ABL   R.F. Harper (ed.), Assyrian and Babylonian Letters, I–XIV, London/Chicago, 1892–1914

AfO   Archiv für Orientforschung

AHw   W. von Soden, Akkadisches Handwörterbuch, Wiesbaden, 1965–1981

AJSL   American Journal of Semitic Languages and Literatures

ANEP   J.B. Pritchard (ed.), The Ancient Near East in Pictures Relating to the Old Testament, Princeton, 1954

ANET   J.B. Pritchard (ed.), Ancient Near Eastern Texts Relating to the Old Testament, Princeton, 1969³

AOAT   Alter Orient und Altes Testament

AOS   American Oriental Series

APOT   R.H. Charles (ed.), The Apocrypha and Pseudepigrapha of the Old Testament, I–II, Oxford, 1913

ARAB   D.D. Luckenbill (ed.), Ancient Records of Assyria and Babylonia, I–II, Chicago, 1926–1927

ARMT   Archives royales de Mari, Textes

BAr   The Biblical Archaeologist

BAs   Beiträge zur Assyriologie

Bagh Mitt Baghdader Mitteilungen

BASOR   Bulletin of the American Schools of Oriental Research

BE   Babylonian Expedition of the University of Pennsylvania, Series A: Cuneiform Texts

Bib Or   Bibliotheca Orientalis

BSOAS   Bulletin of the School of Oriental and African Studies

CAD   The Assyrian Dictionary of the Oriental Institute of the University of Chicago

CT   Cuneiform Texts from Babylonian Tablets in the British Museum

CTA   A. Herdner (ed.), Corpus des tablettes en cunéiformes alphabétiques

190

EJ	Encyclopaedia Judaica, I–XVI, Jerusalem, 1972
Enc Miqr	Encyclopaedia Miqra'it, I–VIII, Jerusalem, 1950–1982
FRLANT	Forschungen für Religion und Literatur des Alten und Neuen Testaments
HSM	Harvard Semitic Monographs
HTR	Harvard Theological Review
HUCA	Hebrew Union College Annual
IDB	The Interpreter's Dictionary of the Bible, I–IV, New York/Nashville, 1962; Supplement, 1976
JANES	Journal of the Ancient Near Eastern Society of Columbia University
JAOS	Journal of the American Oriental Society
JBL	Journal of Biblical Literature
JCS	Journal of Cuneiform Studies
JEA	Journal of Egyptian Archaeology
JJS	Journal of Jewish Studies
JNES	Journal of Near Eastern Studies
JSS	Journal of Semitic Studies
KAI	H. Donner and W. Röllig, Kanaanäische und aramäische Inschriften, I–III, Wiesbaden, 1962–1964
KBo	Keilschrifttexte aus Boghazköi
KUB	Keilschrifturkunden aus Boghazköi
LCL	Loeb Classical Library
LSJ	H.G. Liddell, R. Scott, and H.S. Jones, A Greek-English Lexicon, Oxford, 1968
MDOG	Mitteilungen der deutschen Orient-Gesellschaft
MGWJ	Monatsschrift für Geschichte und Wissenschaft des Judentums
MKNAW	Mededelingen der Koninklijke Nederlandse Akademie van Wettenschappen, afdeeling letterkunde
MSL	Materialien zum sumerischen Lexikon, Roma
MVAG	Mitteilungen der vorderasiatisch-ägyptischen Gesellschaft
OECT	Oxford Editions of Cuneiform Texts
OIP	Oriental Institute Publications
OLZ	Orientalistische Literaturzeitung
OTS	Oudtestamentische Studiën
PEQ	Palestine Exploration Quarterly
PRU	Le Palais royal d'Ugarit
PSBA	Proceedings of the Society of Biblical Archaeology

List of Abbreviations

RA	Revue d'assyriologie et d'archéologie orientale
RAI	Rencontre Assyriologique Internationale
RLA	Reallexikon der Assyriologie, I–II, Berlin/Leipzig, 1932–1938, III–VI, Berlin/New York, 1957–1982
RQ	Revue de Qumran
SBLMS	Society of Biblical Literature, Monograph Series
StBoT	Studien zu den Boğazköy-Texten
TB	Babylonian Talmud
TCL	Textes cunéiformes du Louvre
TCS	Texts from Cuneiform Sources
ThLZ	Theologische Literaturzeitung
TLB	Tabulae cuneiformes a F.M.Th. de Liagre Böhl collectae
TP	Palestinian Talmud
UET	Ur Excavations Texts, London
UF	Ugarit-Forschungen
UVB	Vorläufiger Bericht über die Ausgrabungen in Uruk-Warka
VAB	Vorderasiatische Bibliothek
VT	Vetus Testamentum
VTS	Vetus Testamentum Supplement
WO	Die Welt des Orients
WZKM	Wiener Zeitschrift für die Kunde des Morgenlandes
YOS	Yale Oriental Series
ZA	Zeitschrift für Assyriologie
ZÄS	Zeitschrift für die ägyptische Sprache und Altertumskunde
ZAW	Zeitschrift für die alttestamentliche Wissenschaft
ZDPV	Zeitschrift des deutschen Palästina-Vereins